World Wisdom
The Library of Perennial Philosophy

The Library of Perennial Philosophy is dedicated to the exposition of the timeless Truth underlying the diverse religions. This Truth, often referred to as the *Sophia Perennis*—or Perennial Wisdom—finds its expression in the revealed Scriptures as well as the writings of the great sages and the artistic creations of the traditional worlds.

Treasures of Buddhism appears as one of our selections in the Writings of Frithjof Schuon series.

The Writings of Frithjof Schuon

The Writings of Frithjof Schuon form the foundation of our library because he is the pre-eminent exponent of the Perennial Philosophy. His work illuminates this perspective in both an essential and comprehensive manner like none other.

English Language Writings of Frithjof Schuon

Original Books
The Transcendent Unity of Religions
Spiritual Perspectives and Human Facts
Gnosis: Divine Wisdom
Language of the Self
Stations of Wisdom
Understanding Islam
Light on the Ancient Worlds
Treasures of Buddhism (In the Tracks of Buddhism)
Logic and Transcendence
Esoterism as Principle and as Way
Castes and Races
Sufism: Veil and Quintessence
From the Divine to the Human
Christianity/Islam: Essays on Esoteric Ecumenicism
Survey of Metaphysics and Esoterism
In the Face of the Absolute
The Feathered Sun: Plains Indians in Art and Philosophy
To Have a Center
Roots of the Human Condition
Images of Primordial and Mystic Beauty: Paintings by Frithjof Schuon
Echoes of Perennial Wisdom
The Play of Masks
Road to the Heart: Poems
The Transfiguration of Man
The Eye of the Heart
Form and Substance in the Religions
Adastra & Stella Maris: Poems by Frithjof Schuon (bilingual edition)
Autumn Leaves & The Ring: Poems by Frithjof Schuon (bilingual edition)
Songs without Names, Volumes I-VI: Poems by Frithjof Schuon
Songs without Names, Volumes VII-XII: Poems by Frithjof Schuon
World Wheel, Volumes I-III: Poems by Frithjof Schuon
World Wheel, Volumes IV-VII: Poems by Frithjof Schuon
Primordial Meditation: Contemplating the Real

Edited Writings
The Essential Frithjof Schuon, ed. Seyyed Hossein Nasr
Songs for a Spiritual Traveler: Selected Poems (bilingual edition)
René Guénon: Some Observations, ed. William Stoddart
The Fullness of God: Frithjof Schuon on Christianity,
ed. James S. Cutsinger
Prayer Fashions Man: Frithjof Schuon on the Spiritual Life,
ed. James S. Cutsinger
Art from the Sacred to the Profane: East and West,
ed. Catherine Schuon
Splendor of the True: A Frithjof Schuon Reader,
ed. James S. Cutsinger

Treasures of Buddhism

A New Translation with Selected Letters

by

Frithjof Schuon

Includes Other Previously
Unpublished Writings

Edited by
Harry Oldmeadow

Treasures of Buddhism:
A New Translation with Selected Letters
© 2018 World Wisdom, Inc.

Translated by Mark Perry and Jean-Pierre Lafouge

Published in French as
Trésors du Bouddhisme, 1997 and
Images de l'Esprit: Shinto, Bouddhisme, Yoga, 1961, 1982

Library of Congress Cataloging-in-Publication Data

Names: Schuon, Frithjof, 1907-1998, author. | Oldmeadow, Harry, 1947-
editor.
| Perry, Mark, 1951- translator. | Lafouge, Jean-Pierre, 1944- translator.
Title: Treasures of Buddhism : a new translation with selected letters /
edited by Harry Oldmeadow.
Description: Bloomington, Indiana : World Wisdom, 2018. | Series: The
writings of Frithjof Schuon | "Published in French as Tr?esors du
Bouddhisme, 1997 and Images de l'Esprit: Shinto, Bouddhisme, Yoga,
1961,
1982." | Includes bibliographical references and index. |
Identifiers: LCCN 2018008596 (print) | LCCN 2018018174 (ebook) |
ISBN
9781936597598 (epub) | ISBN 9781936597581 (pbk. : alk. paper)
Subjects: LCSH: Buddhism. | Buddhism--Japan.
Classification: LCC BQ4012 (ebook) | LCC BQ4012 .S3813 2018 (print) |
DDC
294.3--dc22
LC record available at https://url.emailprotection.
link/?aQIGj4lOvUgMGIEdjJ2U_yFmWwJ1b54v7TRd5g7Btmug~

Cover:
Wat Phan Tao, Chiang Mai, Thailand

Printed on acid-free paper in the United States of America

For information address World Wisdom, Inc.
P.O. Box 2682, Bloomington, Indiana 47402-2682
www.worldwisdom.com

CONTENTS

EDITOR'S PREFACE

Treasures of Buddhism could only have come from the sovereign meta-physician of our era, "one of the greatest exponents ever of the perennial wisdom; . . . one who is equally at home—and in a masterly fashion—in all of its many and varied and historic forms".[1] This compilation of Frithjof Schuon's essays on Buddhist themes provides a conspectus that fully respects but transcends the exoteric religious understandings of the various schools and branches of this great tradition. It presents a peerless exposition of many particular doctrines, symbols, and rites as well as illuminating the nature of Shinto and its relation to Buddhism. Furthermore, and most importantly, it brings Buddhism to the reader as a living spiritual force.

Along the way the author banishes many misunderstandings that are widespread in the West amongst both the advocates and opponents of what is understood to be "Buddhism". Consider the salutary remarks opening the chapter "Originality of Buddhism":

> Whoever sets out to define a spiritual phenomenon situated in the still quasi-heavenly era of the great Revelations has to beware of assessing it according to the impoverishing "categories" of a later age or, still worse, those belonging to the completely profane "free-thinking" world. Buddhism, which is so often reduced to the level of a base philosophical empiricism, has in fact nothing to do with an ideology that is purely human and thus devoid of any enlightening or salvific quality; to deny the celestial character of Shakyamuni and his Message is tantamount to saying that there can be effects without a cause, and this remark applies moreover for all *Avatāra*s and all sacred institutions (p. 15).

The status of this tradition, so to speak, is a subject that has caused untold confusion—amongst the adherents of other religions, amongst those who champion atheism and agnosticism, amongst

---

[1] William Stoddart, Foreword to Harry Oldmeadow, *Frithjof Schuon and the Perennial Philosophy* (Bloomington, IN: World Wisdom, 2010), p. vii.

many Western converts, and even, in these later times, amongst practitioners within the Buddhist homelands whose thinking has been adulterated by modern influences. No doubt these misapprehensions arise from many sources, but four are readily apparent: firstly, from a Hindu vantage-point Buddhism presents itself as a heterodoxy; secondly, Buddhism is problematic in the perspective of any exoteric theism; thirdly, the spiritual methodology of Buddhism rests on the metaphysic of the Void, misunderstood as a kind of nihilism of which the doctrine of "no soul" (*anatta*) is seen as another scandalous instance; lastly, many Westerners attracted to Buddhism, often unaware of its close affinities with the Christian tradition which they have repudiated, laud it as "rational", "empirical", "scientific", "humanistic", and the like, and disavow its religious "trappings". They sometimes claim that Buddhism is a "way of life" or a "philosophy" rather than a "religion". What does Frithjof Schuon say about these matters?

On the question of Buddhism's relation to the Hindu tradition out of which it emerged:

> The first question to be asked concerning a doctrine or tradition is that of its intrinsic orthodoxy; that is to say one must know whether this tradition is in conformity, not necessarily with another given traditionally orthodox perspective, but simply with Truth. As far as Buddhism is concerned, we will not ask therefore whether it agrees with the letter of the *Veda* or if its "non-theism"—and not "atheism"—can be reconciled in its expression with Semitic theism or any other, but simply whether Buddhism is true in itself; which means, if the answer is in the affirmative, that it will agree with the Vedic spirit and that its "non-theism" will express the Truth—or a sufficient and efficacious aspect of this Truth—whereof theism provides another possible expression, opportune for the world it rules (p. 16).

No doubt, from a certain viewpoint, Buddhism might be understood as a reaction against various excesses, corruptions, and degenerations within the Brahmanical tradition, just as Christianity can be seen as a reaction against Judaic legalism and pharisaism. But to think of the Buddha as a "reformer" is to misunderstand him and his message. The

Buddha is "renunciation, peace, mercy, and mystery", the last being "the essence of truth, which cannot be adequately articulated through language" (p. 10). As to Shankara's refutation of Buddhism, this, precisely, "does not show why Buddhism is false but why Hinduism cannot admit it without nullifying itself" (p. 181).

On the vexed question of Buddhism's non-theism and its "negative" metaphysic, Schuon writes that

> If one accepts that "the kingdom of Heaven is within you", then one cannot logically reproach Buddhism for conceiving the Divine Principle in this respect alone. The "Void" or "Extinction" is God—the supra-ontological Real and Being seen "inwardly"—within ourselves; not in our thought or in our ego, of course, but starting from that "geometrical point" within us whereby we are mysteriously linked to the Infinite.
>
> Buddhist "atheism" consists in a refusal to objectivize or exteriorize the "God within" in a dogmatic form (p. 19).

Buddhism's non-theism, its emphasis on "the mystery of immanence" (p. 188), is one expression amongst many of the Truth, one that is not only possible but necessary:

> Buddhism, inasmuch as it is a characteristic perspective and independently of its modes, is necessary: it could not but come to be, given that a non-anthropomorphic, impersonal, and "static" consideration of the Infinite is in itself a possibility; such a perspective had therefore to be manifested at a particular cyclical moment and in a human setting that rendered it opportune, for the existence of a given receptacle calls for that of a given content (pp. 16-17).

Moreover, Buddhism is "a 'Hinduism universalized', just as Christianity and Islam—each in its own way—are a Judaism rendered universal, hence separated from its particular ethnic milieu and made accessible to men hailing from all origins" (p. 17). Whilst it is true that Buddhism rests on a metaphysic which is not essentially different to that of the *Vedānta*, it would be a grave mistake to infer that thereby it "does not represent just as spontaneous and autonomous a reality as do the other great Revelations" (p. 17). Dialectically and methodically, it is founded on the experience of human suffering; it is a spiritual way directed to the cessation of such suffering:

> the doctrines of the Buddhas are only "celestial mirages" intended to catch, as in a golden net, the greatest possible number of creatures plunged in ignorance, suffering, and transmigration, and that it is therefore the benefit of creatures and not the suchness of the Universe that determines the necessarily contingent form of the Message; . . . Buddhism, within the framework of its own wisdom, goes beyond the formal "mythology" or the "letter" and ultimately transcends all possible human formulations, thus realizing an unsurpassable contemplative disinterestedness as do the *Vedānta*, Taoism, and analogous doctrines (p. 87).

It follows that the claims sometimes made by Orientalists and Western converts that Buddhism is simply a "philosophy" or "natural religion" have more to say about modern prejudices than about Buddhism properly understood.

Buddhism comprises an immense spiritual universe in which we find an encyclopedic range of religious forms and practices, evident in the very different inflections given to the Buddha's saving message in the *Theravāda*, *Vajrayāna*, Zen, and Pure Land branches of the tradition. On these great branches and their various schools and sects, Schuon has written with characteristic percipience. The author moves freely through "the vast and varied extension" (p. 25) of the Buddhist world, sometimes taking a lofty overview, at others focusing sharply on a particular subject—but always attuned to both the universal and the distinctive features of this tradition. We need hardly add that the author is immune to those modernist prejudices that have marred so much of the Western literature on Buddhism. Schuon's writings are all the more illuminating, and sometimes startling, given that Buddhism has received comparatively little attention within the perennialist school inaugurated by the works of René Guénon, but given its fullest and most authoritative expression by the author of the present volume. No less a figure than Guénon himself for many years harbored the notion that Buddhism was no more than a Hindu heterodoxy until he was set right by Ananda Coomaraswamy and Marco Pallis, who, after Schuon, are the two foremost perennialist authorities on this tradition.

It only remains to make a few passing remarks about Shinto, the mythological and shamanistic Japanese tradition which can readily be included in a book such as this because "Japanese civilization can be said to stem, both structurally and in its particular genius, from the synthesis between Shinto and Buddhism" (p. 137). Firstly, it is as well to disown the common supposition that Shinto ancestorism replaced the Divinity with the ancestors, which overlooks the fact that "the Divinity itself is conceived in the Far East as a kind of Ancestor, and one's human ancestors are like a prolongation of the Divinity, or like a bridge between ourselves and it" (p. 141). It is for this reason that "the ancestor is at once the origin and the spiritual or moral norm" (p. 142):

> he is, for his descendants, the essential personality, that is to say the substance of which they are like the accidents; and piety consists precisely in viewing him thus and in seeing in him but the bridge connecting them—his descendants—with the Divine. . . . Ancestors are the human imprints of angelic substances and, for that reason, also of divine Qualities; to be true to them is to be true to God (pp. 142-143).

The cult of the Emperor is a particular expression of the same principle.

The spiritual affinities between Shinto and other forms of "Hyperborean Shamanism" are manifest in "many mythological, cultural, and even vestimentary similarities", in the cult of Nature, and, amongst their practitioners, in "their thirst for freedom, their contempt for luxury, their taciturnity, and other similar characteristics" (pp. 143-144); the comparisons with the American Indians are too obvious to need laboring. These affinities also go to explain why Shinto was so easily able to assimilate Far Eastern forms of Buddhism (especially the ideal of the *Bodhisattva*), also remembering that "To pass from one Asiatic tradition—Hinduism, Buddhism, or Taoism—to another is in effect no great matter, seeing that the metaphysical content is everywhere quite apparent".[2]

[2] Frithjof Schuon, *Gnosis: Divine Wisdom: A New Translation with Selected Letters* (Bloomington, IN: World Wisdom, 2006), p. 6.

It was Marco Pallis who first suggested that Schuon's writings on the Buddhist and Shinto traditions might form a companion volume to *Understanding Islam*, hitherto the only book by Schuon focusing on a single tradition. Pallis was a widely-respected author on the *Vajrayāna*, which he had experienced at first hand during his many sojourns in Tibet at a time when the traditional Buddhist culture was still more or less intact. Schuon's *In the Tracks of Buddhism* appeared in 1968, published by George Allen & Unwin and translated by Pallis. Twenty-five years later a revised and also retranslated version of this compilation was published by World Wisdom as *Treasures of Buddhism*. It included nearly all the material from the first edition, and added several new articles, most of them written since 1968. The present edition follows the format of the first World Wisdom edition and is newly translated from the original French sources by Mark Perry and Jean-Pierre Lafouge.

Treasures of Buddhism is the latest in the World Wisdom series of freshly translated works by Frithjof Schuon. It includes detailed editorial annotations and a full glossary of foreign words and phrases, of which there are necessarily many in a work dealing with the great Oriental traditions. Like other works in the series, it also includes pertinent excerpts from Schuon's correspondence and other previously unpublished writings; these more informal reflections often provide a different angle of approach to some of the questions explored throughout.

Harry Oldmeadow

PART ONE

Treasures of Buddhism

Treasures of Buddhism

When we contemplate a landscape, we perceive its main features without being distracted by details which, if they were too near, would enclose us in their own particularities; similarly, when we view one of the great spiritual traditions by placing ourselves at a vantage point enabling a panoramic view of its distinctive aspects, then none of its essential features will escape us and, at the same time, none will eclipse the others.

Thus, when contemplating the spiritual system[1] that is Buddhism, we can discern at its base a message of renunciation and at its summit a message of mystery; and in another, so to speak "horizontal", dimension we see a message of peace and one of mercy.

The message of renunciation is like a framework for the other messages; it appears as the very body of Buddhism, while the element of mystery is its heart; this message of mystery has found its most direct expression in the Tibetan, Chinese, and Japanese forms that derived from the original *Dhyāna* teaching. As for the message of peace, it pervades the entire Buddhist tradition; its central and culminating crystallization is the sacred image of the Buddha, which is found in the Buddhism of the South as well as in that of the North and, within the setting of the latter, in Tibetan as well as in Sino-Japanese Buddhism. The message of mercy, for its part, finds its general expression in the doctrine of the *Bodhisattva*s, and a particular and quintessential expression in the doctrine of the Buddha Amitabha;[2] this is the message of "the faith that saves", providing a complement of fervor or intensity that harmoniously rejoins the serene detachment Buddhism displays from the outset; the opposition between detachment and fervor exists in appearance only, for all spiritual realities are united in their common root.

---

[1] We mean this word, not in the sense of a purely logical elaboration or coordination of items, which therefore would be a completely outward and profane assessment, but in the sense of a homogeneous ensemble of spiritual precepts, ordered according to a metaphysical perspective. While a traditional doctrine is never narrowly systematic, it nonetheless constitutes a system, like every living organism does or like the universe.

[2] Amida in Japanese.

Because modern men live almost entirely for the things of the senses and, as a result, remain ignorant of the human condition considered in its totality and in its ultimate purpose, it is difficult for them to comprehend the meaning of an attitude seemingly as negative and senseless as that of renunciation; they will regard it merely as a superstition that goes against nature. In reality, renunciation is not obviously self-explanatory; far from being an end in itself, it is only the provisional support for the development of an awareness that goes infinitely beyond our ego. Renunciation would be without purpose were it not a case of grasping with our whole being—and not with the mind alone—what we really are, and above all what total Reality is—that "something" by virtue of which we exist, and from which we cannot escape. Renunciation aims at preventing man from becoming imprisoned in an ephemeral illusion, from identifying himself with it, and finally perishing with it; it aims at helping man to free himself from the tyranny of dreams that lead nowhere. A sage never loses sight of the universal context of life; he does not yield to fragments of consciousness such as agreeable or disagreeable, joyful or sad events, for he is perpetually conscious of the whole, so much so that in the end the question of "renunciation" no longer exists for him; he does not commit himself to fragmentary experience, does not allow himself to get locked into it, does not become it, nor is he burned by it. It might be objected here that man cannot avoid psychic or sensual experience given that he is a living being; the answer is that in spiritual "alchemy" there always is, and necessarily so, sufficient room for the "consolations of the senses", and this in two ways or for two reasons: firstly, all life and therefore all effort is subject to rhythm; everything proceeds in waves, by repetition, alternation, and compensation, in the soul as in the world; no path can afford to be purely negative, for an overstrung bow will snap. Secondly, when a certain degree of awareness of total Reality or of the "Void"[3] has been reached, things themselves will allow that Reality to shine through them, in spite of themselves. The "consolations of the senses" can conceal Truth and lure us away from it, but they can equally well reveal it and draw us nearer to it, and cannot help but do so depending on the spiritual quality of our "per-

---

[3] According to Asanga, the Nagarjunian "Void" is pure "consciousness" (*vijñāna*); to say consciousness is "pure" means that it is situated beyond the polarity "subject-object", that it is "thusness" (*tathatā*).

4

ception". This is true, not only of the beauties of nature or of sacred or even simply traditional art, which speak for themselves,[4] but of bodily satisfactions too, at least inasmuch as they do not upset the bounds ruling the equilibrium between Heaven and the Law.

The notion of peace—of inward and transcendent peace—is no more accessible to the mentality predominating in our epoch than the notion of renunciation. The message of peace refers metaphysically to Pure Being, of which we are as the foam; Pure Being is the Substance, we are the accidents.[5] The canonical figure of the Buddha shows us "That which is", and that which we "should be", or even that which we "are" in our eternal reality: for the visible Buddha is what his invisible essence is; he is in conformity with the nature of things. He is active, since his hands speak, but this activity is essentially "being"; he has an outwardness, since he has a body, but it is "inward"; he is a manifestation since he exists, but he is "manifestation of the Void" (*shūnyamūrti*). He is the personification of the Impersonal and yet, at the same time, he is the transcendent or divine Personality of men;[6] should the veil be torn, the soul returns to its eternal Buddha-nature, just as light refracted by a crystal returns to undifferentiated unity when no object is there anymore to break up its ray. In each grain of dust there is pure Existence and it is in this sense that it can be said that a buddha, or the Buddha, is to be found in it.

What lies at the heart of things is peace and beauty. Things as such are situated "outside themselves"; if they could be completely "within themselves" they would be identified with the Buddha, in the sense

---

[4] Traditional profane art never loses all contact with the sacred; in the prints of a Hokusai or an Utamaro, there is still a contemplative and rigorous element reminiscent of Zen and Taoism; the same holds true—*a fortiori*, perhaps—for tools, clothing, houses, where the sacred and profane are often intimately linked. The primitive tool is always a revelation and a symbol and therefore also a "spiritual instrument".

[5] Albeit with the difference that in the macrocosmic order the accidents do not in any way affect the Substance.

[6] In their esoteric meaning, the words "God", "divine", "Divinity" signify none other than the terms *Shūnya* and *Nirvāna*, even though they can also refer to the Buddhas and the *Bodhisattvas*. That the Buddhist Absolute is not "nothingness" pure and simple is self-evident: "For some, *Nirvāna* is a state in which there could be no memory of the past and present, it would thus be comparable to a lamp whose oil is being consumed or to a kernel of grain that one burns or a fire that is dying, for in these cases there is a cessation of all substrata. . . . But this is not *Nirvāna*, for *Nirvāna* is not simply destruction and emptiness" (*Lankāvatāra Sūtra*, XIII).

that they would be immutable and blessed Substance; immutable because escaping all opposition, all causal constraint, all becoming; and blessed because enjoying the essence of every conceivable beauty and every happiness. The natural symbol of the Buddha is the lotus, this contemplative flower open to the sky and resting on water unruffled by any breath of wind.

To speak of peace is to speak of beauty. Beauty is like the sun: it acts without obliqueness, without dialectical intermediaries, for its ways are free, direct, incommensurable; like love, to which it is closely related, it can heal, release, soothe, unite, and deliver through its mere radiance. The image of the Buddha is like a drop of the nectar of immortality fallen into the world of forms, or like the sound of a celestial music that could charm a rose tree into flowering amid the snow; such was Shakyamuni—for it is said the Buddhas bring salvation not only through their teaching but also through their superhuman beauty—and such is his sacramental image.[7] The image of the Messenger is also that of the Message; there is no difference between the Buddha, Buddhism, and universal Buddha-nature. Consequently, the image indicates the path, or more exactly its conclusion, or the human setting for this conclusion, in the sense that it displays for us the "holy sleep", which inwardly is wakefulness and clarity; by its profound and wondrous "presence" it suggests, to quote the words of Shankara, "the stilling of mental agitation and the supreme appeasement".

Such was Shakyamuni, we were saying. There are two opinions that are inadmissible: to claim that the life of the Buddha is merely a "solar myth",[8] and to claim that knowledge of the historical Buddha is without importance; in both cases, this is tantamount to admitting that there can be effects without a cause. Historically, the life of Shakyamuni is situated in a past that is too close to us, and is far too important to be dismissed as a mere legend; the analogies it shares with more ancient symbolisms serve only to confirm its sacred

[7] If there are no known statues of the Buddha older than those of Gandhara, it is because the first effigies of Shakyamuni were made of wood, and for this reason could not be preserved like stone statues, which came later and were Hellenistic in style. Indeed, according to tradition, King Prasenajit of Shravasti—or King Udayana of Kaushambi—had a statue of the Buddha made of sandalwood during the very lifetime of the Master.

[8] While a solar myth is certainly no small thing, its function is other than that of a founder of religion. A myth is a doctrinal content and not a concrete spiritual force, a "saving emanation".

character. The fact that the Hindus themselves regard the Buddha as an *Avatāra* of Vishnu is further evidence of his transcendent nature, without which there could be no question either of the efficacy of his Law or the saving power of his Name. Traditions emerge from the Infinite like flowers; they can no more be put together by man than can the sacred art that is their witness and their proof.

To speak of peace is to speak of beauty; the image of the *Tathāgata*—together with the metaphysical and cosmic aspects deriving from it—shows that beauty, in its root or essence, is composed of serenity and mercy; formal harmony appeals to us because it bespeaks both profound goodness and inexhaustible wealth, both appeasement and plenitude.

Like a magnet, the beauty of the Buddha gathers all the contradictions of the world and transmutes them into radiant silence; the image deriving therefrom is like a drop of the nectar of immortality fallen into the chilly world of forms and crystallized under the aspect of a human form, a form accessible to men.

Our first encounter—intense and unforgettable—with Buddhism and the Far East took place in our childhood before a great Japanese Buddha of gilded wood,[9] flanked by two images of Kwannon.[10] Suddenly faced with this vision of majesty and mystery, we might well have paradoxically paraphrased Caesar by exclaiming: *"Veni, vidi, victus sum."* We mention this reminiscence because it serves to highlight this emotionally overwhelming embodiment of an infinite victory of the Spirit—or this extraordinary condensation of the Message in the image of the Messenger—represented by the sacramental statue of the Buddha, and represented likewise, by reverberation, in the images of *Bodhisattvas* and other spiritual personifications, such as

---

[9] In an ethnographical museum. Such masterpieces—to say the least—certainly do not belong in a museum of this kind; but what should one say about the thousands of specimens of Buddhist art scattered—and profaned—among antique collectors and galleries? Nothing could be more arbitrary than art criticism with its absurd and, in many cases, iconoclastic classifications.

[10] Kwan-Yin, in Chinese; Avalokiteshvara, in Sanskrit.

those Kwannons who seem to have emerged from a celestial show-ering of golden light, silence, and mercy.

The gesture of the Buddha and the *Bodhisattvas* expresses con-templation and teaching, whatever forms it may take;[11] it conveys both light and radiance; esoteric tradition insists on this character, at first luminous and then salvific, of the nirvanic Substance, and tran-scribes this idea through many different symbolisms.[12] The sun is light and heat, and similarly the inner nature of things is truth and mercy; these two qualities are to be found in all that exists, since all that exists is found in them and lives through them: in a sense, they constitute the Buddha himself, his wisdom, his peace, his compassion, his saving beauty. He is the gateway to the blessed Essence of things, and he is this Essence itself.

Mercy, ultimately, is nirvanic beatitude, which through refraction, has fallen into the "existent nothingness" that is the world. The salvific descent of mercy into the soul depends on our faith, and in turn our faith depends on our distress, or rather on the degree of our aware-ness of our distress. Our faith, or our trust, thus has two sources: the one situated "below" is our incapacity to save ourselves from our wretchedness, and the other source, situated "above", is the will to save of Amida Buddha—or of the Buddha in his Amida aspect. We must know, on the one hand, that we cannot save ourselves, and,

---

[11] For these *mudrās* are infinitely diverse, such as in the rites, dances, and sculptures of India.

[12] But keeping in mind the following difference, namely that the distinction between "light" and "radiation" corresponds to that between the *Pratyeka-Buddha* and the *Samyaksam-Buddha*, the first being enlightened "for himself" and the second hav-ing the function of enlightening others through preaching the *Dharma*, which makes one think of the respective roles of the *Jīvan-Mukta* and the *Avatāra* or—in Islamic terms—of the *Walī* and the *Rasūl.* Moreover, the *Samyaksam-Buddha* should not be confused with the *Bodhisattva* who, himself, has not attained *Nirvāna* and whose cosmic movement, in keeping with his particular vocation, is "spiroidal" and not "ver-tical". The *Bodhisattva* is, in his human aspect, a *karma-yogī* completely dedicated to charity towards all creatures, and in his celestial aspect, an "angel" or more precisely an "angelic state", whence his function of rescuer and "guardian angel".

on the other, we must have the certitude that divine Mercy not only "can" but "wants" to save us according to the degree of our faith. Faith springs from the abyss of our misery and derives its sustenance from the infinitude of Mercy.

Buddhism in its most general, as well as in its most intellectual and esoteric, aspect is based on "power of self";[13] however, since "power of the other"[14] is a possibility in its own order, Buddhism—as a universal message—cannot overlook it; hence the path of "power of the other" will be like a "compartment" in the spiritual structure of the *Dharma*. It is pointless and even impossible to have recourse here to the hypothesis of borrowings from other traditions, for Truth is one and man is everywhere man; the fundamental spiritual possibilities belonging to man cannot but manifest in some fashion or other within a framework as vast as that of a great Revelation.[15] If there are in Buddhism some seemingly "Christian" elements, then there are likewise some seemingly "Buddhist" elements in Christianity,[16] and there is also some "Christianity" in Hinduism, and so forth; it is inconceivable that things could be otherwise. All the essential aspects of Truth and of the Path will necessarily be found in a Buddhist climate, each with their particularities of emphasis as dictated by that tradition; not one of these aspects can be dispensed with on pain of jeopardizing the universality of the Message. The sacred scriptures inform us that the Buddha makes use of every means to save creatures and that he speaks to each being in a language it can understand, if only it will listen.[17]

---

[13] In Japanese, *jiriki*. This point of view is—*mutatis mutandis*—common in *Theravāda* Buddhism and in Zen.

[14] *Tariki.*

[15] We mean this term "Revelation" in an entirely general and not specifically "theistic" sense; *Bodhi*, although not being the gift of a "divinity" conceived "objectively", is nonetheless a supernatural "unveiling"—intellectual, not rationalist in style—of absolute Reality, which itself appears as a "void" in relation to the world of forms and substances.

[16] Notably in *gnosis* and in contemplative quietism. According to a solidly established prejudice typical of a certain kind of scholarship, there are no coincidences: every text resembling another must have been influenced by the other, no matter how implausible; this is an entirely mechanical logic, going completely against the nature of things.

[17] We have stressed that sacred images constitute such a language; it should be added that their absence, notably in Zen, is another. In total truth there is always an aspect that allows the burning up of all forms; only the Absolute—the "Void"—is beyond all

The Buddha, we said, is renunciation, peace, mercy, and mystery. Mystery is the essence of truth, which cannot be adequately articulated through language—the vehicle of discursive thought—but which may suddenly appear as an illuminating flash through a symbol, such as a key word, a mystic sound, or an image whose suggestive hint may be scarcely graspable. This explains the elliptical and paradoxical character of the *kōan*s in Zen—verbal symbols designed to provoke an ontological breach in the hardened shell of our ignorance—and which also explains the mysterious and transparent atmosphere of Taoist and Zen landscapes; the spirit of Zen and that of Taoism meet in this unrivaled art, as also, be it said in passing, the ethnic genius of China and Japan. On this plane of visual contemplation—or contemplative vision[18]—the genius of the Chinese and Japanese is one and the same;[19] there are no other peoples who have been more successful in visualizing the mystery of things.

While the element of "mercy" has flowered in *Jōdo* and *Shinshū*[20] and its Chinese prototype—and doubtless also in the *Nichiren* school, in a certain way[21]—the element of "mystery" for its part is perpetuated in Zen, as we have seen, but it is equally present in *Kegon, Tendai,* and *Shingon* as well as in their mainland prototypes or equivalents,

infringement. In this regard, Zen possesses some highly paradoxical formulas, which present-day iconoclasts—who never understand the symbols they disdain—have made the great mistake of taking literally, because these truths are not for them.

[18] A vision moreover to which the beauty and richness of Chinese ideography bears witness. Outside the Far East, there are scarcely any but the Muslim peoples who possess equivalent calligraphies, thanks not only to the richness and plasticity of the Arabic characters, but also to the focus—due to religious reasons—of the pictorial instinct on writing alone.

[19] Their differences are affirmed on other planes. Compared to the sumptuousness and gaiety of colors used by the Chinese, Japanese art—in the broadest sense—is conspicuous in general for a kind of sobriety and ingenious simplificatFion, and also for a greater accentuation on the role of nature. But these differences are for the most part rather relative.

[20] The mission of Shinran, founder of the *Shinshū*, was not only to continue and reinforce the work of his master Honen, founder of *Jōdo*, but also to bring about a junction of incantatory Amidism with pure metaphysics, hence with the element "mystery" or "absolute Buddhism". For Shinran, the "power of the other" (*tariki*) is in the final analysis the transcending of the opposition of the two "powers" (*tariki* and *jiriki*).

[21] This school, like the two preceding ones, essentially takes account of the spiritual weakness of mankind in our era of final decadence.

not to mention that storehouse of esoteric science found in Tibetan *Mahāyāna*. *Kegon* lays stress on the ontological and spiritual homogeneity of the world and on the omnipresence of the Buddha-Light, which can be taken as corresponding with the *buddhi* of Hindu doctrine, at least when considered as immanence; *Tendai* proclaims that "all things can become Buddha", which is one way of affirming—to use Vedantic language—that "all things are *Ātmā*" (or *Nirvāna*) or in other words: the world, since it is not nothing, is all—namely, it is the Buddha, or "Buddha-nature". As for *Shingon*, it is a metaphysical synthesis as well as a *mantra-yoga* and is thus related in type to Lamaism.

The foregoing considerations must not leave the impression that *Theravāda* Buddhism is being underestimated here; this form of the tradition is all it should be and we must be thankful that it exists both in its own place and among the totality of the supernatural institutions.[22]

The Buddha, in his kind of perfection and canonical image, represents or suggests for many an "asocial" ideal, an eremitic ideal as a matter of fact; and the hermit, again in the eyes of many, is seen as evading his "responsibilities" in order to dedicate himself to an "egotistical" ideal, and so forth. Now, to begin with, it is absurd to try to define man on the basis of his social value, for a human being is neither a bee nor an ant; if fate casts him on a desert island, he will not thereby cease being a man. Furthermore, social "responsibilities"[23]—provided they are not imaginary—are obviously a relative matter, whereas man's ultimate ends coincide with the Absolute; it is precisely those ultimate ends that the hermit, the contemplative, and the Buddha incarnate. Every human attitude is "egotistical", metaphysically speaking, except the

---

[22] Not a few contemporary Buddhists would tell us that the excellence of Buddhism is to be "natural" or "human", but this betrays a misunderstanding of terminology. Buddhist "naturalism" is "supernatural", just as the *Tathāgata*'s "humanity" is "superhuman".

[23] One will note the hypocritical nuance of this word. In reality, the "useful" man is not annoyed about having to remain "in the world". If eremitism is an "escape", social moralism is so as well; everything depends on knowing what one is escaping from.

transcending of the ego;[24] the egotism of the species, so marked in the animal world, is no more transcendent than that of the individual, though it takes precedence over the individual biologically and morally. Moreover, it must not be forgotten that the ego, as a natural factor, has a positive side like any other phenomenon of nature, for the injunction to "love thy neighbor as thyself" implies that it is permissible and even necessary—and in any case inevitable—to love oneself; it would be the height of hypocrisy for the protagonists of the "social imperative" to deny the existence of this self-love. This entire complex of positions, so easily reducible to the absurd, is overcome only in *Nirvāna*, where there is no "my-self" left to love, nor indeed an "other"; it was in this sense that Sri Ramana Maharshi was able to say: "Is the dreamer, when he awakens, supposed to wake all those of whom he was dreaming?"

When the reproach of "egotism" emanates from those who believe neither in the transcendent Absolute[25] nor in the hereafter, the controversy becomes like a dialogue between the deaf and the mute; but when that same reproach is formulated by professing "believers" it is perhaps worth reminding them that the "good" the individual can do for society is situated—just as society itself and the individual as such—on a cosmic plane that engenders "evil" and cannot but engender it. Suffering, in its nature, is no more opposed to salvation than pleasure or wealth is opposed to perdition, if one may allow oneself a truism which, unfortunately, religious "believers" themselves contrive to overlook by every means possible. Suffering is not merely some kind of unfortunate fate that can be eliminated by dint of "progress" and done so, furthermore, after thousands of years of mysterious impotence. One can transcend the *Samsāra*, but one cannot abolish it. It is more worthy to save souls than to save bodies, though the latter activity is far from insignificant and indeed can be integrated into the former, but only on the express condition that the superior claims of the former task always be clearly maintained. Now, to save others one must first be able to "save oneself", if we may so

---

[24] To transcend the ego is to transcend the human, although one could say, from another point of view, that this transcending is "human" in the sense that it constitutes the specific excellence of man, or his supreme goal.

[25] This qualifier is necessary because mathematicians and physicists also speak of an "absolute", which in regard to total Reality is but a still blind and contingent element.

put it;[26] there is no other way of conveying the "absolute good" before which, moreover, the distinction between a "self" and a "not-self" becomes virtually meaningless. Finally, one cannot save a soul as one would pull someone out of the water;[27] one can only rescue those who are willing to be rescued,[28] and that is why it is ridiculous to reproach the religions for not having succeeded in saving the world.

What the hermit embodies most visibly is contemplative solitude, hence the frequent reproach that he represents a maximum of "uselessness";[29] in reality, nothing is more useful than to demonstrate in concrete form the worth of the Absolute and the painful vanity of transient things. The hermit exercises the greatest possible charity since—apart from the question of his own Deliverance—he points the way towards that which has the highest value and, in the final analysis, the only value. It may be objected: what would then become of society if everyone decided to be a hermit? The answer is: firstly, that the question of what would become of society is of secondary importance, since society does not carry within itself its own justifying cause and does not represent in itself an unconditional value; and secondly, if everyone were to follow the hermit's example, or were disposed to do so, the world would in any case be saved, for subsidiary concerns would then be ordered according to what is essential; thirdly, to consider the question more concretely, we should remember that there have always been saints engaged in the affairs of the world, men such as Shotoku Taishi,[30] Hojo Tokimune,[31] Shonin Shinran, and Nichiren;[32]

---

[26] We cannot take account of all the nuances and reservations that ought to be considered here.

[27] Only the Buddhas can do so, in a certain fashion, and exceptionally.

[28] The word "rescue" necessarily possesses only a relative meaning here, yet sufficient to justify our thesis.

[29] Or a "lack of productivity", to use a still more basely barbaric term.

[30] The holy Prince Regent who introduced and consolidated Buddhism in Japan.

[31] The governor who resisted the Mongol invasion, one of the greatest figures of Japanese history and of Zen.

[32] Or in the West: Charlemagne, Saint Louis, Joan of Arc, Saint Vincent de Paul, to cite but a few names. As for Nichiren, his violent hostility in regard to other Buddhist schools neither prevents his interpretation of the *Saddharmapundarīka Sūtra* ("Lotus of the Good Law")—in virtue of the decadence of the "last days"—from being perfectly valid, nor his school from being intrinsically orthodox.

none of these ever dreamt of blaming hermits—to say the least—and indeed could never have done so, in view of the example offered by so many solitary contemplatives. The hermit's message does not concern rocks and trees, it concerns detachment from the impermanent and attachment to the Eternal; the hermit exemplifies, not a contingency, but a principle; he demonstrates the superiority of contemplation over action—even if the latter surrounds the former[33]—and of "being" over "doing", of truth over works. Man belongs above all to the Absolute—whether we speak of the Void (*Shūnya*), Extinction (*Nirvāna*), or "God"—and before the Absolute he is always alone. But, from another point of view, it can be said that in the presence of the Infinite there is no solitude.

Nirvāna is Truth in its "pure state"; in it, all relative and partial truths are absorbed. Errors cannot but exist so long as their possibility, albeit altogether relative, has not been exhausted;[34] but from the perspective of the Absolute, they have never been and never will be. On their own level they are what they are, but the silence of the eternal *Ādi-Buddha* will have the last word.

---

[33] As is the case in the *Bhagavad Gītā*.

[34] "When the inferior man hears about the Tao, he laughs at it; it would not be the Tao if he did not laugh at it. . . . The clarity of the Tao is taken for darkness" (*Tao Te Ching*, XLI).

Originality of Buddhism

Whoever sets out to define a spiritual phenomenon situated in the still quasi-heavenly era of the great Revelations has to beware of assessing it according to the impoverishing "categories" of a later age or, still worse, those belonging to the completely profane "free-thinking" world. Buddhism, which is so often reduced to the level of a base philosophical empiricism, has in fact nothing to do with an ideology that is purely human and thus devoid of any enlightening or salvific quality; to deny the celestial character of Shakyamuni and his Message is tantamount to saying that there can be effects without a cause, and this remark applies moreover for all *Avatāras* and all sacred institutions. The Buddha, despite certain appearances, was not a "reformer" in the current sense of the word—which implies heterodoxy—and could not be such. A reformer has but one concern, that of bringing back the religion to which he adheres, or thinks he adheres, to its "original purity"; and he does this by rejecting essential elements rather like a man who, wishing to bring a tree back to its root, would saw off all its branches and even its trunk. The reformer—whose idea of "purity" is entirely external and in no way transcendent—fails to perceive that the branches normally and legitimately contain the root and even the seed; that the sap is the same throughout the tree down to its smallest shoot; that every organism has its laws of growth, determined not only by its own particular nature but also by the setting in which it is meant to expand; that time is irreversible and that the qualitative differences of temporal cycles necessitate for any given tradition readaptations in a more explicit and more differentiated sense, just as happens with the tree, analogically speaking, the branches of which are more complex than the trunk. The Buddha, being a direct manifestation of the Spirit, had both the power and the right to place himself outside the tradition in which he was born; he was not concerned with the purity of Hinduism nor did he think of reforming it; the pre-existing frameworks—which moreover were humanly decadent in his time—represented for him no more than the symbols of formalism as such, of a pharisaism "the letter of which kills".[1]

---

[1] We say "formalism" and "pharisaism", not "form" and "orthodoxy"; it is a ques-

The first question to be asked concerning a doctrine or tradition is that of its intrinsic orthodoxy; that is to say one must know whether this tradition is in conformity, not necessarily with another given traditionally orthodox perspective, but simply with Truth. As far as Buddhism is concerned, we will not ask therefore whether it agrees with the letter of the *Veda* or if its "non-theism"—and not "atheism"—can be reconciled in its expression with Semitic theism or any other, but simply whether Buddhism is true in itself; which means, if the answer is in the affirmative, that it will agree with the Vedic spirit and that its "non-theism" will express the Truth—or a sufficient and efficacious aspect of this Truth—whereof theism provides another possible expression, opportune for the world it rules. Moreover, one particular spiritual perspective or another is usually discoverable somewhere within the framework of a tradition that excludes it; thus "theism" reappears in a certain sense within the framework of Buddhism, notably in the form of Amidism, despite the "non-theism" characterizing this religion; and, in its turn, this "non-theism" can likewise be found in monotheistic esoterisms in the conception of the "impersonal Essence" of the Divinity; the above examples show us that there is nothing exclusive about such "frameworks" , and that the question always comes down to one of emphasis or of spiritual economy.[2]

What has just been said means implicitly that Buddhism, inasmuch as it is a characteristic perspective and independently of its modes, is necessary: it could not but come to be, given that a non-anthropomorphic, impersonal, and "static" consideration of the Infinite is in itself a possibility; such a perspective had therefore to be manifested at a

tion of abuses and not of the things themselves that have been abused, although the Buddhist perspective, precisely, had no need to make this particular distinction in regard to Hinduism. Orthodox reformers exist, such as Tsongkhapa in Tibetan Buddhism and, in the West, Saints John of the Cross and Teresa of Avila, not forgetting Savonarola; but in their case it was never a question of invalidating any principle of the Tradition, indeed quite the contrary.

[2] The occasional use, by the Buddha, of terms proper to Brahmanical theism clearly shows that the Buddhist perspective has nothing in common with atheism properly so called. "Extinction" or the "Void" is "God" subjectivized; "God" is the objective "Void". If Buddhists—except in their perspectives of Mercy—do not objectivize the Void or the Self, this is because they have nothing to ask of it, given their own anti-individualist point of view; if nevertheless there are certain "dimensions" where things are otherwise, this is because the "objective aspect" of Reality is too much in the nature of things to pass unperceived or not to be highlighted in some fashion.

cyclical moment and in a human setting that rendered it opportune, for the existence of a given receptacle calls for that of a given content. It has sometimes been remarked that the Buddhist perspective is not distinguishable in any essential way from particular doctrines or paths found in Hinduism; this is true in a certain sense—and all the more likely given that Hinduism is characterized by an uncommon wealth of doctrines and methods—but it would be wrong to conclude from this that Buddhism does not represent just as spontaneous and autonomous a reality as do the other great Revelations; what has to be said is that Buddhism is a "Hinduism universalized", just as Christianity and Islam—each in its own way—are a Judaism rendered universal, hence separated from its particular ethnic milieu and made accessible to men hailing from all origins. Buddhism extracted as it were from Hinduism its yogic sap—not through a borrowing, of course, but through a divinely inspired "remanifestation"—and imparted to this substance an expression that was simplified in certain respects, but at the same time fresh and powerfully original; this is what Buddhist art demonstrates in a dazzling fashion, the prototypes of which are doubtless found in the sacred art of India and in the yogic postures, or again in dance which, for its part, is like an intermediary between *yoga* and temple statuary; Buddhist art—and here we have in mind above all images of the Buddha—seems to have extracted from Hindu art, not such and such a particular symbolism, but its contemplative essence. The plastic arts of India evolve in the last analysis from the postures of spiritual recollectedness that the human body can assume; in Buddhism, the image of this body and of this visage has become an extraordinarily prolific symbol and a means of grace unsurpassable in its power and nobility;[3] and it is this artistic crystallization that

---

[3] The genius of the yellow race has added to the Hindu prototypes something of a new dimension; new, not from the point of view of symbolism as such, but from that of expression. The image of the Buddha, after undergoing the Hellenistic aberration of Gandhara—providentially no doubt, for it is a question of the transmission of some secondary formal elements—attained an unparalleled expansion among the yellow peoples: it is as if the "soul" of the Divinity, the nirvanic Beatitude, had entered into the symbol. The *Chitralakshana*, an Indo-Tibetan canon of pictorial art, attributes the origin of painting to the Buddha himself; tradition also speaks of a sandalwood statue that King Prasenajit of Shravasti (or Udayana of Kaushambi) had made during the very lifetime of the Buddha, and of which the Greek statues of Gandhara may have been stylized copies.

most visibly brings out what Buddhism comprises of absoluteness and therefore also of universality. The sacred image transmits a message of serenity: the Buddhist *Dharma* is not a passionate struggle against passion; rather, it dissolves passion from within, through contemplation. The lotus, supporting the Buddha, is the nature of things, the calm and pure fatality of existence, of its illusion, of its vanishing; but it is also the luminous center of *Māyā* from whence arises *Nirvāna* become man.

From the doctrinal point of view, the great originality of Buddhism is to consider the Divine, not in relation to its cosmic manifestations as ontological Cause and anthropomorphic personification, but on the contrary in relation to its acosmic and anonymous character, hence as supra-existential "state", which will then appear as Voidness (*shūnyatā*) seen from the point of view of the false plenitude of existence (*samsāra*); the latter is the realm of "thirst" (*trishnā*). This perspective will stress the unconditional character of the "divine" Goodness, or rather of the "nirvanic" Grace that projects itself through a myriad of Buddhas and *Bodhisattvas* into the round of transmigration, even down to the hells; faith in the infinite Mercy of the Buddha—being himself an illusory appearance of the beatific Void—already constitutes in itself a grace or a gift. Salvation consists in escaping the infernal circle of "concordant actions and reactions", and in this connection, morality will appear as a quite provisional and fragmentary thing, and even as inoperative in the sight of the Absolute, since it is itself still involved in the indefinite chain of actions and the existential fruit of actions. Forms such as Zen and Amidism are particularly suited for allowing one to sense the subtle relationships, made of imponderables and paradoxes, which separate or connect the world of transmigration and Extinction, of *Samsāra* and *Nirvāna*.

—— ·:· ——

Buddhist "non-theism" offers the advantage of avoiding the impression of a self-interested God; quite obviously, this advantage is relative and conditional, but not unimportant given certain types of mentalities; moreover, Buddhists are of the opinion that the religious dissensions of the monotheistic world result from dogmatic and anthropomorphic theism as such: no God without a party, no party without struggles against another party. Needless to say, this view represents but a partial truth, which is compensated by theism's own intrinsic values.

If one accepts that "the kingdom of Heaven is within you", then one cannot logically reproach Buddhism for conceiving the Divine Principle in this respect alone. The "Void" or "Extinction" is God—the supra-ontological Real and Being seen "inwardly"—within ourselves; not in our thought or in our ego, of course, but starting from that "geometrical point" within us whereby we are mysteriously linked to the Infinite.

Buddhist "atheism" consists in a refusal to objectivize or exteriorize the "God within" in a dogmatic form. Nevertheless, such an objectification does occur, in a "provisional" sense, in the merciful message of Amitabha, and it is precisely the possibility of such an objectification that proves Buddhism is in no way "atheistic" in the restrictive sense of the word.[4]

The fact that Buddhism is founded, dialectically and methodically, on the experience of suffering has given rise to criticisms of a kind to be expected in our time, such as the accusation of being "purely negative", or "unnatural", and so forth; and this makes it necessary to denounce a double error, firstly that suffering is meaningless, and secondly that suffering can be, not transcended, but abolished on its own level, the level of desire and life. For anyone who views things in this manner, all religions will evidently appear as attempts at "resignation" or "flight"; but who can miss the inanity and hypocrisy of these reproaches, since those who express them are likewise forced to resign themselves before some things and to flee before others: they have to resign themselves to the fate of birth, old age, death, and existence itself; and, just like the religious believers they despise, they flee before the forces of nature that threaten them and that they are powerless to oppose; the only difference is that these people do not know that certain things are ruled by fate whereas other things are mortal dangers from which it is possible to escape and from which the believer does escape, precisely. It is self-evident that one has no motive for resigning oneself to a situation that one believes one can

---

[4] The symbolism of the "Pure Land" or of other Paradises would not be possible in Buddhism if those "Lands" were not reconcilable with the intrinsic nature of *Nirvāna*, or in other words, if they did not describe in manifested, "exteriorized", and "diversified" mode the ineffable Reality of the Self.

and should change, and one also has no reason to flee from a peril of which one is quite unaware; however, one can doubtless always disguise one's ignorance with an icy and embittered moralism that gives itself heroic airs, according to the fashion of the time. If the "zeal of bitterness leads to hell", as Saint Benedict said, this is because it is based on pride; and indeed, there is no worse form of pride than this insolent presupposition: namely that all the Prophets, all the sages, all the saints were simpletons, a fact that Mr. X or Mr. Y—who alone are "heroic" and "sincere"!—have at long last come to recognize, after thousands of years gone to waste.

Buddhism has sometimes been described as a philosophy or as a "natural religion". To assert that Buddhism is "natural" makes sense only if this is intended to mean that, unlike the Semitic religions, it is anchored in the existential mystery of things—at least in some of its aspects[5]—or that in a certain way it extracts the Divine from our "nature", even as flint produces fire: which means, precisely, that what we call nature is not exclusively nature, namely that it is not located outside the divine mystery since, in the final analysis, "each thing is *Ātmā*"; this is what is expressed by certain schools of Buddhism, which teach that Buddhas reside at the "center" of every speck of dust; other schools render this same idea by saying that "every stone can become Buddha". This aspect of "nature" also explains not only a certain apparently "rational"—not "rationalist"—character of Buddhism[6] but also the human side of the youthful Gautama's experience; this experience proves, not that Buddhism is not supernatural and supra-rational, nor that Shakyamuni was not an *Avatāra*, but solely

---

[5] This reservation is necessary because it would be possible to speak also of the "intellectual mystery" of existence, to which Buddhism essentially refers, given that "Extinction" or "Voidness" is none other than "Selfhood".

[6] According to the Buddha himself, his doctrine, far from being a philosophical ratiocination, is on the contrary "profound, difficult to realize, difficult to understand, ungraspable by reason". Highly significant also is this gesture: the Buddha picks up a handful of leaves and explains to his disciples that just as these leaves are but a small thing compared to the forest, so also the doctrine he preaches is but a minute portion of what he knows; of this knowledge he will reveal only what is useful for Deliverance.

that the Buddhist perspective possesses a certain "nature-centric"—not "naturalistic"—character, namely that the launching point for the Path to *Nirvāna* starts from the empirical nature of things. The Buddha had to demonstrate, by the unfolding of his own experience leading to *Bodhi*, the "way out" of this world of suffering; to see in this a proof of imperfection, as some have done, is as illogical as to apply a similar reasoning to Jesus, who let himself be baptized and who fasted in the wilderness even while "being God".

The rationalizing aspect of Buddhist dialectic leads us to make two observations here, which may seem to digress from our main subject: firstly, Eastern wisdom resides not only in its doctrinal formulations, the simplicity of which readily lends itself to the contempt of philosophical minds, but it resides also, and essentially, in the way these formulations are envisaged and their contents assimilated in their fullness; in order to understand the value of any form of wisdom it is obviously necessary to know how to place oneself at the viewpoint of those to whom its message is addressed and to possess the intelligence—or the kind of intelligence—it presupposes.[7] The second observation we

---

[7] The contradictions Father Henri de Lubac (in *Amida* [Paris, 1955]) believes he has discovered in the doctrine of the *upāya*s (the "divine stratagems" in view of Truth or Deliverance) do not correspond to any psychological possibility among the men to whom he attributes them, otherwise Buddhism itself would have self-destructed from the beginning. This author draws his argument—as if it were a question of unmasking contradictions, which however are excluded from the outset—from the fact that the Paradises, and the Buddhas and *Bodhisattva*s themselves, are presented in the *Mahāyāna* as illusions; but he forgets to add the essential point, namely that man and the terrestrial world are even much more illusory. To say that without man there would be no Buddha does not mean that the Buddha is less real than man—one finds, moreover, analogous formulations in Eckhart, Silesius, Omar Khayyam— but solely that, without a given receptacle, there would not be a given form of content: water exists without a pitcher, but the form or color taken by the water depends on the pitcher; the sun exists without water, but the appearance its reflection takes depends upon the surface of this element, which may be calm or rough. The fact of using the *upāya*s as arguments to impugn the Buddhist message entails so flagrant a contradiction that it is sufficient in itself to destroy the thesis in question; if this thesis were true and if it were necessary to take the formulations of the Void and the metaphysical indistinction of phenomena literally and nihilistically, how could one explain not merely twenty-five centuries of spiritual effort, but even the slightest moral initiative on the part of Buddhism? What is disappointing in dogmatism as such is precisely its incapacity of seeing itself as a "mirage", that is, of changing its angle of vision; thus, the Buddhist formulas Father de Lubac cites—as "incriminating evidence"—amount for us as so many reasons for in fact accepting the *Mahāyāna*. The same author defines "the

wished to make is the following: there exists no proof, not indeed for the supernatural as such, of course, but for a particular version of the supernatural treated as unique and exclusive. If it be objected that the Buddhist claim to the supernatural—namely, to the divine origin of the Buddha's message and to its salvific efficacy—might be a mere illusion, the Intellect being a "human thing" and miracles proving nothing in themselves, the answer is that this is a two-edged argument, since it is always possible to claim logically—materialists have no compunction in doing so—that the alleged proofs of divinity result simply from a vast objectification of purely human aspirations; in which case, one can always argue that the keys to the evidence are illusory, that even the eye can be deceived and that nothing is ever certain; all that is left for us then is to refer to the certitude of Grace, but if such an argument is irrefutable, then it is equally so for foreign perspectives which one likewise seeks to refute.

But there is yet another side to this question: some modernizing defenders of Buddhism like to emphasize, this time out of an apologetic urge to reinforce the argument of the "purely natural" and "non-obscurantist" character of this tradition, that the Buddhist reality resides "only in our mind"; yet, once again, this is an evolutionist distortion of an esoteric truth, for they carefully avoid to add that what is really at stake is not just some mental fiction but the transcendent inwardness of the human mind, hence, in the final analysis, that of the Self; and given that the Buddha is the Self, he is with all the more reason our mind, in the sense that there can be no Intellect apart from

Pure Land that all the devotees of Amida greet as their hope" as "a myth devoid of substance" and as "a great thousand-faced dream spawned from human nostalgia"; and he goes on: "And would we still be 'Christ-bearers' if we were not able to say to those who have fashioned this dream—like so many other pursuers of fantasies— that the shore that attracts them is but a snare, that it holds a definitive disillusion for them if it does not prefigure the one the Lord has prepared in his love?" (*Amida*, "Foreword"). We would very much like to know what this love is that condemns millions of sincere souls to a vain faith and a sterile fervor, and this for millennia; a love whose means are so ineffective that after so many centuries the overwhelming majority of these souls are still cut off from truth and salvation—unless we concede that these souls, these innumerable "natural mystics" of Asia, are unworthy in proportion to their abandonment; the sheer implausibility of this hypothesis requires no demonstration. If religious ostracism were right, we would have to conclude that for all these "natural mystics", the "love of the Lord" is an even bigger "trap" than all the *upāya*s that are ridiculed with such disconcerting ease.

Him. But at the same time—and this is another aspect of the question—the Buddha appears in our intelligence as a concept, otherwise he would be ungraspable, in which case we would not be able to speak of him in any way. Obviously, one can say that this Buddha, not being the Buddha as such but only a provisional and inevitable perception thereof, resides in our mind like any other concept; this means, not that the Buddha does not possess a relatively "objective"— or "supra-subjective"—reality apart from us, but simply that we are incapable, in our false plenitude, of grasping in a direct way the "suchness" of Buddhahood.

Since we touched upon the evolutionist prejudice above, it will be permissible to mention here a few more words on the subject: evolutionism would be justified if a tree could produce something other and better than what is contained in its seed; it would be justified if the fruits of the tree were, not the manifestation of what the seed already contains, but the result of an evolution that is unforeseeable and variable according to circumstances, or if it were a matter of chance whether an apple tree bears apples and not figs. The phenomena of evolution and transmutation exist within the limits of certain contingencies, otherwise the seed would never become a tree and a plant would never modify its shape under given conditions, such as a change of soil or climate; but these two factors—evolution and transmutation—are altogether secondary with respect to the principle of the qualitative anticipation of effects within their own cause. These truths take on a particular importance when it is a question of Revelations and traditions, for the slightest error on this plane can be devastating to the soul and to the intelligence.

These considerations provide us with an opportunity to denounce another prejudice common to the modernist and evolutionist mind, namely the claim to a maximum of "freedom" for the human animal or, in other words, the ideal of a quasi-total absence of constraints with regard to man, that is to say of man considered apart from his content or quality and also apart from his metaphysical end; now the only freedom proportioned to our nature is that which opens the gates towards the eternal Freedom we bear in the depths of our being, and not to that which delivers man's weakness—especially collective man's—over to the powers of dissolution and spiritual suicide. In India, the Brahmin is at once the most independent and the most obedient of men, which means that he who is socially the freest must be inwardly the most bound—leaving aside the question of liberation through Knowledge. Two things are certain: firstly, that in an integral society everyone cannot be free in the same way; and secondly, that a society, like any cosmos, cannot avoid the approximations and errors ensuing from its condition, that it to say, there will always be exceptions positive and negative, miracles and abuses. It is only on the spiritual plane that the pure norms, and with them perfect justice, are to be found. When spirituality has become darkened, it is vain to wish to establish an ideal justice, this being impossible to implant among men who themselves are devoid of justice; and it is even far more vain to seek to establish this justice at the expense of principles which, even though badly applied in fact, are nevertheless the only concretely possible application in a given human setting.[8] It is totally legitimate to adapt a traditional principle to new circumstances, insofar as these are unavoidable, but one cannot reject this principle in its very substance.

[8] The abuses of the French Revolution—to cite but one instance—were certainly not less than those of the decadent monarchy, quite the contrary as a matter of fact; what should have happened is that, instead of overthrowing the monarchical and theocratic principles, these should have been restored to their full meaning, which was a religious one; this is exactly what the nobility neglected to do from the time of the Renaissance. In order to maintain the people in their religious faith, or to maintain a common equilibrium founded on faith, one has to prove that one possesses faith oneself; injustice towards the people—and the consequent injustice of the people in regard to principles and their human representatives—always derives from a prior injustice with regard to God.

Message and Messenger

In order to understand Buddhism in all its vast and varied extension, it is necessary to distinguish, in the Buddha himself, between the element doctrine and the element being: the doctrine—that of suffering, the salvific way, and *Nirvāna*—and his being, which first is manifested in the visible form of the Buddha—subsequently crystallized in sacred images—and then in the sermons from the latter part of his life, those on which the *Mahāyāna* is founded.

What we have called "the Buddha's being" refers to the merciful[1] and at the same time esoteric contents of his Message; this feature is even discernible in Theravadic Buddhism—despite the fact that it remains closed to the Mahayanic *sūtras*—be it only in the sacred image of the Buddha, the cult of which is prevalent in all countries of the Far East.

From a purely logical point of view, one might assume that there is a contradiction between the fundamental teaching, which rejects all cult of the person itself of the Blessed One—the Law alone being regarded as the agent of salvation—and all the other elements which, on the contrary, crystallize around this person, his body, and his name, the spiritual heritage of this cult being predominant in Northern Buddhism. Both points of view, however, are equally legitimate for if it is true that logically the Message takes precedence over the Messenger, it is also true that the latter can be identified with the former and that the very instrument of the Revelation possesses the salvific virtue of the Message; that said, a certain relative opposition between two complementary dimensions of one and the same truth is in the nature of things. Here one will recall the following saying of Christ: "It is expedient for you that I go away", and the fact that neither the Eucha-

---

[1] The *Gītā Govinda* of Jayadeva, an orthodox Hindu text, says of the Buddha: "Through pity (for living beings), thou hast not observed the Vedic prescriptions for (blood) sacrifice, when thou sawest how the animals were killed; Keshava (Vishnu), Thou within the body of the Buddha, Thou art victorious, Hari (Vishnu), Lord of the universe!" Seen from this standpoint, the Buddha's message makes one think of the abolition of human sacrifice by Abraham, if one may express it thus; but the basis of the idea here is that Buddhism comprises a message of mercy or "non-violence" (*ahimsā*) and this is the aspect by which Hinduism can "situate" it.

ristic sacrifice nor the descent of the Holy Spirit would be conceivable without the departure of Jesus; what we wish to say is that the Buddha while still living on earth may reject all personalism, but that the Buddha once "departed" must be all the more "present"; henceforth the Law and the Person, the Message and the Messenger are one.

To understand the teaching of the Buddha the following must be borne in mind: that this perspective is based *a priori* on the concrete fact of human experience in general, namely under its most immediate and tangible aspect, while leaving out provisorily every element that does not enter directly into that experience; now the Buddha, as spokesman of this perspective, could not exteriorize his own salvific nature on the very plane of a Law which, by the logic of things, confers the entire initiative of Deliverance onto man himself.[2] This salvific nature is evident, since there must be a sufficient cause to account for the fact that it is he, Shakyamuni, and not just any other man, who found the opening leading out of the karmic wheel of births and deaths—or rather that particular opening which is specifically Buddhist and which alone is in question here—and that it is he alone who "has broken his existence like a breastplate"; and this uniqueness of function or miracle—which, not being its content, must at first efface itself before the Law—had to, in its turn and in its own nature, assert itself in its quality as divine gift; and this it did, firstly under the form of the monastic initiation[3] and then through the final sermons.[4] These sermons are distinctly different from those embodying the Law; they reveal the metaphysics of the Void, which will subsequently take on a doctrinal aspect with Nagarjuna and a purely "experimental"

---

[2] In an analogous way, did Christ not say: "God alone is good", and did he not pray, like a mere mortal, despite his divinity? Did he not at first restrict his Message just to the people of Israel? For anyone who knows Christianity, there is no difficulty here—any more than in the fact that Christ was baptized and that he fasted. But a certain logical contradiction nonetheless remains, and a Buddhist could draw an argument from it, were he interested in doing so, as a Christian could, conversely, make something of the "Buddhist contradiction" in order to deny the supernatural character of Buddhism; the fact that, contrary to what happened with the Buddha, Christ declared his divinity and even made it the pillar of his Message, only accentuates certain difficulties, at least from a very outward point of view.

[3] This obviously presupposes an initiatic power and consequently a "divine nature".

[4] It should not be forgotten that some of these Scriptures belong not only to the *Mahāyāna*, but also to *Theravāda* Buddhism.

aspect with the school of *Dhyāna* or Zen, whose great initiator was Bodhidharma; meanwhile, the "Flower Sermon", a silent gesture, is obviously independent of any written doctrine. Yet another expression of the "personal reality" of the Buddha is the saving invocation of the name of Amitabha, and lastly, as we have said, the sacramental image of the *Tathāgata*, true "manifestation of the Void" (*shūnyamūrti*) and "expression of the inexpressible". All these elements derive from the aspect we have called—to distinguish it from his general and more or less "outward" doctrine—the Buddha's being.

— ·:· —

The "Great Vehicle" (*Mahāyāna* Buddhism) possesses a mysterious dimension known as the "Adamantine Vehicle" (*Vajrayāna*); in order to grasp its meaning, one has first to understand what we have termed at various times the "metaphysical transparency of the world", that is to say one has to base oneself on a perspective according to which—to quote an expression of Pascal's we are particularly fond of—Reality is "an infinite sphere whose center is everywhere and its circumference nowhere": it is this "circumference" and this "center" that are represented, in the adamantine doctrine, by the Buddha Mahavairochana (in Japanese Dainichi Nyorai)[5] who is at one and the same time—in Vedantic terms—*Ātmā*, *Īshvara*, and *Buddhi*; that is to say Supraontological Essence, Ontological Essence, and Universal Intellect. This metaphysical transparency restores everywhere the effect back to the Cause without, however, doing away with the irreversibility of the causal relationship; the Absolute is in nowise causal in itself, since in reality nothing can be outside It, but it is causal from the point of view of the cosmos that is real only as effect, and in virtue of the metaphysical reduction of the effect to the Cause; hence "all is *Ātmā*", or all is *Shūnya* ("Void") or Vairochana—or "solarity" if we bear in mind the etymology as well as the symbolism of this Sanskrit name—but no thing is in itself, in its accidentality, the "Self" or the "Void" or the "solar Buddha".

---

[5] The Japanese heir to this current is *Shingon*—founded by the illustrious Kobo Daishi, one of the fathers of Japanese civilization—and also *Tendai*, whose founder was Dengyo Daishi.

We may specify what the structure of this metaphysical "vision" is through recourse to the following symbol: the spider's web, formed of warp and weft threads—or of radii and concentric circles—represents the Universe under the twofold relationship of essential identity and existential separation; the synthesis of these two relationships will be indicated by the spiral. From the point of view of the radii, a given thing "is" the Principle; from the point of view of the concentric circles, a given thing only "represents" It; from the point of view of the spiral, however, we shall say that a given thing is an "emanation" or "manifestation", therefore that it is neither the Principle as such nor simply an image of It. *Grosso modo*, it can be said that the "West"—namely European philosophy and Semitic exoterism—is attached more to the second relationship, that of concentric circles and of existential discontinuity or separation, whereas the "East"— namely Semitic esoterism and Asian metaphysics—will prefer the first relationship, that of radii and identity of essence, therefore of "metaphysical transparency". It is an error—inevitable in exoterism[6]—to believe that "creation" is an absolutely closed and quasi-autonomous system; that it is "absolutely creation" in the same way God is "absolutely God"; God is "absolutely Himself", but the world is only "relatively world" because, while there is a "relatively absolute", there can never be, conversely, an "absolutely relative"; it is true that creation "as such" is entirely created, but precisely these words "as such" neither exhaust all its nature nor explain its possibility. But to return to the spider and its symbolism: this, with the solar form of its web, evokes Being—or the Self—which draws forth the cosmos from itself and "eats" the beings found within it; "deification" means to be assimilated by God.

The great truth—or the great experience—the *Vajrayāna* represents is to show that each thing, each energy, by the very fact that it exists—and that, in existing, it is "something" of That which makes it exist—constitutes a possible "entry" towards the Real and Deliverance; "universal Buddhahood" implies that each consciousness, being essentially Buddha, can "become That which it is". If one may define esoterism as a "shortcut" not within reach of every mental structure or every degree of intellectual scope, the "Adamantine Vehicle", with

---

[6] That is to say, exoterism cannot avoid choosing a "lesser truth" in view of a "lesser evil".

its perspective of "ubiquity" and its quasi-theurgic method of *mantra*, provides a particularly convincing example of what constitutes an esoteric method.

In connection with this, it is worth recalling here a highly suggestive comparison once made to the author by a Japanese Buddhist: the sound of Christian bells, so he told us, draws man upwards and takes him out of the world; but the heavy and deep sound of the Buddhist bell leaves us motionless, making us descend into ourselves, into our supra-personal Center. There is in this an instructive confrontation of two "spiritual rhythms" which, however, has nothing exclusive about it: on the one side there is "dynamic elevation", sublimation of "becoming", while on the other there is "static profundity", essence of "being".

The Question of Illusion

The idea of "universal illusion" or the "unreality" of the world, of *Māyā*, constitutes something like an insurmountable barrier between Western "personalism" and Oriental metaphysics: Hindus are reproached either for denying the world or, on the contrary, for identifying the world with God, and Buddhists are blamed for denying the soul—as if *Nirvāna* were not the prototype of the soul and its summit. But in so doing the would-be critics do not ask themselves what part is played in all this by the contingent aspect of terminology; all too often discussion begins about attributes before there has been any agreement about the things themselves. Buddhists deny the "soul", it is said, and yet they essentially admit the "karmic" continuity—or, if one prefers, the moral causality—of that living and conscious nucleus that is the ego.

Individuation occurs to the degree that the motion of the cosmic wheel is rapid: just as water when agitated becomes dispersed into innumerable drops, so likewise the Self becomes segmented as it were—but in illusory mode and without being thereby affected in its immutability—into innumerable particular subjects: the current of forms becomes the cascade of souls. The current of forms is at once motion and division; there where the rotation of the cosmic wheel takes place, there also occurs the dispersal of souls, namely individuation with its countless modalities; the ego is a quasi-"physical" consequence of this universal rotation. Where there is calm, there also is access to the immutable and indivisible Self; there where the center is, there Unity is. And as the cosmic wheel is "not other" than the Self, on pain of non-existence, so also the Self can emerge everywhere as a saving miracle.

The very "absurdity" of the plurality of "egos" proves that this cannot be other than a question of an "optical illusion" on the macro-cosmic scale, of an existential disequilibrium which, as such, cannot continue indefinitely; each ego is a flagrant contradiction, a "scandal" that reason butts up against just as it does against the "finite infinity" of time and space. The empirical "I" is nothing but a shifting web of images and tendencies; when the ego of an individual at eight years old is compared with the ego of the same individual at eighty years of age one may well ask oneself where the real "I" is; and if a man could live for a thousand years, what would remain of that which was his

"I" in the first century of his life? Beings and events would flee about him like leaves scattered by the wind, the sky itself would end by becoming a crushing burden, his body would be like a coffin—unless this man were to surmount his ego and thereby perceive the Face of God in all things, like a new sky whose infinity stabilizes and liberates; but then this very world would no longer be "of this world" for that man; it would be a kind of hereafter. Man becomes attached to his scanty memories because he confuses these in practice with his own self, as if there were not to be found outside him, and before and after him, impressions, destinies, and memories fairer or richer than his own and to which he will never have access; and as if a mental image, whatever its value, could forever be identified with one's immortal personality. Man is incapable of viewing an object from all sides at once or under all its aspects; it is impossible for him to enjoy at the same time every aspect of a precious thing or of a beloved being; in carnal ecstasy, the creature can no longer enjoy any visual perception of form, and this is an impoverishment even while foreshadowing the extinction of the soul in God. Bliss is possible only beyond all those formal crystallizations to which passion clings; this is why in earthly pleasure one thing excludes another, why all is measured out in space and time, and why one happiness always implies the forgetting, if one may so put it, of a thousand other possible happinesses.

The foregoing considerations bring us closer to the Buddhist— and the Vedantic—idea of the non-reality of the world;[1] so as to render this idea more familiar, we can appeal to a certain imaginative power by posing the question in reverse: what then is the meaning of the common belief that the world is real, absolutely real? How can one—without the slightest attenuation of meaning—term "real" phenomena that are reduced to almost nothing, not in their immediate surroundings of course, but as soon as space and time are considered in their fullest extension? No one denies the relative reality of a given tree, a fleck of foam, a dream; but what does that tree represent on

[1] Sufism, as is known, comprises the same doctrine, as is borne witness to by this passage of the *Gulshan i Raz* of Mahmud Shabistari: "The world is an imaginary form, a diffused shadow of the Infinite . . . the imagination produces objective phenomena having no real existence; in the same way, this world has no substantial reality, but is only a play of shadows or a game. All is penetrated by absolute Being, in its infinite perfection. There are many numbers, but only One alone counts. . . . The house has been left empty, except for the Truth, because the world disappeared in an instant."

the scale of the galaxies and what does its brief life mean, even if it lasts for centuries, in relation to geological periods that themselves, in their turn, are reducible to mere instants? What is the reality of a tiny drop of water beside the ocean and its thousands of years of existence? People will no doubt retort that all the world knows in some way that time is relative, but that is not the question, for there is knowledge and then there is knowledge: who then can concretely "experience" both the simultaneity and the evanescence of things, to the point of being able to transcend himself and thus grasp the quasi-dreamlike character of the current of forms? But there is also ignorance on the plane of naturally simultaneous things, that is to say the inability of most men to "be" the others, to as it were live two lives, or all lives at once: if man feels so much at ease within his limits, this is because his imagination does not allow him to be conscious of what is happening to other people, on other continents, in other spiritual worlds; in fact, a lack of imagination is for many people a condition of happiness since it helps to confer that easy assurance that most men need in order to feel happy, failing a happiness of a higher order gained on the ruins of a previous equilibrium; it might almost be said that man needs errors in order to be able to sleep peacefully.

The Divine Intellect, being free of all infirmity, knows things both in their succession and in their simultaneity: it beholds the logical unfolding of things as well as their overall possibility; knowing the substances, it knows *ipso facto* the accidents, at the level of reality—or unreality—that is theirs. Some man in the Middle Ages is walking in some town and thinks he is living "at this present moment", in which supposition he is of course not more deceived than we ourselves are; now if that man, while crossing his street, thinks deeply of God, he will immediately shed the aspect of temporal and spatial illusion that separated him from us; the street, in its false "actuality", no longer limits him; he has stepped out of the deceptive instantaneity of his corporeal, spatial, and psychological situation; in thinking of God he is at our side, and not only that: he is everywhere, at the side of all men, in all worlds; he is in a sense wherever one has thought of the Absolute[2] and wherever it will be thought of; and maintaining himself

---

[2] This could refer to an "Absolute" still relative in itself, but this "relative Absolute"—which is creative and saving Being—is absolute in relation to man as such; it is relative only *in divinis* and in the Intellect.

thus in the center, he is like a witness of all things; any question of unconsciousness—or of "lack of imagination"—no longer counts then, for it is as if he were endowed with a consciousness of everything from the moment that his mind is directed on the divine Void and thereby becomes situated at the center of space and time.

But there is not only the question of the unreality of the cosmos; there is also the question of its relative reality, therefore of the identity of essence—a mysterious and almost ineffable identity—between manifestation and the Principle, or between symbols and their Prototype; in "such and such" a light or "such and such" an intelligence, we encounter Light or Intelligence "as such", therefore all the light and intelligence "that is"—the term "such and such" expressing first particularity or accidentality, then expressing, in the formulation "as such", essence or reality, the divine "Suchness". That which is not different is identical; the world—macrocosm or microcosm—is "neither divine nor non-divine", or it possesses both qualities at once. Formulations of this kind, apparently simplistic or even unreasonable—as commonly happens with antinomic expressions—require more than simple logic for their understanding, they call into play that which is most mysterious in the intelligence, according to the saying: "He (God) set his eye upon their hearts to shew them the greatness of his works" (Ecclesiasticus 17:8).

Before proceeding further, we would like to allow ourselves a brief digression. The common illusion of an "absolutely real" within relativity gives rise to philosophical sophistries and in particular engenders an empiricist and experimental science wishing to unveil the metaphysical mystery of Existence;[3] those who seek to enclose the Universe within their shortsighted logic fail to see, at least in principle, that the sum of possible phenomenal knowledge is inexhaustible and,

---

[3] With the aid of giant telescopes and electronic microscopes, if need be. Goethe, when he refused to look through a microscope because he did not wish to wrench from Nature what she is unwilling to offer to our human senses, displayed a most just intuition of the limits of all natural science, and at the same time the limits of what is human.

consequently, that present "scientific" knowledge represents a total nothingness beside our ignorance—in short that "there are more things in heaven and earth than are dreamt of in your philosophy" (Shakespeare) and that in order to extend our means of investigation to fit the scale of the total cosmos, we would have to begin by multiplying our human senses in mathematical progression, which brings us back to the limitless, therefore to the inaccessible and the unknowable. In all this desire to accumulate knowledge of relative things, the metaphysical dimension—which alone takes us out of the *circulus vitiosus* of the phenomenal and the absurd—is expressly put aside; it is as if a man were to be endowed with all possible faculties of perception minus intelligence; or again, it is as if one believed that an animal endowed with sight was more capable than a blind man of understanding the mysteries of the world. The science of our time knows how to measure galaxies and split atoms, but it is incapable of the least investigation extending beyond the sensible world, so much so that outside its self-imposed limits, but without recognizing those very limits, it remains more ignorant than the most rudimentary magic. It will doubtless be objected that modern psychology, for its part, is not a science riveted to matter, but this plea misses the merely empirical character of that science: it is a system of observations and hypotheses, compromised in advance by the fact that those who practice it are ignorant of the profound nature of the phenomena they endeavor to study. A science, in order to be deserving of that name, owes us an explanation of a certain order of phenomena; now modern science, which claims to be all-embracing by the very fact that it recognizes nothing outside itself as valid, is unable to explain to us, for instance, what a sacred book is, or a saint, or a miracle; it knows nothing of God, or of the hereafter, or of the Intellect, and cannot even tell us anything about phenomena such as premonition or telepathy; it has no idea about the principle or possibility by which shamanistic procedures may cure illnesses or attract rain.[4] All of modern science's

---

[4] There is a singular irony in the indignation of those who consider that belief in sorcerers and ghosts is incompatible with the science of the "atomic age", whereas this age is precisely—and utterly—ignorant of the meaning of said "beliefs". Only that which can be verified "with laboratory clarity" is held to be true, as if it were logical and objective to demand, in the name of truth, conditions that may be contrary to the nature of things, and as if it were a proof of being endowed with imagination to deny the very possibility of such incompatibilities.

attempts at explanations regarding things of this order are impaired at their very base by a kind of error of imagination: everything is seen in terms, firstly, of empirical "matter"—even when defined by some other name—and, secondly, of the evolutionist hypothesis; instead of conceiving before all else the principial and "descending" emanation of "ideas" and the progressive coagulation of substances[5]—in conformity with the principle of individuation, on the one hand, and of demiurgic "solidification", on the other—one tries to explain "horizontally" that which is explainable only "in a vertical sense"; it is as though we were living in an ice world where water was unknown and where only the Revelations mentioned it, whereas profane science would deny its existence. Such a science is assuredly fitted to the measure of modern man who conceived it and who is at the same time its "product"; like him, it implicitly claims a sort of "immunity" or "extra-territoriality" in the face of the Absolute; and like him, this science finds itself cut off from any cosmic or eschatological context.

We would like to add to the above considerations the following: science—like the machine—has inverted the roles by turning its creators into its own creatures; it escapes the control of intelligence as such the moment it claims to define the nature of intelligence "from the outside" and "from below". Our timeless cosmic environment has been deprived of its instructive function now that it has been replaced with a "backstage setting"; the stellar vault has been turned into the extension of a laboratory, bodily beauty is reduced to the mechanism of natural selection. People no longer sense the fact that the quantitative wealth of a knowledge—of any kind of knowledge—leads necessarily to an inward impoverishment, unless accompanied by a spiritual science that re-establishes unity and preserves equilibrium; the average person, if he were able to travel through interplanetary space, would come back to earth drastically impoverished, or with his reason stricken by sheer terror. This brings us back to the forbidden tree of Genesis, the drama of which is repeated at wide intervals down to our own times; "decentralized" man, whose mind is oversaturated with discontinuous facts, is appallingly destitute, which explains

---

[5] When the *philosophia perennis* says "Principle, emanation, substance", modern science will say "energy, matter, evolution". As far as emanation is concerned, it is necessary to stress its principial and discontinuous character: emanation "takes nothing away" from the Principle: the world is not a "part" of God.

moreover all the nihilistic and anguished philosophies so prevalent in our epoch. The ancients no doubt did not know how to prolong lives despite the fact that they had a meaning; the moderns know how to prolong lives that have none; but the ancients, by the very fact that they gave a meaning to life, also gave one to death. If life is but a faint glow between two nights or two naughts, and if we are only meaningless biological accidents in an absurd universe, what then is the use of all these efforts and, more especially, what is the use of this scientistic faith that is even more absurd than the senseless universe that men explore with no hope of exiting? And of what profit to us are accurate observations if in fact—for in principle they are innocent[6]—they deprive us of all that is essential, namely the knowledge of that whereof natural phenomena are but fragile exteriorizations? Far from being unknowable in themselves, these higher realities can be perceived through phenomena, which are metaphysically transparent;[7] but these higher realities also reveal themselves through the great prophetic, messianic, or avataric manifestations that are addressed *a priori* to collective human receptacles in order to communicate to them that which, in fact, these collectivities have become incapable of knowing directly. God, as Intelligence, is like the "absolute Subconscious" of all beings:[8] just as the subconscious of any man, provided it be actualized through some cause, is able to reveal things unknown in space and time, so too does this "absolute Subconscious" reveal to men—through divinely inspired Messages or through the Intellect, as

---

[6] This point must be stressed. No science is evil on account of its contents; but a demonstration of anatomy, possibly very useful to an adult, might ruin a child's soul.

[7] The "solidification" of this perspective leads to idolatry; there are several stages between idolatry and symbolism, some harmless and others dangerous. When idolatry has become a collective attitude, the only way out is through a theology seemingly abstract in its character.

[8] This word is used here provisionally and in a purely extrinsic sense in order to highlight a functional analogy seen "from the outside", for clearly one should be speaking rather of "supra-consciousness" here; the divine Self is infinite Knowledge, whereas the subconscious of the psychologists can be anything at all. The subconscious covers all that of which we are not actively conscious, whether higher realities or psychic complexes; but in fact, what people ordinarily understand by "subconscious" is merely the lower psychism, as is moreover consistent with its etymology whenever *sub* is opposed to *super* or *supra*. If the word "infra-conscious" were a current term, it would serve to indicate, not that of which we are poorly conscious, but rather that which is poorly endowed with consciousness.

the case may be—that which they need and in fact have an infinite need of. This possibility of an actualization of the universal "Subconscious" is given by the very nature of the human species, and in this sense it can be asserted that the mere existence of religions proves both the Absolute and immortality, although this is but a manner of speaking, since a "proof" of the Absolute can never be more than an indication; a metaphysical argument triggers intellection or actualizes a pre-existing and immanent "remembrance", which is to say that one cannot prove the Absolute outside itself, and also that one cannot prove the existence of light to blind men.

Modern science blithely rejects the different traditional wisdoms without being aware of the fact that this rejection takes no account of the impossible disproportion between the intelligence of the believers, on the one hand, and the hypothetical absurdity of their beliefs, on the other; or that this rejection goes against the no less impossible disproportion between the intelligence of the sages and the supposed absurdity of their convictions and their innermost motives. Man is intelligence, and therefore he is wisdom and contemplation, and consequently tradition; to detach man from tradition, far from rendering him independent, is to dehumanize him.

In an analogous vein of thought, we would like to answer here the following question: why did Providence leave man in ignorance of certain things—on the plane of the sensible world—which he was bound to discover in the long run? For if "an ounce of prevention is worth a pound of cure" then Heaven could not but foresee the disastrous repercussions—material as well as psychological—of modern discoveries and inventions; Heaven had therefore every interest in speaking to man about paleontology and molecular physics, and to situate these things in relation to the Absolute and immortality. The chief answer— and moreover we have already provided it, we believe—is that it sufficed that Revelation, always concerned with "the one thing needful" and conscious of the uselessness and harmfulness of a purely outward and quantitative knowledge, would not provide the example of what it wished to avoid, or the advent of what at least it wished to delay; but there is yet another reason to be considered, one that is no doubt less fundamental but no less plausible from our point of view: it was indeed necessary—since "it must needs be that offences come"—that the men of the "latter times" should find in their surroundings reasons for believing themselves superior to their ancestors and too intelligent

for Revelation; consequently it was necessary to save for later a possible form of knowledge—but one that is a matter of spiritual indifference—which would corroborate and feed the illusions of the Dark
Age, the age when the Law of the Buddha shall be "forgotten", after
having been "imitated" in the preceding age. All this refers, in short,
to this saying of the Buddha, which we repeat from memory: "And
why have I taught you nothing about the world? Because this would
be of no use to you for the knowledge of the causes of suffering, for
the cessation of suffering, for *Nirvāna.*"

Buddhism produces a decisive argument against any science pur-
porting to be an end in itself and therefore—by principal anticipation—against contemporary Western scientism: namely that the fact
of becoming "objectively" preoccupied with the phenomenal world
inevitably draws man into a quagmire of conjectures and illusions and
therefore away from Deliverance; hence, the wish for "exactitude"
professed by this science[9] is far from constituting a guarantee of
intrinsic value and spiritual legitimacy. "They do not understand that
the objective world derives from the Spirit itself" (the Universal Intellect)—says the *Lankāvatāra Sūtra*—"and do not grasp that the whole
system of thought likewise derives from the Spirit; but, in attributing
reality to these manifestations of the Spirit, they examine them, senseless people that they are, and become attached to dualities such as: this
and that or to be and not to be—without realizing that there is but a
single Essence."

---

[9] The "exactitude" in question is jeopardized in advance by the most monstrous beg-
ging of the question: scientism, by denying the Intellect and the Absolute, rejects the
measure of all knowledge.

Cosmological and Eschatological Viewpoints

Between the Hindu and Buddhist cosmologies, there are significant divergences: the *kalpas*, *manvantaras*, and *mahāyugas* of Hinduism are replaced in Buddhism by *mahākalpas*, *asankhyeyas*, and *antarakalpas*, that is to say by altogether different cyclic divisions;[1] the Buddhist conception, as compared with the Hindu, seems to be determined by a perspective that is in some way dynamic; it is as if one were comparing a spiral, which is "in motion", with a system of squares or triangles, which are static. But our intention here is not so much to enter into the details of analogies and divergences as to take the opportunity of developing a few considerations of principle regarding the eschatologies and their profound concordances. If religious doctrines about the universe and the hereafter can differ so much between themselves, this is due, on the one hand, to the diversity of viewpoints and aspects,[2] therefore of positions both subjective and objective and, on the other hand, because one is dealing here with a realm that is impossible to describe exhaustively in human language; but total truth is nevertheless one. The macrocosm—the totality of worlds and cosmic cycles—is an inexhaustible realm, in keeping with the indeterminate nature of universal Substance; therefore it cannot become the object of any scientific investigation claiming to lead to a polyvalent and definitive result; in other words, the macrocosm is neither our visible world, nor is it God: we can know creation and the Creator, or the "I" and the "Self"—with all the appropriate reservations and conditions, depending on the case—but it is not possible for us to know the totality of the phenomena of the Universe because it cannot be grasped either by the mind, which is above all made for knowing our world, or by the Intellect, which is above all made for knowing the

---

[1] For example, the year can be divided into twelve months, but it can also be divided into four seasons or fifty-two weeks, or again into 365 days, without any of these divisions being wrong. The Sanskrit terms just cited denote quasi-incalculable cyclic periods.

[2] In a certain respect, each religion is right versus all the others, otherwise exoterism would be no more than a snare; but precisely, exoterism cannot by definition be aware of the "relationship" which, at one and the same time, justifies and yet limits it.

Absolute.³ Consequently, man has to content himself with fragmentary insights, or with symbolic syntheses and elliptical formulations that will never satisfy every type of curiosity and that it would be vain to wish to complete by means of logical operations that are inevitably pre-condemned to failure; for, let it be said once again, the indefinitely diverse—or inconceivably complex—is not the normal and ultimate content of human intelligence.⁴ Many of the contradictions found in sacred texts only serve in reality to circumscribe indirectly things that in fact are indescribable; if Heaven does not hesitate to use language that seems absurd, this is because absurdity—which is unavoidable in the case we are considering—is nonetheless able to convey fragmentary but indispensable indications concerning the interlinking series of worlds and cycles, and even much more than this.

Be that as it may, it is certainly not venturing too far in this domain to confine oneself to schematic viewpoints and to point out, for example, that the various traditional notions of cosmology and eschatology—creation or manifestation, flood, last judgment, resurrection of the body, renewal of the world, heavens and hells, transmigration, cosmic days and nights, and so forth—refer to the universal rhythms or, if one may so put it, to the "breathing of the Self", together with all the principal and secondary phases of affirmation and negation, "exteriorization" and "interiorization", "projection" and "reintegration", comprised in these rhythms. The origin and likewise the end of the world, of matter, of life—already hard enough to express in the symbolical language of the traditional doctrines—are inaccessible, *a fortiori* and in an absolute sense, to the investigations of a science that is purely rational and experimental; the error of such a science is precisely that it lends to matter a fixed character and makes of it an unvarying basis,⁵ when in fact physical substance—in its "current" and "post-

---

³ It is for reasons of this order that no one can know the "moment" of the end of the world, and that no calculation, even one established on serious bases, can lead to anything close to a precise result.

⁴ This is not unrelated to the Islamic idea that the seat of the devil is situated—subjectively, not objectively—between man and God, that is to say in the imagination which, like the *Saṃsāra*, is "shifting" and indefinite.

⁵ Some will no doubt object that modern physics is perfectly prepared to admit the variability and evolution of matter-energy, or rather, that it has gotten beyond the naive notion of "matter", replacing it with "motion"—or with the ternary "mass-space-time"—but this means nothing, since this same physics does not accept either the non-material or the supra-sensible.

Edenic" state—is in reality but a kind of "accidental" crystallization of "subtle" substance (the *sukshma sharīra* of the Hindus); whatever its consistency or its quality, it is nothing other than the extreme limit or ultimate "point of precipitation"—for our sensible world—of the demiurgic process of manifestation. The Universe is woven of "worlds" and "cycles"; outside our human cosmos, space and time stop, or rather they are replaced by other conditions of existence—analogous conditions no doubt, since Existence is one, but unimaginable for us.

The human microcosm is like a circle, the center of which is situated on the circumference of a larger circle, namely the sensible macrocosm, and the center of this second circle in its turn is situated on a still larger circumference, representing the total Macrocosm. A cosmos or a cycle is essentially something that becomes and that ceases to be; for man, there are three cosmoses or cycles to consider, namely firstly the soul, then the world, which is its medium of manifestation, and finally the Universe, of which this world represents but a minute fragment. The difference between the "particular judgment" and the "Last Judgment", or between death and the end of the world, consists in the fact that at the time of death only the soul—and not the body, which belongs to our own world—is reabsorbed in the direction of the Principle in order to be "judged", whereas at the time of this world's ending it is the world itself that is thus reabsorbed; but there is yet a third and ultimate reabsorption that takes place, the one marking the end of all manifestation: for the "elect", this is not an ending but an exaltation in the "uncreated Light."[6]

Concerning the remembrance Buddhas have of their "past lives", it is important not to lose sight of the fact that the Buddha possesses or encompasses all destinies; furthermore, it must not be forgotten when considering the innumerable "incarnations" of the same soul—or to be more precise, of the same "karmic" nexus—that the chances of attaining Deliverance are very slight in the majority of states to be traversed; the Christian concept of "limbo"—or of the "existential state" of the dead before Christ's coming and outside his fold—is like a symbolical expression of the same idea. In order to understand well the differences in language of traditional doctrines, it is necessary to take

---

[6] In Hindu terms, this is the *mahāpralaya*, the great return into undifferentiation—*pralaya* being this return when applied to our world alone—and doubtless such is also the meaning of the apocatastasis of Western Antiquity and of certain gnostics.

account of the following: a perspective centered on the Absolute, and therefore belonging to pure intellectual contemplation, will tend to emphasize the relativity of the cosmos, whence doctrines such as that of transmigration; whereas a perspective that considers the Absolute in relation to man and that consequently "humanizes" it—in which case it will be a question not of the pure Absolute but of Being—will readily attribute an absolute character to certain relativities, doubtless marked by the Absolute but nonetheless belonging to the cosmic order. By a paradoxical compensation, the directly metaphysical perspective will sometimes seem to erase the "hiatus" between the Absolute and the relative, whereas the cosmological and religious perspective will, on the contrary, appear to maintain the "purity" and "transcendence" of the Divine, even while "relativizing" it, and even while affirming the "compact" reality of the cosmos.

From the monotheistic and Western point of view it may seem strange that Buddhism—as also Hinduism—takes only scant account of the possibility of obtaining what the Confucio-Taoist tradition calls the state of "longevity"; the explanation lies in the fact that these perspectives, being metaphysical and not "humanist", envisage Deliverance primarily outside of any and every world; thus they start out from the alternative "Existence-Deliverance" and not, as in the Judeo-Western perspectives, from the alternative "damnation-salvation". In other words, they have no interest *a priori* in "individualistic" solutions; they do not wish to compromise Deliverance by lingering over solutions that still pertain to the realm of *Māyā*, although in a secondary way they do in fact admit such solutions, for example in the case of Vishnuism or of Amidism; but in the present context it is the general and determining form of the doctrine that is at issue. As far as Judeo-Western monotheists are concerned, the apparent absurdity of their eschatology[7] can be explained precisely by a wish to concentrate all of man's energy on his immediate final ends—therefore without exiting the human sphere—and so as not to paralyze man's efforts by raising considerations that are in fact inopportune, given the psychological conditions of the sector of humanity in question; there is always to be found, both in the insistences as well as in the silences of the traditional teachings, an initial concern for steering man in the

---

[7] Eternal heavens and hells; creatures—and states—having a beginning but no end; relative acts having absolute consequences, and so on.

direction—and with the means—best suited to his nature, be it only at the starting point.

Human logic derives from Divine Wisdom and not inversely; "divine logic" may therefore follow "procedures" that totally elude man's ordinary understanding; the differences between religions—irreconcilable outwardly—provide examples of this that are even more disconcerting than any of the apparent inconsistencies within the same sacred text. The "mythological" wording of a traditional perspective is essentially determined by a spiritual and social interest, which coincides in the end—and by definition—with the truth; the sacred wording "contains" in its own way the infinite Truth, otherwise it could not serve any interest concerning it.

We have seen that the various eschatologies, whether Buddhist or Judeo-Christian or other, can never entirely accommodate their contents to human understanding. For example, "it must needs be that offences come", but nevertheless "woe unto that man by whom the offence cometh": this cannot be solved by ordinary logic, which is incapable of reconciling antinomic realities for much the same reason as the eye is incapable of fixing its gaze on two different planes at once; but this fact does not warrant our denying that our own limitations exist or claiming that Revelation is wrong, for even the physical realm displays examples of antinomies that are rationally insurmountable. We do not have much choice but to believe that space and time are limitless—for it is contradictory to posit a spatial limit to extension or a temporal limit to duration—yet it is impossible for us to picture this; and the fact that we can conceive of this intellectually—or are able to represent to ourselves a situation in which, after traversing all space, supposing this were feasible, we would return in the end to our point of departure—solves nothing from the viewpoint of concrete imagination.[8] Thus on the physical plane, and despite our incapacity to

---

[8] Space is "round", therefore it is limited, but not spatially so; it would be impossible to reach its outermost limits otherwise than in an indirect way, given the fact that our faculties of sensation cannot under any circumstances step outside the spatial condition. As for time, it is "spiroidal" and irreversible, whence its cyclical rhythm.

"understand" it in an immediate manner, we can "believe" something that is apparently absurd—because the absence of a limit regarding a dimension that in itself is measurable is an absurdity—since the very elements of the problem oblige us to such conclusions; but if such is true of the physical realm, then by what right will we summarily deny the apparent contradictions in the metaphysical realm as propounded by Revelation? We must resign ourselves to recognizing that human reason has its limits, just like our faculties of sensation, which are the first to commit inconsistencies;[9] as for the pure Intellect, which escapes these limits "from within",[10] it allows us to grasp the "limited limitlessness" of space and time and the internal homogeneity of the universal antinomies, but it does not allow us to "see" these things, that is to assimilate them humanly, so to speak; for man as such, Existence will always comprise an element of "scandal" or mystery. Once again, the enigmas of the holy Scriptures are neither any the less understandable nor any the more absurd for the rational mind than is the absence of limitation characterizing the existential conditions in which we live; the antinomy between necessity and freedom, or between ontological "good" and the "evil" that results from it as an incidental consequence, is encountered in all the traditional doctrines.

Now, if we start out from the idea that, metaphysically speaking, there is no "evil" properly so called and that all is simply a question of function or aspect, we shall then have to specify: an evil being is a necessary fragment of a good—or an equilibrium—which exceeds this being incommensurably, whereas a good being is himself a good, so that any evil in him is but fragmentary. Evil, then, is the fragment of a good, whereas the good is a totality containing some evil but neutralizing it by its very quality of totality.

One question that gives rise to many difficulties in the consciousness of present-day man is that of damnation, even when rendered less absolute by some obligatory metaphysical reservations: how can a human being merit such a disgrace and what interest can God have in chastisement? The answer is that immortality, whatever its contents—or its risks—is the measure of man's quasi-divine majesty:

[9] They commit them due to the existential prejudice embodied by the ego, the subject.

[10] "Externally", on the plane of formulations, the Intellect inevitably adopts the restrictive boundaries of reasoning and language, and this gives rise to the opinion, radically false, that intellection belongs to the same order as profane "thought".

noblesse oblige. It is, to say the least, strange that those who are the most jealous about their own autonomy, whether real or illusory, wish to be treated like irresponsible people as soon as there is any question of paying the price of their liberty. Man will openly proclaim his freedom and independence in front of Heaven—which reveals norms and gives orders—and consequently, in doing so, he acknowledges his responsibility; yet he declares himself to be irresponsible and throws the blame back onto nature and destiny, hence onto God—"it is not I who created the world"—as soon as Heaven begins to speak of judgment or as soon as there is a question of "concordant reactions", of immanent justice, of *karma*. One thing that should cause men to think—but that pride, using intelligence as an excuse, prevents them from taking into consideration—is the fact that for thousands of years and without undue difficulty, men have accepted the idea of posthumous chastisements, which can be explained by their still having had a sufficiently intact sense of the godlike majesty of the human being; they felt that there is something absolute in man, and also that God knows us better than we know ourselves and therefore that He cannot fail to make due allowance for any real irresponsibility comprised in our nature. But modern man lives beneath himself and would like to impose on Heaven his own arbitrary and convenient evaluation of the human condition; he would like, as Voltaire put it, "to sit under his own fig tree and eat his own bread without asking himself what is in it"; now, in order to do this, there is no need to be a man; any animal achieves as much, effortlessly so. It is our theomorphic nature that dictates our behavior; our real nature is that which God asks of us, or that which, in the sight of the Absolute, is our true destiny. The fact that the best of human beings—to say the least—have never merely "eaten their bread under a fig tree without asking themselves any questions" proves that the Voltairian man is mistaken, that his dream is unrealizable, and that he alone will have to answer for it; because Plato, Virgil, and Saint Augustine have existed, it can no longer be said of man that he is a goat or an ant.

It has been said that modern man has lost the sense of sin;[11] but it should be specified that the kind of attitude in question can best

---

[11] In former times, people might have said, "we are sinners, incapable, lacking"; but today one readily declares that "religion is bankrupt". Where previously a man would have said, "I am not intelligent enough to understand Thomism", today he will say that "Thomism is obsolete". It is the same thing but expressed differently.

be described by saying that man no longer has a sense of his own smallness,[12] or that he has become insensitive to all the violations brought about by the decadence of his nature, in short, that he has become insensitive to the point of being pleased with himself and of no longer having any awareness of the ambiguity of his human condition. The empty shadow of this awareness he calls "anguish", and he hates all those who, still possessing this awareness and accepting the positive consequences this awareness entails, are safe from this "anguish" and are thereby also safe from the risk of "revolt"; and he wants to believe that these two complexes, those of anguish and revolt, are universally shared, because it is in man's nature not to want to go to perdition alone.

Responsibility may be total, but not absolute; this is what explains the intervention of Heaven's Mercy; this Mercy is amply sufficient to satisfy the argument of our fragility. There is a point, however, where man is always entirely responsible: when he refuses Mercy; and nothing more surely brings about a fall into the infernal states than this refusal, which is a distant echo of the pride of Lucifer. Moreover, what really stands in judgment over us is our own norm, which we bear within ourselves and which is an image at once of the whole cosmos and of the divine Spirit shining at its center; the impious man thinks all he has to do in order to escape it is to close his eyes and pretend not to be human, in a word, to live below himself; he does not want to know that to be a man means to pass through the narrow gate, and he refuses the Mercy that wants to open a passageway for him.

The metaphysical importance of Mercy is apparent in the fact that Buddhism, while being non-theistic and thus seeming to abandon man to his own initiative and to the logic of an ineluctable *karma*, nevertheless contains an entire mythology of Pity, if one may so say, and a whole method of prayer and trust referring to it, namely Amidism or the way of Amitabha, a way in which Mercy even takes on, in keeping with its nature, the aspect of a personal and saving Divinity.

---

[12] This does not run counter to what we said a moment ago, for the actual smallness of man is one thing—a smallness of fact, not of right, though relatively "real" because of the Fall—and quite another is the smallness that man attributes artificially to himself and into which he plunges in order to escape the terrors of his own divineness; this whole attitude could well be termed the illusion man has of being able to claim some kind of spiritual "extraterritoriality".

In a certain sense, divine Mercy is the measure of human relativity. The acceptance of Mercy is like the pinnacle of our liberty.

— ∴ —

The considerations that follow do not have a direct relationship with our general subject, but nevertheless can and must find their place here.

Matter, as was pointed out before, is nothing else but the extreme limit or ultimate "point of precipitation" in the process of manifestation, at least for our world; consequently, it is what is "lowest" within the reality that concerns us; but is not this lowest point, one might ask, on the contrary a "consciousness", namely the principle of evil, that very Mara who tempted the Buddha, or Satan who tempted Christ? This difficulty is resolved if one distinguishes in the cosmos two poles, one existential, which is blind and passive, and the other intellectual, therefore conscious and active; matter is the ultimate point of precipitation with respect to the existential pole alone, whereas the intellectual pole gives rise, again at the extreme limit of the process of flight from God, to the "personifiable" force—or that perverted "consciousness"—that is Satan or Mara; in other words, matter is the state of existence most remote from pure Being, and the devil is the state of consciousness most remote from the divine Intellect; and given that this remoteness can only be, on the intellectual plane, subversion or opposition, the intelligence that is most distant from the Absolute will be the one that denies the Absolute as "intelligently", or rather as "consciously", as possible. Existence—the *materia secunda* or *natura naturata*—in drawing away from pure Being becomes both "hardened" and segmented: matter is the "heaviest" and the most discontinuous existence there is, the most "broken"—seen always from the point of view of the human state, for there are other worlds and other limits of manifestation—and Satan is the most subversive, the most perverse intelligence; yet compared with Satan, matter—although both hardened and corrupted—remains innocent. But stupidity should not be confused with Satanism, nor vulgarity with materiality: while there is a consciousness that suffers diminishment through the pole "matter", and this is unintelligence, be it human or otherwise, there is an existence that is enhanced by "intelligence"—if indirectly—and this is the nobility of material substances, whether of noble metals and precious stones or—passing through the vegetable order—of the bodily beauty of living beings. Intelligence, in drawing away from the Self, is not necessarily diabolical, for it can sink passively, becoming diminished but without subversion; and existence, in drawing away from Being, is not exclusively hardness and undifferentiated inertia, it can be accompanied by qualities that bring it near to the pole "Spirit", and in this sense one may assert that the diamond displays more "intelligence" than some stupid man.

Before proceeding further and even at some risk of repetition, let us once again summarize the question of the limitation of matter and of a science that restricts itself to matter, or—what amounts to the same—the question of the reality that lies "behind" the material plane. Modern science is strictly "horizontal" and "linear"; at no point does it extend beyond the plane of sensible manifestation. Magic, for its part, enters into another "dimension", a dimension of "depth", one might say: unlike modern science, it does not restrict itself to reducing the phenomenon of "matter" to "energies" or "movements", which are both equally physical, that is to say, which are comprised within the post-paradisial "solidification" of the terrestrial or spatial substance,[13] but it goes beyond the material shell "in the direction of the inward" by penetrating into the underlying subtle or animic substance—whence its power of "dematerialization" and transformation. Now, this power is denied by official science, which does not see the subtle intermediary realm situated between the contradictory phenomena of magical translocations and metamorphoses. Nor does this science perceive—*a fortiori*—the dimension of "height" anymore than that of "depth", namely the spiritual world, although magic may also be unaware of this dimension; now it is this spiritual dimension that explains theurgy and miracles. Seen from the vantage point of the spiritual dimension, the subtle or animic world, that of magic and spiritist

---

[13] One will find in *Le règne de la quantité et les signes des temps* by René Guénon an explanation of the qualitative inequality between the temporal phases or periods of history; this doctrine is of the highest importance and this no doubt is why it is shunned, with a kind of unerring instinct, by all modernistic proponents of spirituality, both West and East, who evidently have every interest in holding equivocal opinions or in deluding themselves about the possibilities of their epoch since they believe in integral and indefinite progress.

empiricism,[14] is a "shell" in its turn, just as matter is a shell from the standpoint of the subtle world; or rather the subtle substance should be compared to a heavy liquid like blood, and the spiritual or supraformal substance to air or vapor. Metaphysically, it is necessary to add yet another dimension: the "divine dimension"[15] whereof the "spiritual dimension" is but the cosmic reflection or "angelic" emanation.

When speaking of matter, we are well aware that the Buddhist point of view conceives of it in a "subjective" and empirical sense, but this consideration lies outside the question we have been discussing; the fact that matter can interest us as a phenomenon of consciousness is in fact independent of the relatively "objective" content of that phenomenon.

The above considerations—and a few of the following ones—have no direct bearing on the general topic of this chapter; nonetheless, they can and must find their place here.

Much could be said about the close and almost complementary relationship between matter and the ego. The one pole gives rise to the other: matter, in all its heaviness, opacity, and separativity is what individuation, in the end, wanted; a pseudo-Self calls for a pseudo-Being, which in turn determines, attracts, hardens, and dissipates the soul all at once. Pure intelligence transcends both matter and the ego; therefore, to postulate a relationship between intelligence as such and pride is a contradiction in terms: the intellectual element is poles apart from that living and breathing absurdity called "me", as it is also from that blind and mortal coagulation called matter; it is in the very nature of the intellect to correct the "optical illusion" of individuality and to break free from the deceptiveness of earthly things. Intelligence leads us away from matter because it perceives its painful limitations, which presupposes that intelligence not be steeped in those limitations and

---

[14] An empiricism that operates blindly and is equipped with a false doctrine, although this does not prevent phenomena from being real.

[15] Or "nirvanic", from the Buddhist viewpoint. The three "dimensions" we have just described are represented in the most diverse of traditional symbolisms by earth, fire, and light respectively.

therefore that it be entirely itself; and intelligence leads us away from the ego because it is universal, whence its nature devoid of all possible partisanship.

Reason is intelligence that is intrinsically individualized, while passion is intelligence that is intrinsically materialized or sense-bound; we say "intrinsically" because every mental formulation, even when its contents belong to a supra-rational order, amounts to a kind of "individualization", just as every pleasure of the senses, even when entirely non-passional and merely experienced, is in some degree a "materialization" of the soul, a projection into the sensible order. It is true that both reason and passion can turn towards God, but it is not reason that will understand God nor passion that will reach Him: reason must allow itself to be enlightened by the divine Intellect to the point of perceiving its own limits through a direct act of knowledge, and passion must be transmuted, by Mercy, into a supernatural love.

If metaphysically all is "empty", this means that, cosmologically and by way of consequence, all must needs "return to the Void". Is there anything more self-contradictory than this mixture of life and death making up our world? Living death and dying life: here is the whole terrestrial condition and, like all contradictions, it calls for a solution on a superior plane, the very one from which it was issued in the wake of a downward crystallization; by this we mean that matter will have to be reabsorbed into its celestial origin like a wave which, having reached the limit of its expansion, withdraws from the shore; matter must return to pure Life. This image allows one to glimpse what is meant by that "naturally miraculous"[16] transmutation that is the resurrection of the body, where "death is swallowed up in life", as Saint Paul said. This great reabsorption of the sensible world—but not implying the least fusion—will be heralded by cataclysms on a cosmic scale that will be like the cracking of the shell of our existence; matter, by passing through fire, will be "vaporized", not in the physical sense of the word, which would in no way take us out of the

---

[16] The miraculous is that which is due to a direct, hence "vertical", intervention of a heavenly Power, and not to a "horizontal" unfolding of causality. If one extends the notion of "nature" to all that exists, miracles too are "natural", but in that case words would lose all meaning, as it would then be impossible to make the distinction, which is so essential, between blind or unconscious causes and the supra-conscious Cause, the source of all consciousness and of all power. Scientists confuse the miraculous with the unreasonable and the arbitrary.

material domain, but in the sense that it will "decompose" towards the "inward", in the direction of the subtle and principial order and will rejoin, in due course, the protomatter of the terrestrial Paradise, that of the non-evolutive creation of species; death, moreover, is nothing other for the human microcosm than what this same regression is for the macrocosm.[17] In both cases, man has every interest in "being ready";[18] he must be at the level of his new condition, failing which he will be clothed in the very form of his own insufficiency or of his own internal contradiction—or, shall we say, of his "sin"—and his separation from his norm or prototype will then make itself felt as an inextinguishable fire.[19] It is because Adam at the time of the fall was no longer at the level of the paradisial ambience that the state of semi-death that is post-Edenic matter came to be produced; we die because this matter is in itself a substance of death, an accursed substance; our state is something like that of fishes unknowingly enclosed in a block of ice.[20] Revelation is then the ray of Omniscience that

---

[17] This is the distinction between the "particular judgment" and the "general judgment".

[18] "He who dies before he dies, does not die when he dies" (Old German proverb).

[19] "Hypocrisy, arrogance, vanity, fury, insolence, and ignorance belong to him who is born, O Partha, for a demonic destiny" (*Bhagavad Gītā*, XVI, 4). According to Shankara's commentary we are to understand by "hypocrisy" (or ostentation) the claim to be just (without defects); by "arrogance" is meant pride in erudition, wealth, or social status; by "insolence", the affirmation that the blind see, or that the ugly is beautiful, opinions that amount finally to a contempt for truth, a falsification of facts, and the inversion of normal relationships; by "ignorance", is meant a mistaken notion of our duties.

[20] According to a Pali text, the *Agganna Sutta*, the progressive materialization of man and his surroundings is due to the fact that the primordial and "prematerial" men—who used to shine like stars, glided through the air, and fed on Beatitude—began to eat the soil at the time when the terrestrial surface emerged from the waters; this primordial earth was colored, scented, and sweet, but men, by feeding on it, lost their radiance; then it was that the sun and moon appeared, days and nights, therefore also the external light with its alternations and with measurable duration. Later the soil ceased being edible; it was limited to producing edible plants; still later, only a small number of plants could be eaten and man had to nourish himself at the cost of hard work. Passions and vices, and with them adversities, increasingly entered the world. Myths like this one, describing the hardening of the primordial substance—parallel to the hardening of hearts—are found everywhere and constitute, like all the fundamental traditional precepts, a testimony the traces of which are lost in the night of time; this is tantamount to saying that they form part of man himself.

teaches us that this ice is not everything, that there is something else around it and after it, that we are not the ice and that the ice is not us; Omniscience teaches us all this because it is in our nature to learn it, even as it teaches the swallows to fly southwards and the plants to turn towards the light. The religions present inestimable truths in the form of symbols and they have good reason—corroborated by thousands of years' experience—for presenting them in this manner. We cannot exist in opposition to Being nor can we think in opposition to Intelligence; we must tune our rhythms to those of the Infinite. When we breathe, one part of the air is assimilated, another part is rejected; the same is true of the reabsorption of universal manifestation: only that remains with God which conforms to His nature. Everything is finally "breathed in" by the Source of all good—a blazing Source, but ever merciful.

The manifested Universe comprises two rhythms, the one horizontal and the other vertical: the cosmic cycles follow each other in an incommensurable coming and going, but all this coming and going, all this manifestation will disappear in its turn; it will ultimately be "breathed in" by its immutable Cause.

Insights into Zen

The interest in Zen manifested in Western countries results from an understandable reaction against the coarseness and ugliness prevalent in the world today, and also from a certain weariness with concepts judged, rightly or wrongly, to be inoperative, to say nothing of the current philosophical disputes over words; but this interest is all too easily mingled with anti-intellectual and falsely "concretist" tendencies—as was to be expected—which deprive it of all effective value; for it is one thing to place oneself beyond the mental level and it is quite another to remain below that faculty's highest possibilities, while imagining one has "transcended" things about which one does not understand the first word. He who truly transcends verbal formulations will be the first to respect the ones which have shaped his thinking in the first place and to venerate "every word that proceedeth out of the mouth of God". There is a country proverb which says that only the pig overturns its trough after emptying it, and the same moral teaching is to be found in the well-known fable of the fox and the grapes. If Zen is less doctrinaire than other schools, this is because its structure allows it to be so; it owes its continuity to factors that are perfectly rigorous, but not easily grasped from the outside; its silence, laden with mystery, is quite other than a vague and convenient muteness. Zen, precisely owing to its direct and implicit character—marvelously suited to certain possibilities of the Far Eastern soul—presupposes so many conditions by way of a mentality and ambience that the slightest lack in this respect risks compromising the result of any effort, however sincere; moreover, we must not forget that an elite Japanese individual is himself, in many respects, a product of Zen.

But there is also a reverse danger, this time concerning Far Eastern people themselves: followers of Zen in the course of their scholastic and academic contacts with the West find it hard to resist overdoing what is, in a sense, the adogmatic character of their tradition, as if the absence of dogmas bore the same meaning and coloration for a contemplative Asiatic as for a Western agnostic. Similar mistakes of this kind are found in the realm of art, where contemporary "abstract" productions have been confused, in Japan, with works inspired by Tao-Zen, at least as regards their spirit; and one should also mention the confusion made by European psychologists between drawings by insane patients and Buddhist *mandalas*; in this case, just as in the case of "adogmatism", people discover equations between appearances that in reality are poles apart from one another, which is precisely why they are confused.[1]

In an altogether general way, one must be on guard and implacably vigilant about the inclination to reduce the spiritual to the psychic, a practice that has become commonplace, so much so that it characterizes Western interpretations of traditional doctrines. This so-called "psychology of spirituality"—or "psychoanalysis of the sacred"—is the breach through which the mortal virus of modern relativism infiltrates the still living Oriental traditions.[2] Now, even though spirituality is essentially determined by the supra-individual order, there is no question of denying here that it also comprises secondary modalities of a psychic order given that it necessarily engages "all that we are". But a "psychology of the spiritual" is a contradiction in terms that can only end up in the falsification and negation of the Spirit; one might just as well speak of a "biology of truth" and indeed one can be certain that someone has already done so. Similarly, some people confuse the supra-logical with the illogical and inversely, depending on the case; and as soon as a logically impeccable demonstration happens to disturb them in some fashion, these same people will hasten to qualify it as "Aristotelian", or even "Cartesian", in order to emphasize the artificial and outdated character they attribute to it.

---

[1] In an encyclopedia on Japan (*Le Japon illustré*, Paris, 1915) one finds the following sentence intended to comfort Western readers: ". . . This neo-Buddhism has ceased to be an ultra-metaphysical, ascetic, anti-natural religion; it is a kind of lay religion, purely moral, deriving its justification from its national and social advantages." That says it all, nothing is missing! And thank you for the "justification".

[2] According to Jung, the figurative emergence of certain contents of the "collective unconscious" is accompanied empirically, as its psychic complement, by a noumenal sensation of eternity and infinitude; such an assertion insidiously ruins all transcendence and all intellection. According to this theory, it is the collective unconscious—or the subconscious—that is the origin of "individuated" consciousness, for it posits that human intelligence has two components, the reflections of the subconscious on the one hand and the experience of the external world on the other. However, since experience is not in itself intelligence, then intelligence will necessarily have the subconscious for its substance, so that one ends up trying to define the subconscious on the basis of its own ramification; this is the classical contradiction of all subjectivist and relativist philosophy.

Much has been made of the reputed "adogmatism" of the Buddhist teachings; but one has to be extremely circumspect how this thought is to be expressed, for it is pointless to assert—out of contempt for dogmatic forms—things that could never be, or to let oneself be drawn to conclusions that may be quite logical, perhaps, but erected on bases that are false and contrary to reality. We are always astonished with what frivolousness some people, disdaining dogmas for allegedly spiritual reasons, forget to consult tradition concerning a given order of possibilities, while blithely claiming for example that their little personal recipe is going to inaugurate at long last a better world where everyone will be happy, however steeped in illusion they may be, while overlooking the fact that no less than the Buddha himself did not succeed in accomplishing this, even supposing he might have wished to; one finds here, apart from the sheer inanity of such a project, a fundamental ignorance regarding the qualitative differences between historical phases; this is to say that people wish to invent rules about things situated in the universe without having the least notion of the laws governing it, and with a total contempt for the traditions revealing those laws. "Adogmatism" applies in reality only to the mental crystallizations of partial truths but confers no *carte blanche* at all against Truth as such: although closing the door against any fixation of half-truths, it opens no door to error. Modernizing spiritual seekers, however, take advantage of this "adogmatism" as a license to do anything they please,[3] and do so in the name of a tradition to which they remain paradoxically attached out of atavism, or out of sentimentality, or simply out of lack of imagination.

---

[3] According to the *Lankāvatāra Sūtra*, the being who has entered into the state of a Buddha accomplishes mysterious actions which are "impossible to conceive" (*achintya*) and which are "carried out without purpose" and "outside any feeling of usefulness" (*anābhoga-charyā*); this statement is at the opposite end of a utilitarian, if not materialistic and democratic Neo-Buddhism. Like other men, a Buddhist can certainly busy himself with some useful activity that either good or bad circumstances may warrant, but he will do so only on condition of not forgetting that outward activities have in themselves no connection to Buddhahood and Reality, and that they are not situated outside the *Samsāra*, nor forgetting that these activities cannot counter illusion; and above all he will do so on condition of not claiming to add anything whatsoever to tradition or to sanctity, as if these had been lacking in some essential quality that at long last has been discovered thanks to Kant or Rousseau after countless centuries of inadequacy. Relativities cannot be grafted onto what is absolute.

—— .:. ——

Since we have been speaking about Zen, it will be appropriate to add a few words about the mysterious practice conventionally known as the "cult of tea". Contrary to the opinion of some "specialists" who take their wishes for realities and for whom the norm is situated in decadence and in flattening everything, certain Japanese followers of Zen have told us that the tea ceremony contains on the contrary "a very deep meaning": tea, they explained, represents the "Essence", and mastery in the art of tea requires that the act be accomplished, not by the ego, but by the "Void" or the "Self". To prepare tea with meticulous perfection and sobriety of gesture or with elegance is nothing, although the technical perfection is obviously both a condition and a result—in different respects—in the enactment of this symbolism. If one famous master, in answer to a disciple who claimed to know how to do a thing as simple as preparing tea, was able to say, "Then I become your disciple", this was precisely in order to insinuate, not without irony yet with a perfect logic, that this particular know-how implies in reality a radical stripping away of the individuality, therefore something great and difficult.

Some people will not fail to object, against this esoterism of tea and other analogous esoterisms,[4] that the Buddha never prepared tea, that he did not practice archery, nor arrange flowers; the response to this kind of objection is that the manner of acting counts more, spiritually speaking, than the material content of the act, at least in certain respects and provided the activities in question are legitimate in themselves. Being a man, the Buddha had to act; accordingly, all his actions were imbued with the same supernatural quality, or imbued with the same "Buddhahood"; after him, all kinds of other symbolical activities could be integrated into the tradition, thanks to the fact that they had been practiced by saints who thereby "consecrated" and "sacralized" the activities in question.[5] Moreover, one must not lose sight of the

[4] Those who deny esoterism fancy that it is an invention, because they are obviously unaware of what is at stake; the man who is ignorant of what a religion is believes he is capable of founding one himself.

[5] "The monks gathered before the image of Bodhidharma and drank tea out of a single bowl with the profound solemnity of a holy sacrament. This Zen ritual finally devel-

fact that originally every act of life partook of the nature of a rite, as Guénon noted; one must therefore conceive of the case where an art already ritual by virtue of its origin has been "reconfirmed" in a fresh light and thus assimilated into a given tradition. However, since practically everything can be debased down to the level of what is now called "culture", even a "spiritual art" may be turned into a simple aesthetic pastime and a game of virtuosity devoid of conscious content or efficacy; nevertheless, even then such a practice is "better than nothing", for it preserves at least the memory of what it should be, suggesting thus a whole world of the Spirit.[6]

This question of the tea ceremony provides an opportunity for observing, in quite a general way, that the now widespread depreciation of the "picturesque" is basically aimed against the notion of form as such, against the human visual faculty in its primordial function, against images in their capacity of "natural sacraments"; this goes hand in hand with contempt for speech and the word: in both cases it

---

oped into the tea ceremony of Japan in the fifteenth century. . . . Our legends attribute the first flower arrangement to those early Buddhist saints who gathered flowers scattered by the storm and, in their infinite solicitude for all living things, placed them in bowls full of water. . . . We see them (the master-florists) indicate the Directive Principle (Heaven), the Subordinate Principle (Earth), the Mediatory Principle (Man), and any arrangement that did not incorporate this principle in the flowers was considered sterile and dead. They also attached great importance to the art of showing a flower in its three different aspects: the formal, semi-formal, and informal" (Kakuzo Okakura, *The Book of Tea*, J. E. Tuttle, 1906). "It is possible to say many things about the art of flowers; and yet, whatever one can say about it, there always remains, beyond the tangible realizations which are visible for everyone, the mystery of its principle in unfathomable Being. . . . That which is at the basis of floral compositions and which finally can only be experienced is in itself formless and only takes form in a visual and symbolic representation. This formless and spiritual form is precisely the 'Idea' of the art of flowers. There the incommensurable is merged with the visible in order to shine forth and become apparent through the most modest forms of the sensible world" (Gusty L. Herrigel, *Der Blumenweg*, Otto Wilhelm Barth-Verlag, 1957).

[6] The influence of the "spirit of the tea ceremony" in Japanese civilization cannot be underestimated. "Manifold indeed have been the contributions of the tea masters to art. They completely revolutionized classical architecture and interior decorations, and established the new style . . . to whose influence even the palaces and monasteries built after the sixteenth century have all been subject. . . . All the famous gardens of Japan were laid out by tea masters. . . . It is in fact impossible to find any department of art in which the tea masters have not left marks of their genius" (Kakuzo Okakura, *The Book of Tea*).

amounts finally to a devaluation or profanation of the symbol under the double relationship of container and content.

Zen is a wisdom that readily draws inspiration from the image, the thing seen, be it only for the reason that it originates from the vision of a flower in the Buddha's hand.

The question of knowing which among the many Buddhist schools is the truest to original Buddhism could have no meaning for us; it is as if one were to ask which of the branches of a tree is truest to the root. Regarding the manifold forms of traditional Buddhism, the only question worth asking is that of their orthodoxy or heterodoxy: all that is orthodox today, whatever the unfolding of its forms, was contained in Buddhism from the beginning. All orthodox Buddhism is the "real Buddhism"; the unfolding of a more or less subtle aspect of the *Dharma* is not an "evolution" in the progressivist sense of the word;[7] inspiration is not invention[8] any more than a metaphysical perspective is a rationalist system. To declare that the primitive *Dharma* was "practical" and not "speculative"—the *Sūtras* are there to prove the contrary—amounts to reducing it to a purely individual experience without any possible radiation. Knowledge of a doctrine cannot be fully adequate except on the basis of the notion of orthodoxy.

One has heard it said that Buddhism, just as it needed at a certain moment in its history to find a "new form", namely the *Mahāyāna*, should likewise in our day be "rejuvenated" in a manner in keeping

---

[7] With Asian authors, Western terms are often employed carelessly though without an erroneous intention; but in that case it is the Western reader we must forewarn, who otherwise will not fail to make the association of ideas implied in the terms involved.

[8] This makes us think of an avant-garde theologian who, in order to prove that "tradition" means "progress"—and not "immobilism"—went so far as to maintain that Saint Paul, in order to formulate given truths in his Epistles, "had to invent". It was doubtless a question of annexing "progress" to Christianity and of aligning in one and the same glory the Apostles and the inventors of machines, serums, and explosives. Not to be intelligent enough to understand the Scholastics is called "being in tune with one's time", and to deceive oneself thus about one's own limitations by erecting them as a norm will no doubt be described as "humility".

with "the spirit of our times",[9] a statement—need one say it—that is false twice over: firstly, because the *Mahāyāna* was not put together by men, nor did it seek to render itself pleasing to any "age" whatsoever, and secondly because it constitutes, for the humanity to which its message is addressed,[10] the definitive expression of Buddhism, valid therefore until the end of the world and the coming of Maitreya. If our age—not because of its hypothetical superiority, but on the contrary because of its wretchedness—requires a certain readaptation of the Eternal Message, this has been effected long since: *Jōdo*, Pure Land,

[9] The same phenomenon is seen in the Catholic world as indeed everywhere else. Without pausing to ask what the value is of this pseudo-absolute one calls "our time", without considering its tendencies, its structures, its situations, in short without asking the question of knowing whether a world without God or hostile to God can be accepted as a normal or even as a good world, it is decreed by some that it is for religion to change, that religion must become "social", existentialist, and surrealist in order to be "up to the level" of present-day humanity; what is totally forgotten is to look at this question the other way round, according to the normal order of relationships. We are living in a world bereft of measures.

[10] Concerning the scission between Buddhism of the "North" and of the "South", and also the different—if not divergent—paths that Buddhism offers in general, we cannot do better than to quote the following words of Honen, one of the great saints of Japanese Buddhism: "We find in the many teachings that the great Master (the Buddha) himself promulgated during his lifetime, all the principles for which the eight Buddhist sects, the esoteric and exoteric and the Greater and the Lesser Vehicles (*Mahāyāna* and *Hīnayāna*) stand, as well as those elementary doctrines suited to the capacity of the masses, together with those intended for men capable of grasping Reality itself. Since then there have been many an exposition and many a commentary has been made on them such as those we dispose of presently, with their multitude of diverse interpretations. Some expound the principle of the utter emptiness of all things; some bring us to the very heart of reality; while others establish the theory that there are five fundamental distinctions in the natures of sentient beings; and still others reason that the Buddha-nature is found in them all. Every one of these schools claims that it has reached the goal through its perspective, and so they berate each other reciprocally, each persisting in saying that its own perspective is the most profound and the most perfectly true. The fact, however, is that what they all say is exactly what the *Sūtras* and *Shāstras* say, and corresponds with the golden words of Nyorai (the Buddha) himself who, according to men's varying capacity, taught them at one time one thing and at another time another, as circumstances required. . . . If we but attend to our religious practices as the *Sūtras* teach, they will all help us to pass safely over the sea of births and deaths to the other shore . . ." (*Honen, the Buddhist Saint*). The end of this passage evokes the famous formula of the two *Prajnā Pāramitā Hridaya Sūtras*: "Gone, gone; gone for the other shore; attained the other shore; O Enlightenment, be blessed!" (*Gāte, gāte; pāragāte; pārasamgāte; Bodhi, svāhā!*).

Elementary Remarks on the Enigma of the *Kōan*

Anyone who has taken however minimal an interest in Zen Buddhism knows that the *kōan* is a formula rendered absurd by design because intended to provoke a kind of liberating rupture in the mind of the person meditating on it—the mind being considered in this instance with regard to its hardness and blindness. All too frequently, however, the *kōan* has been represented in a rather regrettable manner: people like to pretend, not without a hint of relish with regard to common sense in general or to allegedly "Western" logic in particular, that *kōan*s are there to confer a new vision of the world and life, an aim completely devoid of interest as such; or else they make out that Zen is an integral part of a practical type of life of the most everyday sort, a view that takes no account of spiritual values. We do not say that such assertions or praise are totally groundless, we are simply emphasizing that they do not constitute definitions and that if they did they would not be of the kind to convey a lofty idea of Zen spirituality.

Obviously it is quite inadequate to declare that the purpose of the *kōan* is to produce a particular mental change of some kind or another, and that this is achieved by its very absurdity; such an opinion fails to explain why one *kōan* differs from another, nor does it account for the trouble taken to assemble a collection of *kōan*s—a traditional work deriving all its canonical authority from the fact that the *kōan*s were given by the greatest masters. Were it enough for a *kōan* to be absurd so as to provoke in the end a state of enlightenment, one could simply declare that two and two make five, and there would be no need to resort either to a traditional *kōan* or to one *kōan* rather than another.

The fact that *kōan*s do not deliberately contain an insight into metaphysical doctrine and that it is impossible to explain their meaning verbally does not imply that they have no meaning at all: people are not made century after century to meditate on absurdities pure and simple; and the traditional character of the *kōan* as well as its enlightening result prove that this formula is not just anything. But if the *kōan* possesses no intentional doctrinal content, what can its content be? Both the specific character of Zen itself and the replies of the masters provide us with the meaning: the *kōan* expresses the spiritual experience of a given master in a symbolical—and intentionally paradoxical—form, the significance of which is only verifiable by undergoing the selfsame experience. At the moment of the rupture that is *satori*[1] or enlightenment, the *kōan* is suddenly "understood", its contents are identified; and if one *kōan* differs from another this is not because the effect of *satori* is multiple but because its aspects are such. No doubt a *kōan* is bound to have a metaphysical meaning if it has any meaning at all, or since it has a meaning; but its justification lies precisely in its referring to the inexpressible aspect of the experience of Awakening. The objection could be raised that in such a case the *kōan* has no right to exist, having no place in language since language implies intelligibility; this objection is in itself pertinent, but exceptions must be allowed their due, given that paradox can have a catalytic function in the economy of *Māyā*.

The above observations call for some further remarks on the intentions and means of Zen in general. What Zen wants is the supernatural recovery of the perception of things *sub specie aeternitatis* or in the "Eternal Present"; the mind, having neither the ability nor the need to step outside relativity, finds itself henceforth rooted in the Absolute, both intellectually and existentially. But Zen also comprises another dimension, complementary to the first: this is its aspect of "simplicity" or "equilibrium", a returning to primordial nature. The complement of lightning and of rupture, or *satori*, is found in the peace that dwells in the nature of things, as revealed in the stillness of a pond reflecting the moon, or in the contemplative grace, one might say, of the water lily, or yet again, in the calm and precise elegance of the tea ceremony. The nature-loving and somewhat iconoclastic sobriety of Zen is no mere luxury: whoever wishes to bring the human mind back to that "intuition of Eternity" for which it is made, but which it has lost

---

[1] *Satori* is not absolute enlightenment; it amounts already to a degree of *bodhi*, but is not yet the *Samyaksambodhi* of the Buddha. If the profane state is separated from that of the Awakened as the circle is separated from its center, *satori* would be the sudden realization of the ray which, without itself being identical with the center, is as it were a prolongation of it. In relation to the profane state one may say that *satori* "is" Enlightenment in itself; distinctions between degrees of Enlightenment only have a meaning on the spiritual plane, not in relation to the world.

through its decadence—its scattering curiosity and its compressing passion—must also bring the soul and body back to their primordial simplicity by freeing them from the artificial superstructures of civilization.[2] The one thing does not go without the other: there is no content without an adequate container; the lightning's perfection calls for that of the lotus. In this second dimension, Zen was able to profit from the ground prepared by Shinto, just as, with regard to its first dimension, it had been helped by the presence of Taoism. This, however, must not make us lose sight of the fact that all was given from the beginning: by the Buddha's gesture, his smile, and by the flower he held in his hand.

— ∴ —

When one starts from the very basic idea—targeting only a certain effectiveness—that the world is impermanent and nothing else, that it is composed of impermanent and ever-shifting "categories" or "atoms" and that *Nirvāna* alone possesses permanence, one oddly forgets—unless one deems it superfluous to consider it—that escape from impermanence, or even the mere conception of the idea of impermanence and deliverance, would be impossible if no trace of permanence existed within the impermanent, or of absoluteness within the relative. Conversely and *a priori*, there must be an element of relativity in the Absolute, otherwise the relative would not exist, let alone the notion of relativity and escape from the relative; the *yin-yang* symbol represents this in its own particular way, as we have often pointed out on other occasions.

Now this element of absoluteness or of permanence at the very heart of the contingent, or of the impermanent, is precisely our own essence, our "Buddha nature"; to rediscover our own true nature is to realize Permanence and to escape from the "round of existence". It is by basing itself on this idea of immanence that Zen sets out to detach

---

[2] The posture in Zen meditation, *zazen*, is revealing in this respect: erectness and motionlessness; balance between effort and naturalness. Zen has developed an "art of gesture" extending to various crafts, including the profession of arms and all kinds of decorative and more or less feminine activities, and which is poles apart from the fake sincerity of the sloppy casualness and false "naturalness" of our times.

itself, not from tradition of course, since it is Buddhist, but from concepts as such: its very foundation is the fact that everything Revelation offers is to be found principially within ourselves. Zen teaches its disciples, by means of various signs and attitudes, to perceive and to become everything that constitutes the reason for being of words, ideas, and tradition.

We are not Aristotelian, but it goes without saying that Aristotle is a thousand times preferable to a falsified Zen, one divorced from its roots and thus deprived of its justification and its effectiveness; if this point is stressed here, this is because modernistic Zen all too readily overlooks the fact that Zen is "neither with nor without forms" and that, besides rigorous introspection and what may be termed the cult of voidness, it includes an attitude of devotion, of humility, and gratitude, at least *a priori*,[3] which it shares in common with all spirituality worthy of the name.[4] Be that as it may, a spiritual method is not something that is freely available: to the very extent that it is subtle or esoteric it turns to poison when not practiced within the framework of canonical rules, hence "in the name of God", as one would say in the West; in the case of Zen, this framework is above all the triad "Buddha-Law-Community" (*Buddha-Dharma-Sangha*). Zen depends on everything implied by this triad, or else it is nothing.[5]

---

[3] This reservation implies that the devotional virtues are supposed to become absorbed ultimately in an inward extinction that transcends them but without being opposed to them; from another point of view one may also say that in Zen divergent attitudes are found side by side, everything being set in its proper place.

[4] Zen monks recite the *Sūtras* every morning, which proves they are far from scorning texts; they also repeat the prayer of Ta-Hui, which contains a series of spiritual and material demands and is addressed to "all the Buddhas and *Bodhisattva-Mahāsattva*s of the past, present, and future in the ten quarters (of the Universe), and to *Mahāprajnāpāramitā*", the *Shakti* of the *Ādi-Buddha*—Vajradhara—with whom she is sometimes identified. One should also note that every meal is accompanied with prayers and that the main building of the monastery contains an image of Shakyamuni.

[5] Thus there is nothing in common between Zen and the theories of men like Jung or Krishnamurti, or any other type of psychologism.

Nirvāna

According to an error widespread in the West, the spiritual "extinction" Buddhism has in view represents a "nothingness", as if it were possible to realize something that is nothing. Now either *Nirvāna* is nothingness, in which case it is unrealizable; or else it is realizable, in which case it must correspond to something real. It is too easily forgotten that Paradise—not to mention uncreated Beatitude,[1] which is none other than the positive content of *Nirvāna*—can also be regarded as an annihilation, the relationship between formal and non-formal manifestation being analogous to that between manifestation as such and non-manifestation.[2] On the other hand, since Paradise is necessarily

---

[1] According to Saint Macarius of Egypt, "the crowns and diadems that Christians will receive are uncreated". Western theologians tend to ascribe a merely poetical meaning to such expressions, which is absurd, for the Fathers did not write literature; this attitude is explainable, however, by the viewpoint Western theology adopts regarding grace, which, in the final analysis, it views only as something created, whereas Eastern— that is, Palamite, Areopagitic, Patristic theology, which is metaphysically complete— recognizes the "divine Essence" in grace and its modes, therefore its uncreated or divine character. It is true that Latin theology is not altogether wrong in attributing a created character to grace, and Greek theology therefore is not entirely right in condemning the Western point of view: the Latin considers things according to a properly cosmo- logical and hence "horizontal" and distinctive perspective, whereas the Patristic views them according to a metaphysical and hence "vertical", essential, and synthetic perspective; in the first sense, grace is created, which is to say it constitutes an interference of non-formal manifestation within the formal; in the second sense, grace is uncreated for it is none other than the mysterious interference of God in manifestation as such.

[2] If between one level of reality and another there is a parallel analogy with respect to positive contents, there is on the other hand an inverse analogy with respect to relationships: for example, there is a parallel analogy between earthly and heavenly Beauty, but there is an inverse analogy as regards their respective situations, in the sense that earthly beauty is "outward" and divine Beauty "inward"; or again, to il- lustrate this law by symbols: according to certain Sufic teachings, earthly trees are reflections of heavenly trees, and earthly women are reflections of heavenly women (parallel analogy); but heavenly trees have their roots above and heavenly women are naked (inverse analogy—that which is situated below becoming situated above, and that which is inward becoming outward). The three great degrees of reality are: formal manifestation (comprising the gross, corporeal, sensible plane and the subtle, psychic plane), non-formal manifestation (constituted by the universal Spirit, the supreme Angels), and non-manifestation (God, in His Essence as well as in His Word).

a reflection of divine Beatitude—lest it be bad and even non-existent[3]—it cannot but represent, in each of its aspects, a "less" in relation to its divine Prototype, in the same way that the earthly world in which we live is necessarily a "less" in relation to Paradise, which is its heavenly Prototype; were it not so, the earthly world would be indistinguishable purely and simply from the heavenly world, just as that world, were it not a "less" in relation to God, would be indistinguishable from God Himself.[4] Therefore, if the reabsorption of a being in God is viewed as an annihilation,[5] then logically the reabsorption of the earthly being into paradisial existence must also be viewed as a passage from the real to nothingness; and conversely, if Paradise is regarded as an intensification or exaltation of all that is perfect and lovable in this lower world, then the state of supreme Extinction must also be regarded as an intensification or exaltation of what is positive and perfect, not only in the earthly world but in the entire universe. It follows that a higher level of reality—that of non-formal manifestation or, beyond the universe, that of non-manifestation—can be regarded either with respect to the negative aspect that it necessarily presents from the standpoint of the lower plane on which one is situated and whose limitations it negates, or else it can be regarded with respect to the positive aspect it

[3] It cannot be validly objected that evil, since it exists, is also a reflection of God for, firstly, it is not a reflection inasmuch as it is evil, but solely by virtue of its reality, however relative that may be; and, secondly, the fact that evil, by its mere existence, is such a reflection in no way prevents it from not being so with respect to its content. Hence evil is a reflection of God in only one respect, that of existence or container, whereas the good—Paradise, for example—is such a reflection in two respects at once, namely with respect to "that which exists", or content, as well as *a fortiori* that of existence, or container. Thus there is a respect in which evil is in no way a reflection of the Divine. That which is not a reflection in any respect is that which does not exist.

[4] This is an application of the *Shahādah*, the Islamic testimony of faith: "There is no divinity if not The Divinity" (*Lā ilāha illā 'Llāh*). In other words, there is no reality, if not the only Reality; or again: there is no perfection if not the sole Perfection. Christ's saying: "Why callest thou me good? God alone is good", has the same meaning and thus lends itself to the same cosmological and metaphysical applications.

[5] The distinction between *Nirvāna* and *Parinirvāna* does not apply from the standpoint taken here; it will suffice to recall that *Nirvāna* is extinction in relation to the cosmos, and *Parinirvāna* in relation to Being; *Nirvāna* is thus identified with Being, according to a conception that is more initiatic than properly metaphysical, since a "principle" is here represented as a "state"; and *Parinirvāna* is identified with Beyond-Being, that is to say with the divine Quiddity, which, according to Greek theology, "envelops" Being, or which, according to Sufism, "erases all predicates" (*munqat al-ishārat*).

contains in itself and thus also—and *a fortiori*—in relation to the lower plane under consideration. When Christ says that "in Heaven there is no marrying or giving in marriage", He refers to the negative aspect presented by the higher reality when seen from the lower plane; by contrast, when the Koran speaks of the houris and other delights of Paradise, it refers to the positive aspect of the same higher reality, as does every mythological symbolism, Hindu symbolism for example; and this makes it easy to understand that it is pointless to deny the existence of the houris (the Hindu *apsarās* and the Buddhist *dākinīs*) and other delights of Paradise, since the existence of analogous delights in this lower world—which precisely allow the symbolism in question to be established—proves the existence of the heavenly delights, just as a mirage proves the existence of the object reflected.

What has been said above should help us see that whenever confronted with a teaching which, in regard to the summit of all spiritual realization, seems to maintain the insuperable distinction between the creature and God, one is not yet entitled to conclude—in the absence of other criteria—that one is dealing with a limited point of view, namely one that does not go beyond such a distinction; for like every possible distinction, this one has its immutable prototype in the divine Order itself, namely in the distinction—absolutely fundamental in pure metaphysics—between Being and Beyond-Being, or, to use the language of Eastern theology, in the distinction between the revelatory Energies, or Processions (*Proothoi*), and the impenetrable Substratum (*Uparxis*); or again, expressed in Sufic terms, the same distinction is made between the Qualities (*Sifāt*) or Names (*Asmā'*) of God—which alone can be known distinctively—and the Quiddity (*Dhāt*), which eludes all penetration by an individualized intelligence, and thereby eludes all definition; or in other terms, it is the distinction—always in ascending order—between Unicity (*Al-Wāhidīyah*) and Unity (*Al-Ahadīyah*), the second term symbolically expressing Non-Otherness (the *Advaita* of Hindu doctrine).[6]

---

[6] Islam, being pre-eminently the doctrine of Unity, in the sense that it has to insist as expressly and exclusively as possible on Unity, could not designate supreme Reality by a term that would seem to deny Unity, as does for example the Hindu term *Advaita*, "Non-duality"; it must of necessity give this supreme meaning to the term "Unity" and to no other, and it does so by a transposition that confers upon this term the meaning of "Absolute". Moreover, the expression "Non-duality" does have its equivalent in Muslim language, namely in the formula "He hath no associate" (*lā sharīka lahu*) which, depending on one's vantage point, can be applied to Beyond-Being as well as to Being.

If the creature can indirectly contemplate an aspect of God, this is because within God Himself, who is the totality of the Processions and Attributes, the Word eternally contemplates its Essence or, expressed differently, because the Son eternally contemplates the Father—although it goes without saying that there is no common measure between the relationship of the creature to the Creator and that of the Son to the Father. Be that as it may, if it is legitimate to identify the Angels—who are none other than the direct and consequently non-formal, or supra-formal, reflections of the divine aspects or Names—with different Paradises or states of Bliss, then it is *a fortiori* legitimate to identify these aspects or divine Names themselves with states or places of Bliss, and hence with Paradises—whence the expression *Jannat adh-Dhāt*, "Garden (Paradise) of the Essence", used to designate the supreme spiritual realization.

To discuss the question of whether the delivered saints are annihilated in God or whether they remain separate within Him is pointless, since it amounts to knowing whether the divine Names are distinct or indistinct in God; now every divine Name is God, but none is any of the others and, above all, God is not reducible to any of them. The man who "enters" into God can obviously add nothing to Him nor modify anything in Him, God being immutable Plenitude; however, even the being who has realized *Parinirvāna*, that is, who is no longer limited by any exclusive divine aspect, but has become "identified" with the divine Essence,[7] such a being is still and always—or rather "eternally"—"himself", for, quite obviously, the divine Qualities cannot not be inherent in the Essence in some way;[8] they may be extinguished therein, but not lost. In a word, the saints "pre-exist" eternally in God, and their spiritual realization is but a return to themselves; and in an analogous way, every quality, every earthly pleasure is

---

[7] The feeble resources of human language—and we would even say of human thought as such—do not allow the translation of transcendent truths without altering them partially by contradictions that cannot be avoided.

[8] Were it otherwise, it would have to be admitted that the "Son" knows things that the "Father" does not, which is absurd.

but a finite reflection of an infinite Perfection or Beatitude. Nothing, therefore, can be lost; the simple fact that we enjoy something proves that this enjoyment exists infinitely in God. The Koran (*Sūrat al-Baqarah* [2]:25) expresses this in these words: "Every time they (the blessed) receive fruits (of Paradise), they say: 'We have tasted of this beforehand'", which is to say: we become aware of what we have tasted (near God or in God) from all eternity.

According to a saying of the Prophet Muhammad, "the world is the prison of the believer and the Paradise of the infidel",[9] and according to another, "Paradise is peopled with the ignorant". It is in an analogous sense that the Sufi Muadh Ar-Razi could say that "the Paradise of the believer is the prison of the sage", which shows clearly that if metaphysical Deliverance implies the "extinction" (*fanā'*)[10] of every created thing, it does not at all mean that the state of the "extinct" being is a kind of nothingness; exactly the reverse is true, since every created thing—be it heavenly or earthly—is a nothingness in relation to the divine Bliss, or let us say in relation to God without attribute. After extinction, or rather correlatively with it, comes permanence (*baqā'*): this is the reintegration of the saint into his eternal Prototype, a given divine Name, and thereby into God; the term "permanence" shows that the state of a being reintegrated into God is as positive as possible, that is, positive without limits; which is why Christ could say that He is the "Life". There is between two levels of Reality not only a relationship of analogy, but also one of inversion, as we have seen: if Paradise is a life because its divine Prototype is Life, and if for the same reason, the earth also comprises a certain mode of life—a mode whose Prototype is heavenly life and still more so divine Life—the inverse is equally true: the earthly state, like the Heaven of which it is a pale glimmer, is also a death, first that of the terrestrial state in relation to Heaven, and then both earth and Heaven in relation to God; for if God is "the Living" (*Al-Hayy*), no one else but He can be so.

———— ·:· ————

[9] The word "infidel" (*kāfir*) has here the meaning of "profane" or "worldly" and not that of "pagan".

[10] Literally, "disappearance".

Given that the question of *Nirvāna* represents a passage from the world to the Divine Reality, or from manifestation to the Principle, it raises the problem[11] of the continuity—or discontinuity—between the relative and the Absolute; pantheism, a Western philosophical conception, admits this continuity—"from below", of course—in such a way that in fact it amounts to a kind of atheism adorning the world with the name "God"; howbeit, a pantheism that includes a kind of vague theism also exists among "liberal" theologians, as well as among Westernized Hindus, who deduce crude simplifications from the symbolism of their Scriptures. This supposed continuity between God and the world, such as they conceive of it, does not correspond to any reality, needless to say; otherwise there could be no discontinuity in the world itself; now the discontinuity that one can observe everywhere can only be the reflection of the discontinuity separating manifestation from the Principle, or the world from God, and that can be abolished only by the ontological—or spiritual—reduction of the first to the second, or by the supernatural radiation of the Principle into the manifested order. In reality, there is simultaneously discontinuity and continuity between the relative and the Absolute; which is to say that there is continuity in discontinuity and, in another respect, discontinuity in continuity. It goes without saying that discontinuity is conceivable only from the standpoint of illusion—the standpoint of every creature as such—since there is nothing in Reality that could be discontinuous in relation to It; consequently, discontinuity is the product of manifestation itself, and is identified with it in a certain sense.

As for continuity in discontinuity, it is none other than the presence of the Principle in manifestation, according to the appropriate modes, for "*Brahman* is not in the world"; this means that It is not present as *Brahman*, but as reflection, either as *Sattva* and *Buddhi* (existential and intellectual manifestations of the "Holy Spirit")—terms that correspond respectively to *An-Nūr* and *Ar-Rūh* in Sufism—and their particular manifestations, such as the *Avatāra*s and *Yogī*s, or as spiritual Influences quite generally, such as the eucharistic Presence for instance. These realities, while necessarily pertaining to the cosmic order, are nonetheless *Brahman*—or *Allāh*—with respect to essential identity. Light is not the sun, but it is essentially identified with it

---

[11] By "problem" we mean a question that cannot be resolved in the absence of sufficient information deriving from Revelation or Intellection.

and represents the presence of the sun on earth; here too there is simultaneously discontinuity and continuity; however, the essential continuity can never abolish the discontinuity between Principle and manifestation, for this discontinuity subsists independently of the continuity in view, whereas continuity presupposes the exteriorization of God and hence discontinuity. The sun can exist without the earth, but light cannot exist without the sun; Reality is independent from illusion, but the fact that illusion is integrally linked to Reality in no way modifies the absolute transcendence of the latter.

"In the Absolute", said Ramakrishna, "I am not, and you are not, and *Brahman* (in Its personal determination) is not, for It (the Absolute) is beyond all speech and all thought. Yet as long as there still remains something outside myself (that is, so long as I am still on the plane of individual consciousness), I must adore *Brahman* within the limits of my reason, as something outside myself." The fact that a spiritual man who has attained *Nirvāna* can return to his individual modality, and even remain in it parallel with his state of supreme Identity,[12] proves precisely that *Nirvāna*, if it is an extinction, is not an annihilation, for nothing that is can cease to be.

It is sometimes asked how the sensible appearance or the activity on earth of a being possessing supreme sanctity—the Holy Virgin, for example—is compatible with her posthumous state, which, being divine, is thereby beyond all individual determination and hence beyond all form. To this it must be replied that sanctity is effacement in a universal Prototype: being holy, the Virgin cannot but be identified with a divine Model of which she is as the reflection on earth. This divine Model is first of all an aspect or Name of God, and it can therefore be said that in her supreme reality or knowledge the Virgin is this divine aspect itself; but this aspect necessarily has a first reflection in the cosmic or created order: this is the "Spirit", the *Metatron*

---

[12] If *Nirvāna* were a nothingness, how could it be explained that a being such as the Buddha not only returned to his human consciousness after purely contemplative states, but could even manifestly maintain this wholly nirvanic state in a permanent manner, hence even in the state of earthly consciousness?

of the Kabbalah, *Ar-Rūh* or the supreme angels in Islamic doctrine, and also the Hindu *Trimūrti,* or more precisely—since it is the Virgin who is being considered—the feminine and beneficent aspect of the *Trimūrti,* hence Lakshmi who, at the summit of all worlds, is the immediate imprint of divine Goodness and Beauty; from this imprint all created beauty and goodness are derived or, in other words, it is through this imprint that God communicates His Beauty and His Goodness to the world.

Thus the Virgin Mary—regarding what may be termed her post-humous state with reference to her human existence—is at once created and uncreated; whatever self-imposed limitations exoteric theology is forced to assume here for reasons of expediency, we need not take account of them since our point of view is esoteric. Be that as it may, even if exoterism cannot recognize Mary's divine reality without entering into insoluble contradictions—although it admits this reality implicitly at least when, for example, it defines the Virgin as "Co-Redemptress", "Mother of God", "Spouse of the Holy Spirit"—it is nonetheless able, without running the risk of ill-sounding formulations, to recognize that the Virgin is created before Creation; and this amounts to identifying her with the universal Spirit envisaged more particularly in its feminine, maternal, and beneficent function.

This divine imprint in supra-formal or luminous manifestation also comprises, by cosmic repercussion, a psychic imprint—or rather a psycho-physical one, since the corporeal can always issue from and be reabsorbed into the psychic plane of which it is, in the final analysis, merely a mode—and it is this psychic imprint that is Mary in her human form; this is why the universal Prototypes, when they manifest themselves in that portion of humanity for which Mary lived on earth, do so by way of the psychic,[13] hence individual and human, form of

---

[13] In other sectors of earthly humanity, the same Prototype—at once divine and an-gelic—takes the form appropriate to the respective ambiences; it appears most often in the form of a beautiful woman, as is the case in the apparitions of the *Shekhinah* in Judaism, of Durga, "the Mother", in Hinduism, or of Kwan-Yin or Tara in the Far East; similarly, in the Sioux Indian tradition, the Sacred Pipe—the pre-eminent sacred in-strument—was brought from Heaven by Pté-San-Win, a marvelously beautiful celes-tial maiden, dressed in white. But the merciful Principle can also take on—when there is inverse and not parallel analogy—a masculine form, for example that of Krishna or that of the *Bodhisattva* Avalokiteshvara—likened moreover to Kwan-Yin, "Goddess of Grace", in Chinese and Japanese Buddhism—or again, in Islam, the form of the

the Virgin; this form can always be reabsorbed into its Prototypes,[14] as the body can be reabsorbed into the soul, and as the created Prototype—the "Spirit" in its function of Mercy—can be reabsorbed into the uncreated Prototype, which is the infinite Beauty, Beatitude, and Mercy of God.

Prophet, one of whose names is precisely "Key of Mercy" (*Miftah ar-Rahmah*). Let us not forget to add that these manifestations of Mercy sometimes have a terrible aspect, closely related with that of purity. Concerning the Blessed Virgin, the following can be said: she is co-eternally in God—otherwise there would be perfections in the world lacking in the Creator—in two ways: firstly as "existential Substance" or *Materia Prima* (the divine *Prakriti* of Hindu doctrine), and secondly as "divine Quality" (thus an aspect of *Purusha*, the male Principle of the creative act) or as "divine Name"; thus she is the Beauty, the Purity, the Mercy of God; but in being such, she is also, and *a fortiori*, present in the manifested or created divine Spirit, of which she is the merciful Beauty as well as the forbidding Purity; finally, she is incarnated as Mary—and in other human forms, for the Unique becomes of necessity multiple once it manifests itself on the formal plane, barring which it would annihilate this plane—and, owing to her individual and psychic form, she can even appear on the corporeal plane.

[14] We use the plural because all perfection derives from two principal Prototypes, one cosmic or angelic, and the other divine.

Christianity and Buddhism

Christianity and Buddhism present certain remarkable analogies which are all the more striking given that in other respects these two traditional forms appear as very different from each other, to the extent that Buddhism has even been qualified as an "atheistic religion"—an absurd definition, but understandable on the part of people whose idea of God is almost exclusively anthropomorphic. In reality, the Divinity takes on a concrete form in the Buddha just as it does in the person of Christ: indeed, both appear in an expressly superhuman, transcendent, divine mode; the "kingdom" of the Buddha, like that of Christ, "is not of this world"; contrary to the case of other *Avatāras*,[1] Christ and the Buddha are neither legislators nor warriors but wandering preachers; Christ frequents "sinners" and the Buddha "kings", but they do so as strangers and without involving themselves organically in the life of men. Their respective doctrines are characterized—notwithstanding the universality they imply, which contains no limitation—by an exclusive spirit of renunciation, a monastic or eremitical spirit one might say, and hence an asocial one in a certain sense, if one leaves aside the question of charity that here seems to replace all law, but which in reality cannot compensate in practice for the absence of a legislation properly so-called. In one word, these doctrines never consider the here-below as capable of serving as a positive support for the spiritual path, but reject it as an obstacle; which is to say that they consider it, not in relation to its symbolism, which connects all things essentially, qualitatively, or vertically to the divine Prototype, but solely in relation to its character of manifestation, creation, hence of non-divinity, imperfection, corruptibility, suffering, and death.

Another striking analogy consists in the fact that each of the two religions springs from another, which it abolishes for its own purpose

---

[1] We have in mind here Sri Rama and Sri Krishna, both great warriors who outwardly lived the life of the world; and also, as regards the Semitic world, Abraham, Moses, and Muhammad. The universality of holiness implies that it can be clothed in the most varied of modes.

and in relation to which it will therefore appear as heterodox.[2] Needless to say, this does not prevent it from being orthodox from the standpoint of its intrinsic truth; for Christianity as well as for Buddhism, the previous religion serves the symbolic role of the "dead letter"—whence in Christianity the rejection of the Mosaic Law, and in Buddhism, the rejection of the *Veda*. The subjectivism of these negations is to be explained by the evident and necessary opportunism of every specifically initiatic perspective, which is therefore above all methodical. In Christianity the negation has a mystical stamp, whereas in Buddhism it assumes a rational appearance, which however does not imply any rationalist character in the slightest, but on the contrary demonstrates, in its own way, the spontaneity and independence of the Intellect in relation to forms. The new *Avatāra*, far from passing unnoticed in the mother civilization, leaves a deep albeit more or less external mark on it: the imprint left by Christ on the Jewish civilization is particularly important since Judaism henceforth lost its center and thus an essential aspect of its cohesion; likewise, the advent of the Buddha marks a turning point in the history of Hindu civilization, although this was not at all detrimental to its spiritual or traditional continuity.

But the most profound analogy between these two forms of universal Revelation lies in the fact that each possesses—in principle and *grosso modo*—an integrally initiatic character, not one that is *a priori* exo-esoteric like Judaism and Islam. Yet, and however paradoxical this may seem at first sight, it is in this common characteristic that there also lies the greatest divergence between the Christian and Buddhist religions,[3] in the sense that if their intrinsic nature is similar in the aspect we have considered above, the extrinsic consequences of

[2] The great Shankara sees in Buddhism only its extrinsically heterodox aspect; as the providential and inspired spokesman of Hinduism, he was not obliged—any more than the Hindu tradition itself—to take account of the intrinsic orthodoxy of a doctrine for which he had no need. In an altogether general way, it is always illogical to demand of a traditional authority a scientifically objective knowledge of a foreign religion, since the latter assumes in such a case only a symbolic value; it is therefore legitimate to agree with Sri Shankara while at the same time accepting Buddhism in itself.

[3] We are excluding here the doctrinal divergence that results from the different conceptions of the Absolute, Christianity conceiving it as a "Being" and Buddhism as a "State"; both terms have here, needless to say, only a wholly provisional sense, for "God"—in the apophatic sense—is beyond Being, and *Parinirvāna* is no longer a "state" since there is no individuality left.

that nature differ totally, somewhat like the solutions to one and the same difficulty can vary according to circumstances. The difficulty here lies in the fact that while Buddhism and Christianity are initiatic in their structure, they had to meet not only the spiritual needs of an elite but the manifold demands of a total human collectivity, and thus of a society containing the most diverse of minds and aptitudes;[4] if there is a contradiction here, it was nonetheless unavoidable, and it is precisely this contradiction that constitutes the particularity of the two religions. Both of them had to reconcile their character of spiritual path with the demands of a collective equilibrium: Christianity, for its part, had no choice but to veil the esoteric nature of its dogmas and sacraments by declaring them to be "unfathomable" and by qualifying them as "mysteries"; but the difficulty was only apparently resolved, because in reality all that was done was to avoid its implications; the reaction of the "swine" and the "dogs" was bound to occur sooner or later, and in fact the "wisdom according to the flesh" ended up invading everything, triumphing in the form of that unearthed paganism called the "Renaissance" and culminating over time, via a series of secondary subversions, in the extreme negation of all that is "mystery".[5] As for Buddhism, it was able to avoid a similar fate thanks to the rational—and not mystical—appearance of its doctrine; this appearance was eminently suited to neutralizing *a priori* and as it were in the bud, the above mentioned reaction, which—seeing that Buddhism possesses no exoterism properly so-called—would have inevitably occurred without this anticipation. We have said "rational appearance", for it goes without saying that Buddhist "reasoning", just as the Christian "mystery", is in itself not a form of mental elaboration but a symbol meant to act as the vehicle of a wisdom "according to the Spirit"; such a wisdom is never bound by the contingencies of the human mind, but transcends and annihilates them in the absolute plenitude of pure Truth.

---

[4] This is why the Buddha could say: "Three things shine forth openly: they are the sun, the moon, and the doctrine of the Perfect One." This saying also refers to the rational form mentioned above.

[5] There is a prefiguration of this destiny of Christianity in the fact that Christ himself gave Judas the piece of bread intended to designate the traitor; this indicates the necessary and providential character of what in Christianity might appear as an accidental deficiency.

—— .:. ——

Christianity and Buddhism, we have said, had to reject the religions from which they respectively issued; but they made the spiritual store of these religions accessible to many foreign peoples, precisely owing to this rejection—if such a paradoxical formulation is permissible. What had closed monotheism to non-Jewish humanity—we are speaking only of those peoples that were destined by nature to adopt it—was a sacred legislation which, ordered according to the needs of the Jewish people alone, lost its reason for being in other ethnic settings and therefore could not act as the vessel of universal Monotheism; now, neither the monotheist idea nor messianism could remain tied solely to the people of Israel.[6] Likewise, neither could the idea of liberation through Knowledge, nor that of transmigration, which depends on it, remain the prerogative of the Hindu world alone, for they answered too well the needs of peoples outside India; these peoples, however, had no need of the caste system, which was suited to the particular conditions of Hindu humanity,[7] but which was useless and inapplicable to the yellow races, and above all superfluous in the early Buddhist community itself whose character was, as mentioned above, initiatic and not social.

It will perhaps be objected that this function of the universalization of an idea hitherto confined to a form not lending itself to expansion, is not particular to Buddhism and Christianity, that it is notably incumbent on Islam as well; yet the case of Islam is different, for if on the one hand it is true that Islam also universalizes an idea which without its intervention, would not have known the full expansion it is capable of, it does not however present itself at all as

---

[6] We know what Saint Paul says of circumcision "in the spirit", which he opposes to the one "in the flesh". The Buddha's rejection of castes "in the flesh" and their replacement by castes "in the spirit" has the same significance; similarly, Islam replaces the "baptism of men" by that "of God" (*sibghatu 'Llāh*). Heterodoxies often adopt an analogous attitude, out of a need for compensation and due to hypocrisy, but without being able to justify it by any intrinsic truth and spiritual strength; heresies, in fact, always depend negatively on the truths they deny; error is but a shadow, and a shadow has no independent existence.

[7] Other civilizations possessed a caste system, but here in fact it is only the castes of Hinduism that are under consideration.

an initiatic extraction of the religions to which it is related, but much more as an exo-esoteric synthesis, or a sort of Christian Abrahamism, as it were. Consequently, Islam is distinguished from Christianity and from Buddhism—apart from other differences not applicable here— by the fact that it possesses an exoterism revealed as such and not merely adapted *a posteriori*; but it is also distinguished by the fact that it was revealed parallel to the forms it synthesizes in its own way, and not outside these forms as is the case with Christianity and Buddhism, whose Founders were respectively Jewish and Hindu.

As we were saying earlier, pity or charity, or rather a particular manner of stressing this quality, is another feature that brings Buddhism closer to Christianity. One must beware, however, of confusing this charity with a vague and flabby attitude; in other words, charity is not a sentimentalism that causes one to be blind to the objective differences of phenomena, nor is it equatable with a "psychologism" that reduces all culpability to nothing. Indeed, it is one thing not to know how to tell a wolf from a lamb and quite another to recognize their distinction on the plane of contingencies even while perceiving the ontological unity of opposites, and refraining from entering into the impasses of passional illusions and in the mechanism of concordant actions and reactions. As in the case of Christ's Law—requiring that one love one's enemy and turn the other cheek—so also for a Buddhist, it comes down finally to a question of transcending the plane of affective contrasts, and this in view of a reality—or of Reality as such—that contains all things and is situated beyond all things; a Christian would say: "for the love of God". It is a pernicious error to believe that serenity is blind and egalitarian; on the contrary, it is serenity's very lucidity that gives it all of its value: not to "resist the evil one" makes sense only on condition that we remain aware, on a certain plane which concerns us unquestionably as living beings, that an evil person is something other than a good one. Few things are more suffocatingly intolerable than the sentimentalist's attempts "to see only the good everywhere" or "to see evil only in oneself", at the expense of the truth and to the detriment of human equilibrium; for just as generosity has value only if one is strong, so the perception of unity has meaning only for he who is capable of discerning diversity. Charity, in the sense intended here, is to seek to discover in those whom we have to judge the qualities they really possess, and not blindly to attribute to them qualities foreign to their nature or which in no way counterbalance their defects; for charity has no value, in fact, apart from its contents; without the truth it is nothing. It is an outrage to intelligence to want to abolish our capacity for judgment for the sole pleasure of persuading ourselves that we are charitable; now, it is true that such behavior may have a certain ascetic meaning, depending on circumstances, but in that case it is not devoid of a certain selfishness.

And this is important: an outward attitude, whatever may be its usefulness, is never more than an approximation, not a totality; it has a value as a symbol and as a key, not that of a strict adequation, otherwise hypocrisy would not be possible: the moral exteriorization of the letter of the law must not be taken "word for word" anymore than scriptural symbolism, for here too "the letter killeth, but the spirit giveth life". Buddhist charity is above all a spiritual perspective, therefore it is transcendent with respect to its possible forms.[8] The *Tathāgatha* has no vices, assuredly, but he is likewise above virtues.[9]

To love all beings without distinction is to love that Being which is indistinct in all things—it is therefore to love the Divine or the Void whence every creature springs and it is to love, in the creature, the center where it ceases to be itself and where there is no longer anything but "Oneself", without either virtue or vice, or any other determination. However, it is proper to distinguish cleanly between a unitive vision of all beings due to a spiritual realization, and a mental attitude that seeks to anticipate this realization through sentimentalities and mirages.

While we are on the subject, it will not be inopportune briefly to sum up the monotheistic doctrine[10] concerning human charity,

---

[8] Proof of this is that Buddhists never had the idea of abolishing the death penalty—a demented and criminal idea, born moreover from contemporary "psychologism", which forgets not only the charity owed society but also, in the last analysis, the charity owed the condemned person himself.

[9] Virtues, that is to say inasmuch as they are distinctive properties and illusorily conscious. The satanic imitation of this wisdom would be to declare oneself independent of virtues we do not possess.

[10] And universal if one sets aside a certain type of terminology, while taking account of circumstances that actualize the problem.

since this doctrine has become blurred in the consciousness of the majority of people, being replaced by social concepts having no connection whatsoever with traditional truth:[11] what counts in the sight of the Absolute and regarding our last ends is a charity practiced in virtue of the "love of God" and which is accepted for the sake of that same love; for human life has no other meaning, either for him who gives or for him who receives.[12] It can however happen that charity is exercised out of love of God, but on behalf of someone who fails to profit from it in view of God, just as it may happen that someone exercises charity without loving God, but on behalf of another who does profit from it spiritually; in both cases the gain is one-sided, and the other party will have served only as an instrument of destiny. Can one infer from this that charity should be practiced only towards those who are supposed to profit thereby in view of their last ends? If such an alternative is encountered, then yes; otherwise no; but even in a case where a choice is possible, one practices charity towards an "unbeliever" when it seems that this might somehow help to heal his soul and on condition that the "believer" in need is not thereby harmed with respect to a vital interest; and the same holds good when the need of the "unbeliever" is of a more important order than that of the "believer" and when this charity is not harmful in the end to those who exercise it.

One additional point to be noted is the following: poverty, no more than illness or any other misery, does not carry with it in the sight of God any "right" to impiety, displeasing as this may be for religious demagogues who, under pressure of a materialistic and atheistic environment, accept this kind of blackmail; love of the Divine is a "categorical imperative" which, coming from Heaven, cannot fail to take account of the limits of our nature or of our responsibilities and which, consequently, could not depend *de jure* on any social or economic condition. The requirement of recognizing the Absolute is itself absolute, it concerns man as such and not man under a given

---

[11] In fact, this kind of confusion occurs everywhere, in the East as well as in the West.

[12] Likewise for work: far from constituting a merit in itself, work become meritorious only on condition that it is carried out for the love of God, which implies that it be done as well as possible and that its content—when it is a question of a work of art—transmits something of the truth, of the spirit, of that which gives meaning to life.

condition;[13] it is even a fundamental aspect of human dignity—and above all of the intelligence that makes up man—that we accept Truth because it is true and for no other reason.

There is still another analogy we wish to point out, namely the fact that neither Christianity nor Buddhism possesses a sacred and hence unique language, which again is a result of the particular and to some degree exceptional nature of these two religions; in fact, they are founded much less upon a revealed Book than on a more direct or more concrete, a more immediately tangible mode: namely the very Body of the God-Man, which offers an as it were consubstantial participation in the Word. In Christianity, this sacred Body has taken the form of the Eucharist, and in Buddhism the form of the sacramental image of the Blessed One, which image is derived from the very shadow of the Buddha,[14] and was left by him as a "remembrance"[15] for his spiritual

---

[13] What renders religion implausible—notwithstanding the absence of the desire to understand it—is not this or that "standard of living", but the scientist and machine-driven ambience that has made poverty more odious than ever and removes from work any quality of art, all intelligibility, all human character, and as a result all satisfaction. It has to be acknowledged that the abnormal and antihuman nature of industrialism provides some excuse for the materialism of the victims—whether poor or rich—of this state of affairs, but this excuse can never be more than very relative, man being what he is.

[14] The *Chitralakshana*, the Indo-Tibetan canon of pictorial art, attributes the origin of painting to the Buddha, which is quite significant; it will be recalled that the sacred art of Christianity, that of icons, goes back to Saint Luke and the angels. Buddhist tradition tells also of a sandalwood statue, which King Prasenajit of Shravasti (or Udayana of Kaushambi) had made during the lifetime of the Buddha, a statue of which the Greek statues of Gandhara may have been superficial and decadent copies; be that as it may, the spiritual source of the sacramental statues of the Blessed One is the same as that of the paintings, and in any case the symbolic rigor of the forms and proportions of Buddhist sacred sculpture exclude the hypothesis of a Greek influence for this art, although it is not impossible that the Greeks supplied some formal elements of a secondary order.

[15] There comes to mind here the words of Christ on the occasion of the institution of the Eucharistic sacrament: "Go and do this in remembrance of me." In Sufism, the "eucharistic" invocation of a holy Name, under whatever form, is called "remembrance" (*dhikr*); in Buddhism too, to invoke the Buddha is called "to remember the Buddha" (*Buddhānusmriti*).

posterity, hence as a means of grace; as a result, the bodily appearance of the Buddha is said to be a teaching no less than is his doctrine,[16] which explains the central position of the sacred image in the Buddhist system: contemplation of the revealed image of the Buddha is indeed, like Christian communion, an absorption of the sacred Body of the manifested God.[17] Needless to say, one should not look for a strict analogy between this Image and the Eucharist, for the points of view remain nonetheless very different since in the Eucharist it is the aspect of Presence that outweighs the aspect of Symbol, whereas in the image of the Buddha it is essentially through the symbolic form that the real Presence is transmitted. But to return to the liturgical languages of the two religions: what matters almost exclusively in Buddhist and Christian texts is the meaning of the text and not the language that conveys it, since this language does not constitute the sacred materiality of the Revelation. Moreover, the part played in Christianity by the "gift of tongues" suggests that the diversity of liturgical languages, already affirmed by the three inscriptions—Hebrew, Greek, and Latin—on the Cross, has a positive significance in the sense that it denotes in its own fashion the universality of the New Alliance. By contrast, in all the other traditional forms—excepting Buddhism—the language of the Revelation is like the sacred flesh of the divine Word; it is thus the "Body of the Buddha" as well as the "Word made flesh"; and if a book like the Koran may not be read in a language other than that of the Revelation, it is for a reason analogous to that which forbids making the Eucharistic Species from materials other than those prescribed by the Church, or making the sacramental images of the Buddha otherwise than according to strictly established rules.

— .·. —

[16] Tao-Cho, in his work entitled *An-le-tsi* (*The Book of Peace and Happiness*), one of the chief sources of the Pure Land doctrine, says, quoting a *sūtra*: "All the Buddhas save human beings in four ways: 1. By the oral teaching of Buddhism as it is set out in the twelve categories of Buddhist Scriptures. 2. By their physical traits of supernatural beauty. 3. By their marvelous powers, their properties, and their transformation. 4. By their names, which when uttered by beings remove all obstacles and assure rebirth in the presence of the Buddha" (Daisetz Teitaro Suzuki, *Essays on Zen Buddhism*).

[17] Hindu *darshan*—the contemplation of saintly persons—is of the same order.

The four divine gifts bequeathed by the Buddha are: the doctrine of Deliverance, the visible symbol of the Blessed One, his ever-present spiritual Power—or his Blessing—and finally his saving Name. These gifts will be found with Christ in the following forms: the Doctrine of Redemption and of Love, the Eucharist, the Paraclete, and finally the salvific Name of Jesus, as it is invoked in Hesychasm. According to Buddhist teaching, these four gifts proceed from "all the Buddhas", and are to be found in appropriate forms in every divine Messenger.[18]

To conclude, we shall sum up the function or role of Buddhism and that of Christianity in the following terms: each had to reject outwardly the form—with respect to its formal expression, not of Revelation[19]—from which it issued; each presents itself as the spiritual or specifically initiatic essence of the preceding religion, which had become more or less literalist or pharisaical, at least in a transitory and in fact providential manner; finally, each adapted the said essence to the needs of an autonomous and hence integral religious existence, thus making possible an expansion and radiation of certain spiritual treasures far exceeding the possibilities of their original frameworks.

[18] The "celestial" Name of Muhammad is *Ahmad*; when the letter *m* (*mīm*) is removed, which is that of death (*mawt*), what remains is the divine Name *Ahad*, "One". The Prophet expressed his identity with God through the following *ahādīth*: "I am *Ahmad* without *mīm*"; "I am an Arab without '*ayn*"; and "Whoso hath seen me hath seen God" (*Al-Haqq*, "the Truth"). In the second *hadīth*, the word "Arab" ('*arabī*) becomes "my Lord" (*Rabbī*) by the suppression of the letter '*ayn*, which is that of "servitude" ('*ubūdiyyah*, from '*abd*, "servant"), that is, of cosmic, relative, unreal existence. The Prophet also said: "Whoso knoweth his soul, knoweth his Lord"; in this *hadīth*, the truth expressed in the three others becomes a general truth and thereby a spiritual rule of cardinal importance, concerning the realization of "God within us".

[19] A Revelation, as such, comes from God alone; however, just as a man, although he is not the creation of his parents, borrows from them the constituent elements of his earthly form, so a tradition, although it is never the creation of a human ambience, must nevertheless borrow from it certain elements of a formal order.

Mystery of the *Bodhisattva*

There is a side of Buddhism in which it resembles not only Christianity, but also the Semitic religions in general—paradoxically so, considering its non-theistic character—in the sense that its starting point depends on a human point of view rather than on the metaphysical nature of things; indeed, when it is said that Existence is but suffering and that the Absolute is the cessation of suffering, and further that human perfection lies in "compassion for all living beings", this opens up a perspective that corresponds to our human situation and to our ultimate interests, no doubt, but it does not offer from the outset the most direct possible definition of "that which is", if it may be expressed thus when considering both the manifested Universe and that which transcends it. Such an observation is not, however, of a kind that need logically disturb Buddhists,[1] and this for two reasons: firstly, because they are not unaware of the fact that the doctrines of the Buddhas are only "celestial mirages" intended to catch, as in a golden net, the greatest possible number of creatures plunged in ignorance, suffering, and transmigration, and that it is therefore the benefit of creatures and not the suchness of the Universe that determines the necessarily contingent form of the Message; and secondly, because Buddhism, within the framework of its own wisdom, goes beyond the formal "mythology" or the "letter" and ultimately transcends all possible human formulations, thus realizing an unsurpassable contemplative disinterestedness as do the *Vedānta*, Taoism, and analogous doctrines.

Hence the question that Shakyamuni might have asked himself—had he needed to ask one—was: "Which is the most effective way of conveying the saving Truth to men—or to certain men—in these Latter Times?" and not "Which is the most adequate—or least inadequate—formulation of the metaphysical nature of things?" Neither the *Vedānta* nor Neoplatonism include the possibility of addressing all men usefully and of serving as the vehicle of an integral tradition, nor indeed is this their purpose; but Buddhism wishes to and has to include this possibility, and cannot therefore not offer itself first of

---

[1] No more so than the anthropomorphism of the Semitic Scriptures need disturb Kabbalists, Gnostics, or Sufis.

87

all as an *upāya*, a "provisional means", with an aim that is above all charitable, in the broadest and most complete sense of that word. Buddhists, it must be stressed, find it all the easier to recognize this in that they are—especially in Zen—far from claiming that the nirvanic Truth can be enclosed definitively within the mold of any dialectic. Nevertheless, there results from this general situation—apart from any fluctuations of terminology—a certain difficulty in speaking of Knowledge in such a way as to satisfy at one and the same time the metaphysical Truth and the voluntaristic and emotional side of Buddhism.

——— ⸬ ———

Original Buddhism distinguishes extrinsically between a *Samyaksam-Buddha* and a *Pratyeka-Buddha*; the former corresponds to what Hindus would call a major *Avatāra*, having by definition the function of founder of a religion, and the latter to a *Jīvan-Mukta*—a man "delivered in this life"—who has neither the quality of a major or plenary *Avatāra* nor consequently the function attaching to such a one; and not having had a Buddha as master, neither does he have disciples.[2] After this comes the *Shrāvaka*, who is a disciple—or the disciple of a disciple—of the Buddha; like the *Pratyeka-Buddha*, he is an *Arahant* or perfected saint, but in some fashion owing to the direct influence of the Master. Finally there is the *Bodhisattva* who, in principle, is a saint on the way to becoming a Buddha.

Now, when it is stated, as in the *Mahāyāna* writings, that the state of a *Pratyeka-Buddha* is inferior to that of a *Bodhisattva* because the realization of the former is "selfish" and lacks compassion for crea-

[2] It could be that the *Pratyeka-Buddha*s are in fact identified to the Hindu *Yogīs* and *Avatāra*s, of whom nascent Buddhism could obviously not be unaware and whom it needed to "situate" in one manner or another. The saints of Brahmanism indeed "have no master" in the sense that they do not follow the Buddha, and they "have no disciples" because they do not teach Buddhism and do not address the Buddha's followers; but it might also be admitted—and one thing need not exclude the other—that the *Pratyeka-Buddha*s correspond to the category of saints whom the Sufis call "solitaries" (*afrad*, from *fard*) and who likewise have neither masters nor disciples. Be that as it may, the *Sūtra* of the Rhinoceros (*Khaggavisāna Sutta*), where Shakyamuni has a *Pratyeka-Buddha* speak, seems to indicate that this type of sainthood is based essentially on the mystery of solitude, which calls to mind an inscription we once saw in a medieval hermitage: O *beata solitudo, o sola beatitudo*.

tures, it seems to be forgotten—or at least this logical objection comes to mind *a priori*—that *Nirvāna* implies by definition the abolition of all egoism and the realization of total charity. This is an objection that the *Mahāyāna* itself raises in its own way and in its sapiential dimension, without really contradicting itself since it recognizes two truths, the one being relative and provisional and the other absolute and definitive, and since its doctrinal form is essentially apophatic and antinomic. In other words, when it is said that the *Mahāyāna* is "great" (*mahā*) for the sole reason that its aim is the salvation of "all sentient beings"—thanks to the sacrificial ideal of the *Bodhisattva*—and not the salvation of a single individual as is the case with the *Hīnayāna*, then it is proper to object, in accordance with the higher teaching of the selfsame *Mahāyāna*, that the reason adduced carries no weight with respect to *Nirvāna* or, what amounts to the same thing, with respect to Knowledge; not to mention the fact that this world of ignorance and suffering—this *Samsāra*—is metaphysically necessary and need not be considered solely from a volitional and emotional angle.

Be that as it may, the sapiential *Mahāyāna* intends to support the heroic ideal of the *Bodhisattva*, but does so by bringing it back to a strictly metaphysical perspective: it specifies that compassion is a dimension of Knowledge, then it adds that the neighbor is non-real, and that charity must therefore be exercised "quietly when the occasion arises" and without slipping into the dualist and objectivist illusion for, it says, there is no one whom our charity could concern, anymore than there is a charity that could be "ours". Thus, on the very basis of the bhaktic interpretation of the *Bodhisattva*, Mahayanic *gnosis* rejoins as if by a roundabout way the most rigorous and hence the most objective or most disinterested metaphysical positions.

To be as precise as possible, Buddhism can be said to present itself under the following fundamental aspects: first of all, original Buddhism; then *Theravāda* Buddhism, which is its continuation as to form if not to all its content; finally, *Mahāyāna* ("Great Vehicle"), which characterizes the preceding as *Hīnayāna* ("Lesser Vehicle") and which in its general form exalts the heroic ideal of the *Bodhisattva*; then, within the framework itself of the *Mahāyāna*, a sapiential perspective that corrects and counterbalances the specifically bhaktic elements in the Mahayanic ideal; and parallel with this perspective there is another that is devotional and centered above all on the cult of the Buddha Amitabha. Therefore, if we acknowledge the greatness of the "Great Vehicle", this is not because of the altruistic ideal that appears as its mythological mantle and its elementary thesis, but because of the two quintessences just mentioned—the one sapiential and the other devotional—the ultimate crystallizations of which are, in Japan, Zen and *Jōdo*.[3]

While sharing the sacrificial ideal of Buddhism's foundational doctrine, but without following it into what is too literal and too human in its interpretations, sapiential *Mahāyāna* adopts the terminology of this doctrine and projects its own certitudes into it: consequently it will say, not that *Nirvāna* requires charity, but that the state of the *Pratyeka-Buddha* is not *Nirvāna* in the fullest sense, or that it is a *Nirvāna* on a transitory level, comparable no doubt to the *Brahmā-Loka* of the Hindu *Krama-Mukta;* in this case, the use of the designation "Buddha" seems to prove that there has been a change of terminology, for it is *a priori* unusual to call a man "Buddha" when he is placed lower than a *Bodhisattva;* it is, however, possible to justify such a designation seeing that it refers to a state that is already nirvanic, when there is extinction at least in relation to the formal world, and that owing to this fact alone there is no obligatory return to the round of births and deaths.[4]

These considerations bring up the matter of the authenticity of the Mahayanic *sūtra*s, since these supposedly report the discourses of the Buddha, just as do the texts in Pali. Now, it is not the authenticity itself that is in question, but the mode of authenticity: that is to say, these texts, or certain of them, while certainly based on the teachings of Shakyamuni—for otherwise they would not assert this[5]—seem to present developments or commentaries rather than the sermons themselves, and they do so availing themselves of the terminology

---

[3] This juxtaposition may well appear paradoxical to many of the faithful of these two schools, even though both were recommended by the great Nagarjuna himself, and even though Honen, the illustrious spokesman of *Jōdo*, expressly admitted all the forms of traditional Buddhism.

[4] The Mahayanist polemic against the *Pratyeka-Buddha*s should not astonish us unduly on the part of a perspective of sacrificial idealism; the Vishnuite *bhakti* too readily represents the Shivaite *jnānī* as a sterile and dreary rationalist, lacking what is essential until, touched by Grace, he discovers devotional love—as if the latter were not eminently comprised in *jnāna*.

[5] This argument will surprise those scholars who have no idea either of the nature of spiritual inspiration or of the organic laws governing—and guaranteeing—the Tradition.

in use in the environment where they were composed.[6] However, whether it is a question of the Buddha himself or of his inspired commentators, it is well not to lose sight of a principle to which we have already alluded and which finds an application in all sacred Scriptures, namely the distinction between two kinds of truth, the one relative or provisional and the other absolute and definitive,[7] at least inasmuch as there can be anything definitive on the plane of verbal crystallizations;[8] or again, from a more contingent point of view: the Buddha, in his long career, could have presented diverse perspectives to audiences of unequal levels, and could even have used varying terminologies.[9]

As far as the Mahayanic ideal of the *Bodhisattva* is concerned—an ideal of sacrificial compassion in the heroic *Mahāyāna* and a symbol of spiritual totality in the sapiential doctrine—account must be taken of the following fundamental situation: Buddhism unfolds as it were between the empirical notions of suffering and cessation of suffering; now, the notion of compassion springs from this very fact: it is an inevitable or necessary link in what might be called the spiritual mythology of Buddhism. He who speaks of suffering and cessation of suffering speaks of compassion, given that he is not alone on earth; and this is where the *Bodhisattva* intervenes: he embodies the element compassion—this quasi-ontological link between pain and Bliss—just as the Buddha embodies Bliss and just as ordinary beings embody

---

[6] On the other hand, it is not out of the question—or is even probable—that certain particularly homogeneous and concise texts, such as the *Mahā Prajnā Pāramitā Hridaya* or the *Vajracchedikā*, render faithfully, and without development or commentary, the sacred discourse word for word.

[7] When Christ strikes the Temple merchants, he manifests a partial and conditional truth, namely that there are phenomena—of the hypocritical or blasphemous type— that by their nature authorize or call for violence; but when he enjoins us to turn the left cheek to him who smites us on the right, he is teaching a total and unconditional truth concerning, as such, our inner attitude and hence also our general tendency, which means that holy anger and holy patience can and must be combined, the levels being different. The Scholastic distinction between a truth *secundum fidem* and another *secundum rationem* stops halfway between belief and intellection; it is more like a syncretism than a synthesis.

[8] This reservation brings into question, not the immutability of intellectual evidences or of sacred formulations, but the absoluteness of concepts as such from the standpoint of the Divine Selfhood and in the context of direct Knowledge.

[9] For example, in presenting the *Shrāvaka*, the *Pratyeka-Buddha*, the *Arahant*, and the *Bodhisattva*, in the latter sermons, as so many different degrees of realization.

suffering; he must be present in the cosmos as long as there is both a *Samsāra* and a *Nirvāna*, this presence being expressed by the statement that the *Bodhisattva* wishes to save "all beings".[10]

From a more contingent point of view, it could also be pointed out that concern for personal deliverance, while irreproachable in itself, does involve a certain danger of egoism once it becomes the sole motive of a tradition carried by a large collectivity whose tendencies are bound to be exoteric; from this point of view, the intervention of the *Mahāyāna* appears to be providential. At the time when it first asserted itself, the Buddhist tradition had doubtless given rise to all kinds of narrow and pharisaical perspectives; the same had been the case with Brahmanism in the Buddha's time, as also with Judaism at the time of Christ, which does not mean that these crises involved either of these traditions in their entirety or in their subsequent existence; thus there is no need of taking up the polemic of the early Mahayanists against the Theravadins of Ceylon and Indo-China. Or again, in a more fundamental sense concerning religion as such: the very necessity of an emotional element—in the absence of a theism properly so-called and given the conditions of the "Latter Times"[11]—explains the opportune-

---

[10] The Buddhist adage, "May all beings be happy", or the will of the *Bodhisattva*s to save "all sentient beings", has its equivalent in the Islamic "Blessing on the Prophet" (*Salāt ʿalā 'n-Nabī*), which proceeds from above to below in the sense that Muhammad, who is mentioned first, is the center of the cosmos, upon which all other creatures depend, these being designated—in descending order—by the terms "Family" (*āl*) and "Companions" (*sahb*). But even if it were not specified that the blessing extends to the "Family" and the "Companions", the graces would reach the totality—or a totality—of mankind by virtue of the avataric character of the name *Muhammad*, which includes all human beings while at the same time indicating their summit; he is at once summit and circumference. In the Buddhist perspective, the blessing—actualized, among others, by the prayer wheels—concerns all sentient beings without exception.

[11] According to the *Nirvāna Sūtra*: "Those who despise the *Dharma* will then be like the volume of earth of the ten directions, and those who remain faithful to it will be like the crumb of earth that can be put on a fingernail." And similarly according to the *Saddharma Pundarīka Sūtra*: "At the horrible time of the end, men will be malevolent, false, evil, and obtuse and they will imagine they have reached perfection when it will be nothing of the sort." According to the caliph Ali, "The inhabitants of the here-below are nothing but barking dogs and ferocious beasts howling at one another; the strong devour the weak and the great subjugate the small . . ." Under such circumstances, a spiritual treasure can no longer take hold collectively except by means of a sentimental, even a passional, element, which alone is capable of acting effectively in a milieu of this kind.

ness of the cult of the *Bodhisattva* in its connection with the path of works and the path of love; in this respect, the difference between the Buddhism of the North and that of the South is no more than one of style and mythology, without prejudice of course to their supra-formal essences. Be that as it may, it can be admitted that if in the climate of the *Mahāyāna* the Buddha Amitabha is the object of a special cult, this is *a priori* because, as *Bodhisattva*, he was able to accumulate the merits capable of creating a "Buddha-field" and a "Pure Land"; but, quite obviously, it is also possible that this retrospective motive need not concern contemplation, whether devotional or other, especially since the same causal sequence may also be conceived in the reverse direction: in other words, the prime mover is not a contingency like the merit accumulated by an individual, or by a "karmic nexus" if one prefers, but a principle of Mercy that creates simultaneously both the merit itself and the saint who accumulates the merit. The principle of Mercy results from the very nature of the *Ādi-Buddha*, namely the Absolute who is at once Knowledge and Love.

The doctrine of Shinran presents a wonderful synthesis between the devotional and the sapiential paths: to start with, it envisages the "Pure Land", the *Sukhāvatī* Paradise, in its aspect of transcendence, hence of identity with *Nirvāna*; similarly, it reminds us that death, by virtue of universal analogies, can serve to rend the veil of *Māyā*, and hence can be an occasion for Enlightenment and Deliverance,[12] provided we are in a spiritual situation that enables this junction or actualizes this analogy, and this precisely is made possible by the Grace of Amitabha and our trust in it. The whole emphasis is placed here on the element "faith"—partly evoking, *mutatis mutandis*, the *satori* of Zen[13]—and this faith is an attitude of trust which, by its quality, coincides with the forgetting of the ego. The Absolute—which has revealed itself under the particular name of *Amitābha*—is essentially

---

[12] This is the case with the Hindu *Videha-Mukta*.

[13] This comment permits the following remark: it has been possible to say in Zen: "If you meet the Buddha, slay him"; this means, paraphrasing the first sentence of the *Tao Te Ching* ("The Tao that can be grasped is not the real Tao"): the Buddha whom you can meet is not the real Buddha. This is the point of view of the absolute Subject, hence infinitely transpersonal, namely the point of view of perfect non-objectification. It is encountered also in Western *gnosis*, for example when it is said that God could not "live a single instant" without us: what then is meant by "God" is only the mental objectification—hence the relativization—of the Ineffable, which, Itself, is beyond all polarity.

Wisdom and Compassion, Knowledge and Mercy; that is to say, in the symbolism of the Buddha Amitabha, the "original vow" to enter *Nirvāna* only on condition that all those who invoke the sacred Name with faith be saved, is in fact the Absolute's aspect of Mercy; it is as if the Absolute were saying, to paraphrase the vow: "I would not wish to possess Beatitude if there existed between Me and contingent beings an insurmountable barrier preventing them from drinking deeply of my Beatitude"; or again: "I would not be the Absolute were I not blessed and merciful."[14]

But this path of Amitabha of which Shinran, after Honen, was the last great spokesman, likewise includes, at a lower degree than the nirvanic miracle of which we have just spoken, a properly human finality: it leads to the *Sukhāvatī* Paradise where the faithful will await *Nirvāna* till the end of the cycle. This Paradise—which Hinduism, analogically speaking, also knows since that is the condition of the *Krama-Mukta*—is of quite a different order from the ones comprised in the round of transmigration; it is the exact equivalent of the Paradise of the Semitic religions, in which "eternity" means precisely this nirvanic conclusion and the ceasing of *Samsāra*.[15]

A distinction must be made between the personal *Bodhisattva* who is transmigrating and the celestial or universal *Bodhisattva* endowed with ubiquity; the former, if he is not simply a manifestation of the latter, accumulates merits by his virtues and actions;[16] the latter,

[14] In Christianity, the Name of the Virgin, which signifies Mercy, is joined with that of Christ, which is an indirect Name of the Absolute. In Islam, the Name of the Absolute—*Allāh*—is followed immediately by the Names of Mercy, *Rahmān* and *Rahīm*—the one intrinsic and the other extrinsic—in the formula of consecration at the beginning of every Revelation and every rite.

[15] If in the Semitic monotheisms there is no place for the concept of the *Bodhisattva*, it is because these perspectives take into consideration neither what is before birth nor what may be situated outside the human Paradise. The function of the celestial and compassionate *Bodhisattva* is nonetheless represented, in the West, by the "apotropaic" saints or "Holy Helpers" (in German *Nothelfer*), not to mention the guardian or protecting angels.

[16] "A hundred beatitudes of the *Gandharvas* are as one beatitude of the *Devas* who

namely the universal *Bodhisattva*, is the cosmic emanation of a Buddha, or—in Western terms—he is the Archangel who manifests a given divine Quality; his reintegration into *Nirvāna* coincides with the *Mahāpralaya*, the Apocatastasis, which brings about the return of each and every manifestation to the Principle, or the return of all contingency to the Absolute.[17] The human *Bodhisattva* is—to use now Hindu terminology—either a *bhakta* or a *jnānī*: in the former case the path alternates between devotion and compassion—devotion towards the Buddhas and celestial *Bodhisattvas* and compassion towards the creatures wandering in the *Samsāra*—whereas in the latter case, that of the *Bodhisattva* who is a *jnānī*, it is *gnosis* that takes precedence over everything else: compassion is not something added sentimentally to an imperfect mode of knowledge but, on the contrary, this compassion is the secondary dimension or internal complement of a knowledge that is virtually or effectively perfect, because it is situated on the axis of Buddhahood or is identified with Buddhahood itself.[18]

---

have attained to their divinity by the accumulation of meritorious works, and a hundred beatitudes of the *Devas* by merit are as one beatitude of the *Devas* by birth . . ." (*Brihadāranyaka Upanishad*, IV, 3, 33). The samsaric situation of the personal *Bodhisattvas* places them in the category of *Devas* by merit; these have less beatitude than the *Devas* by origin because merit can always be exhausted and cannot be maintained save by means of new merits. As to the *Gandharvas*, they are "celestial musicians", creatures that are more or less "peripheral", and perhaps comparable to our terrestrial birds in certain respects or, on the contrary, incomparable in relation to the things of this world.

[17] Saint Gregory of Nyssa alludes to the Apocatastasis in speaking of the demons: "And these, it is said, the Apostle accounts as subterranean beings, wishing to indicate by this turn of phrase that no creature will remain excluded from the Kingdom of the Good when, after long periods of centuries, all evil shall be destroyed . . ." (*Conversation with Macrina*, IX, 2).

[18] A Buddhist has rightly pointed out to the author that the merits, compassion, and knowledge of the *Bodhisattva* correspond respectively to *karma*, *bhakti*, and *jnāna* and consequently are addressed to those who follow those ways; for each of them the *Bodhisattva* reveals himself under this or that aspect; to use Buddhist terminology, these are the three aspects respectively termed *upekshā* (impassivity), *maitrī* (love of one's neighbor), and *prajnā* (knowledge). In the framework of *gnosis*, however, compassion changes its mode: Jacques Bacot was correct in declaring, in his introduction to *Le Poète tibétain Milarepa*, that "Buddhist pity has no relationship with sensibility. It is entirely objective, cool, and connected with a metaphysical conception. It is not spontaneous, but the outcome of long meditations. The idealism that tends no longer to differentiate between 'me' and 'not-me' is the generator of this pity for all that lives and is the victim of illusion." It is the compassion comprised in *prajnā*.

Some will no doubt object that the *gnosis* of the *Bodhisattva* is not that of the Buddha: namely that the Buddha's compassion is intrinsic in the sense that he carries all things in himself—but at that degree the *Samsāra* cannot oppose *Nirvāna* or be associated with it in any manner whatsoever, which means that the opposition "existence-Void" only becomes meaningful at the degree of existence and is resolved in the principial Void—whereas the universal pity of the *Bodhisattva* is extrinsic and therefore still situated under the sign of duality; but this would not do full justice to the nature of the great *Bodhisattva*s, for the sacrificial sojourn in the world necessarily combines with *Nirvāna*; it is a way of realizing *Nirvāna* in a certain sense also "outwardly", within the samsaric condition itself.[19] This must needs be so, for the simple reason that a being cannot deprive himself, from life to life, of that which constitutes the very meaning and end of all his efforts, all his virtues, and all his merits; it is neither possible to persist in an exclusively negative situation, on the one hand, nor, on the other, to consider the ultimate Wisdom merely as a means of coming to another's aid, which would amount to making a means of the end or a contingency of the Absolute; Knowledge as such cannot be an instrument designed for charity any more than the Real can be subordinate to the illusory.[20] The condition of the gnostic *Bodhisattva* would be neither conceivable nor tolerable if it were not a manner of contemplating the Absolute at once in the heart and in the world; and above all it must be stressed that Knowledge, by definition, has no connection with the quantity of merits or the number of incarnations.[21] Only a bhaktism with an exoteric bias could imagine perfect

[19] This brings to mind the Arabic Divine Names "the Inward" and "the Outward" (*Al-Bātin* and *Az-Zāhir*) and the mystery of the Divine "outwardness" in connection with the concepts of the "metaphysical transparency of phenomena" and the "relatively absolute".

[20] In the opinion of the Tibetan *Arahant* Milarepa, "One should not show oneself rash and hasty in the intention to serve others as long as one has not realized the Truth oneself; otherwise one risks being a blind man leading the blind."

[21] This is what *Dhyāna*—Zen—teaches in the most explicit manner. Texts like the *Diamond Sūtra* or the Chinese *Sūtra of Huang-Po* formulate the decisive truth in the most explicit possible fashion and thereby express—in terms of doctrine—the very quintessence of Buddhism. In the same vein of thought, the *Lankāvatāra Sūtra* and other texts establish a distinction between a progressive realization and a realization that is immediate, the progressive concerning the rooting out of vices and illusions and the immediate the assimilation of nirvanic Light; according to this distinction, there are two kinds of saints or, within the same being, two degrees of sanctity, or two stages.

Knowledge as being the fruit of a process of accumulating elements of one kind or another, even be they sublime from the human point of view;[22] in short there is nothing either quantitative or moral about the Spirit. At the same time, the following should also be emphasized: *Nirvāna* seen or experienced from the standpoint of a formal condition—as is the case with the Hindu *Jīvan-Mukta* and the Buddhist *Arahant*—is not absolutely the same as the *Nirvāna* experienced beyond all form; thus the refusal on the part of the great *Bodhisattva*s to enter *Nirvāna*—and here we have in mind not only their celestial prototypes, where the matter is self-evident—is not a refusal, in itself impossible, of total Knowledge, but a merciful hesitation to cast off one last veil or to leave the formal Universe definitively.[23]

Here one has to insist on the difference between *Nirvāna* and *Parinirvāna*: only death allows of a total reintegration—for those who in their lifetime have realized "Extinction"—in that "supreme Extinction", which is none other than the Vedantic "Self". Living beings, whatever their degree of spirituality, remain of necessity linked with Being, which belongs to the realm of *Nirvāna*, since it represents a perfect transcendence in relation to all manifestation and to the whole cosmic sequence of cause and effect, but which, being still of the realm of *Māyā* whereof it is the summit or quintessence, is not yet the Self. If in a certain respect death brings no change for one who has realized *Nirvāna*—the Hindu *Jīvan-Mukta* or the Buddhist *Arahant*—yet in another respect it nonetheless produces a considerable change, so much so that it can be said that death for the "living liberated one" is neither a modification nor a non-modification, or that it is both at once. However: if we say that the Buddha, in dying, entered *Parinirvāna*, this is again only an earthly way of speaking: in reality, he was always there as *Dharmakāya*, "body of the *Dharma*"; similarly he did not cease to dwell in Heaven in his manifestation as *Sambhogakāya*, "body of Bliss", even while manifesting himself

---

[22] According to the *Lankāvatāra Sūtra*, the *Bodhisattva*s, while holding back from entering into *Nirvāna*, are there already in fact, "for in their love and compassion there is no cause for illusory distinction and consequently no intervention of such a distinction". The *Diamond Sūtra* mentions this saying of the Buddha: "A *Bodhisattva* who would say: 'I will deliver all beings'—do not call him a *Bodhisattva*."

[23] The attitude of the great Hindu *bhakta* Sri Chaitanya rejoins the ideal of the *Bodhisattva*: "Lord, I desire neither riches, nor servants, nor a beautiful damsel, nor the poetic muse. Let me, O Lord, from birth to birth, have only devotion to Thee—a devotion which seeks nothing in return" (*Shrī Shrī Shiksāstakam*).

among mortals by virtue of *Nirmānakāya*, the "body of supernatural metamorphosis". In monotheistic terms, we would say that to every Prophet or *Avatāra* there corresponds an Archangel and, beyond creation, a divine Name, and that each divine Name reflects in its own way the whole Divinity.

A question that might be asked about the supreme *Bodhisattvas*—given the virtually divine cult surrounding them—is the following: are they no more than archangels, that is to say, do they remain at the summit of the cosmos, thus below Being, or can they be situated at the summit of *Māyā*, thus at the degree of Being but below Beyond-Being? The response has to be negative with respect to the latter part of this question, despite certain hyperboles or verbal syntheses that could suggest the contrary; for the "Divine Names" or Qualities of Being are represented, in Buddhism, by the different Buddhas—notably the "*Dhyāni-Buddhas*"—or in other words, by absolute Buddhahood envisaged under the aspect of differentiation, which—being already contingent—is specific to *Māyā*. Let us add that for the celestial *Bodhisattva*, who even while becoming "incarnate" does not leave his Paradise, "to become incarnate" may also mean "to delegate a power", and it is in this sense that a particular saint or great lama may be described as an "incarnation" of Avalokiteshvara or of Manjushri.[24]

Another question that may be asked is this: whence originates the initiative for the coming into being of a *Bodhisattva* and *a fortiori* of a Buddha? Does it come from man or from the heavenly *Logos*? The two things coincide: once the human support is ready, namely once it has attained a degree of perfection, the *Logos* descends upon it and settles in him, just as light automatically settles on a clear and smooth surface; but precisely, the ripening of the human support is in its turn and by anticipation an effect of the *Logos*—which is at once Wisdom and Mercy, Knowledge and Love, light and warmth—so that we are obliged to admit that the original initiative comes from Heaven and that the support was brought forth in the realm of the cosmic play solely in view of the manifestation of the *Logos* and by the *Logos* itself. It is in an analogous sense that it has been paradoxically affirmed, in

---

[24] The terrestrial charity exercised by the celestial *Bodhisattvas* brings to mind a Saint Theresa of Lisieux wanting "to spend her time in Heaven doing good on earth"—symbolized by the "shower of roses"—although in this case the intention is situated in the context of an altogether different eschatology.

the language of various traditions, that the world has been created for the Prophet or *Avatāra* or for the sake of his manifestation. An important point touching the mystery of the "virtual Buddha" is understanding the nirvanic essence of the *Samsāra*: just as we have written upon other occasions that the finite is a sort of internal dimension of the Infinite—an indispensably necessary dimension, obviously, by reason of infinity itself or the intrinsic character of infinity—so too we could define the *Samsāra* here as a sort of dimension of *Nirvāna*, or as an "ignorant" manner (in the sense of the term *avidyā*) of envisaging it, the factor "ignorance" occurring as a result of the very infinity of the divine "Void". The actual substance of this reality in reverse is constituted by those countless "grains of sand" that are the *dharmas*—the elementary qualities—these being like the segmented, innumerable, and "inverted" crystallizations of the Void or of the pure nirvanic Substance. The impermanence of things is none other than their own relativity.

To summarize what has just been explained and at the same time to complete it, it is necessary to distinguish between three *Nirvānas*—or three degrees of Extinction—two of which are still in the order of *Māyā* or contingency, whereas the third, *Parinirvāna*, is the Absolute; if another *Nirvāna* were the Absolute there could not be a question of a *Parinirvāna*. The first *Nirvāna* is ontologically that of the *Bodhisattva*: it is extinction in relation to formal manifestation and corresponds to the degree of the Archangels, Heaven, Existence; we say "ontologically" because the *Bodhisattva* "lives" at this level even if he has already realized the second *Nirvāna*, the one which coincides with the state of the terrestrial Buddha, namely the extinction in regard to universal manifestation, which corresponds to the degree of Being. The third *Nirvāna*, beyond *Māyā*, is that of the celestial or absolute Buddha: this is *Parinirvāna*, extinction in relation to Being or to *Māyā* and which corresponds to the supreme Self of the Vedantists.[25] Now

---

[25] The lowermost tip of what could be called the "nirvanic axis" is the heart or the pure Intellect, or again the mind in a state of perfect truth and purity, or the *mantram*, the *nembutsu*. In monotheistic, or simply theistic, language we would speak of the "heavenly" or "divine axis".

to say that the *Bodhisattva* renounces *Nirvāna* is to say that he intends to remain, not in formal manifestation alone, but in transmigration, whatever the degree of extinction he may inwardly have attained. What the *Bodhisattva* desires is not a divine perfection but a cosmic one, one which will result in the obtaining of a divine message; now this function—that of the *Samyaksam-Buddha*—requires a perfection of cosmic Knowledge that the *Pratyeka-Buddha* does not possess and that moreover is—like the fact of Revelation itself—insignificant with regard to absolute Knowledge;[26] in Islamic terminology, we would say that the Prophet is sublime, not by virtue of his prophetic mission (*nubuwwah*), but by virtue of his perfect sanctity (*wilāyah*), which has led certain people to claim that saints are superior to Prophets, whereas in reality prophecy, without being in itself a degree of sanctity, requires or implies total sanctity.[27] But the *Bodhisattva* can "renounce" *Nirvāna* only on condition of having attained it in the mode accessible within formal existence, and it is only then that his decision to become a *Samyaksam-Buddha* has any meaning; prior to that, his desire even to "become a Buddha" or "to save all sentient beings" is at the same time a stimulus and an obstacle, depending on whether his path is primarily related to *bhakti* or *jnāna*. On attaining *Nirvāna* he will know whether the *Ādi-Buddha*—the supreme Buddhahood, identified with the nirvanic Infinite—has chosen him or not; or in other words whether the universal economy, or the equilibrium or rhythm of the Cosmos, has decided whether he is to be a Messenger or whether he is finally to be integrated—until the exhaustion of the "life of Brahmā"—into the state of an Archangel, such as Avalokiteshvara or Manjushri. All that has just been pointed out implies that the specific Knowledge of the *Samyaksam-Buddha* is "neither superior nor inferior", but simply "other"—although in a certain sense more "ample"—than the Knowledge of the *Arahant*; it is a kind of existential penetration into worlds and creatures, a dilation in the direction of the *Samsāra*, which is as a projected shadow, so to speak, of his

---

[26] Sri Shankara realized this Knowledge without having produced the *Veda*; and in an analogous sense, Mary Magdalene was perfectly holy without possessing the cosmic and quasi-divine greatness of the Holy Virgin.

[27] A further distinction must be made between minor Prophets (*nabī*, plural *anbiyā'*), who have a limited mission within a given tradition, and major Prophets, the "Messengers" (*rasūl, rusul*) who have a universal mission and are founders of a religion.

dilation in *Nirvāna* or *Parinirvāna;* and this is doubtless connected with the "remembrance of former births", for the penetration in question embraces both "time" and "space" simultaneously, symbolically speaking.

The Enlightenment that occurred in the lifetime of Shakyamuni beneath the *Bodhi* tree is none other than what in more or less Western parlance would be called "Revelation", namely the reception of the Message or of the prophetic function:[28] just as the soul descends suddenly on the embryo once it is sufficiently formed—neither before nor after—so *Bodhi* descends on the *Bodhisattva* who has acquired, alongside his Knowledge and his *Nirvāna,* the cosmic perfections required for the prophetic radiation.

At the risk of repetition, it is necessary to return here to a particularly important point: if there is in the *Mahāyāna* an element that may be open to question from the metaphysical point of view, it is not the path of the *Bodhisattva* quite obviously but, what is quite different, the ideal of the *Bodhisattva* insofar as it is polemically opposed to the "non-altruistic" spirituality of the pure contemplative, as if, firstly, all true spirituality did not include charity and, secondly, as if the consideration of some contingency or other could rival pure and total Knowledge. But if the wish to deliver all beings, as expressed under this elementary and even sentimental form, is of necessity opposed to Knowledge—since it is here a question of "interested disinterestedness"[29]—one may well ask what, from the point of view of tradition, can be the profound meaning or the alchemical function of a desire objectively so disproportionate and subjectively so contingent? The answer is that this is a means of channeling certain mentalities towards Virtue and Truth; it is this idealism of heroic abnegation, this heroism at once karmic and bhaktic—and nothing else—which will attract their goodwill and kindle it, and this is a factor that tradition must take into account in its multi-faceted formulation. As for

---

[28] This Revelation is summed up in the highly elliptical formula of the *Bodhi* of Shakyamuni: "This being, that becomes, from the becoming of that which becomes; this non-becoming, which does not become, from the cessation of that which ceases." Here is the commentary on it by one of the Buddha's disciples: "Of those things that proceed from a cause the *Tathāgata* has explained the origin, and likewise their cessation he has explained. This is the doctrine of the great *Shramana.*"

[29] In a parallel and reverse manner, the non-acting solitude of the contemplative could be described as "disinterested interest", at least from a certain point of view.

the *Bodhisattva* himself, his refusal of *Nirvāna*—not of the "nirvanic axis" that passes through him, but of the repose in Extinction—is simply the will to be reborn despite the possibility of no longer having to be reborn; since this possibility exists and presents itself to him, he is entitled to it according to his vocation and destiny.[30] What the *Bodhisattva* then lacks is not the formless, nor even the supra-existential, *Nirvāna*—that which the terrestrial Buddha enjoys—but solely the prophetic mandate that would make him a *Samyaksam-Buddha*, and the retirement into unmanifest, hence extra-samsaric, Reality; the absence of such a mandate is of course involuntary, whereas sojourn in transmigration is vocational and aims either expressly at obtaining the mandate or mission, or else at a state of beneficent and angelic presence in the *Samsāra*. It is this and this alone that is meant by the refusal to enter into *Nirvāna*, for it goes without saying that no-one can prevent—or could wish to prevent—the flowering forth of Knowledge.

Humanly speaking, the *Bodhisattva* is an altogether extraordinary being owing to the acuteness, amplitude, and scope of his faculties, something which, on this scale, cannot be the case with the *Pratyeka-Buddha*, who, while "delivered in this life" and possessing supreme Knowledge to the extent that it can be imparted to one still bound to the earthly or formal condition, may only be endowed with individual faculties that—apart from intellectuality and contemplativity—do not really go beyond the general norm, as seen by the example of a Ramakrishna or of a Ramana Maharshi; when leaving aside their inner realization, their human breadth—which is the sole consideration here—is obviously less than that of a Rama or a Krishna, or of the young prince Siddhartha, the future Buddha; there is here no common measure, and even the mightiest genius disappears next to this order of greatness—speaking uniquely from the point of view of human constitution and without taking account of any posthumous spiritual destiny. Or let us take the example of the Mother of Jesus: tradition tells us that in a natural—or "supernaturally natural"—manner she possessed every virtue and all knowledge in the fullest possible degree of unfolding; this supereminent perfection was indispensable for her role as "Co-Redemptress", but this is a case of

[30] We may recall here the text of Chaitanya, already cited, according to which the saint has one sole desire, to "have only devotion to Thee, from birth to birth".

providential configuration or cosmic prodigality which, while necessarily combined at a certain point with Knowledge, is nonetheless not the prerequisite for it, otherwise it would be pointless to speak of *gnosis* and to teach it to mere mortals. The "superhumanly human" perfection of the *Bodhisattva* is necessary, not for Knowledge as such and hence for departing from this world, but for the earthly manifestation of the Divine Principle, of the liberating Truth, of *Nirvāna*— which is an altogether different matter; far from being exclusively directed towards the unmanifest, the properly angelic human nature of the virtual Buddha on the contrary radiates into the cosmos, as the sun illuminates the night. This, we repeat, is what renders his nature capable of transmitting that crystallization of the Infinite—or that Truth "become flesh"—which is Revelation, the seed and nourishment of a universal and millenary tradition.

To the question of whether this perfection, combined with the *Bodhi* for which it is the predisposed receptacle, constitutes a degree of Knowledge, the answer is both yes and no; in a sense, it is as if one were to ask whether the *Samsāra* is real; the answer can be affirmative or negative, depending on the viewpoint, so long as the absolute truth be acknowledged. "Each thing is *Ātmā*", certainly, but "the world is false, *Brahma* is true", and "there is no divinity save the one Divinity"; what the problem comes down to is that of the "divine nature" of *Māyā*, or the nature of *Māyā* as "modality", "play", "unveiling", or "aspect" of the ineffable Self, of *Paramātmā*. The supreme Knowledge attributed to the *Samyaksam-Buddha* comprises essentially three factors: the unimaginable cosmic unfolding of the perfection of the *Bodhisattva*, then the *Nirvāna* comprised in that perfection, and finally the "celestial weight" of Revelation, of the *Dharma*. As for knowing whether extra-nirvanic factors, however incomparable they may be at their respective levels, add something to *Nirvāna* or constitute an element of principial Knowledge, this seems to us to be a question that metaphysically answers itself.

There is nonetheless a factor that allows one to accept, with the appropriate reservations, the interpretation of the specific Enlightenment of the *Samyaksam-Buddha* as a degree—or as the supreme degree—of Knowledge, and it is the following: in the *Bodhisattva* ready to receive it, Revelation coincides with the "recollection" of the Wisdom "previously" acquired, but temporarily "forgotten" owing to the fact of incarnation. This "forgetting" or this initial perplexity occurs for the simple reason that it is not in this new world of forms that the *Bodhisattva* had acquired his Wisdom. The temporary obscuration in question is moreover comparable, in the natural order, to childhood, which also transitorily veils faculties that are nonetheless pre-existent. Under the *Bodhi* tree there was therefore a twofold Enlightenment: on the one hand the "recollection", which was bound to occur after the inevitably fumbling efforts to find one's way around in a new body and in a new space, and on the other hand the Revelation accompanied by the samsaric Knowledge that characterizes the *Samyaksam-Buddha.* If we admit that the term *Buddha* can have two or more meanings, as the *Mahāyāna* obliges us to do, we must equally admit two or more kinds of *Bodhi;* there is one *Bodhi* that belongs to every Buddha, whether externally a *Bodhisattva* or not, and there is another that concerns solely the Buddha as Revealer and in which an extrinsic dimension is combined with the intrinsic *Bodhi.*[31]

As we have remarked, the *Bodhisattva* who has become Buddha possesses absolute Knowledge not by virtue of his quality of *Samyaksam-Buddha,* but by virtue of his quality of *Arahant* or fully perfected saint, that is to say he can be—but does not have to be—a *Samyaksam-Buddha* because he possesses this Knowledge; we also pointed out that the altogether illusory opposition *Samsāra-Nirvāna* exists only from the point of view of the world and is resolved in and by *Nirvāna* and not otherwise, for there is here no possibility of any reciprocity or symmetry, so that the particular Knowledge of the Buddha in his capacity of Revealer could add nothing whatever to nirvanic Knowledge. Now it must not be lost sight of—and we have already alluded to this—that it is possible to consider the *Samsāra* under its aspect of indirect "Nirvanahood", in other words as an internal dimension of the Void or of the Infinite, and in that case one could, if need be—while observing the proper precautions, which are necessary, albeit relatively so—speak of a supreme Knowledge belonging to the *Samyaksam-Buddha* alone.[32] We will say no more

---

[31] A distinction is made, moreover, between the unconditional *Bodhi* of the Absolute and its heavenly and earthly reflections, the three levels belonging to every Buddha, according to the theory of the three "bodies" of the "Awakened".

[32] *Samyak* means "upright", "perfect", or "whole", whereas the prefix *sam*—as in the Latin words *summum* and *summa* or the German words *samt, zusammen, sammeln*—expresses the related ideas of "summit" and "totality". The scholarly transcription

Samsāra—of the world as an indefinite chain of causes and effects—it must be clearly understood that the kind or style of this knowledge depends on the style of the Revelation that it accompanies: whatever the Revelation enunciates is something the *Avatāra* knows immediately without its being always possible to assign a priority, in the avataric soul, either to the Knowledge itself, or else to the "divine fact" of the Revelation. As for the question of spiritual style, it is for example possible to know space in various ways, starting from different symbolisms or by applying different measures: it can be known in terms of a circle, a cross, a star, or a spiral and it is thus that the *Samsāra* can be known according to diverse perspectives, analogically speaking; but this science will never have anything more than a character of "relative absoluteness", like every reflection of the absolute in the contingent.

Monotheism seems to teach that the world has a beginning and not an end, whereas Buddhism seems to assert, no less paradoxically, that the world has an end, but does not have a beginning. This remark, made by a Buddhist to the writer, calls for the following comment: the answer to both difficulties is contained in the idea of Apocatastasis, which satisfies the demands of both the above metaphysics by bringing creation to an end—but without annihilation, quite the contrary—and by realizing the humanly impossible ideal of the *Bodhisattvas*. When Buddhists admit that the *Samsāra* will come to an end thanks to the *Bodhisattvas* and Buddhas who will have saved "all sentient beings" down to the last one, they implicitly attribute the final reintegration to the *Ādi-Buddha*, the universal or divine Buddha whose Act is in effect identified with the transmutative *Logos;* in other words, the Apocatastasis or *Mahāpralaya* is the *Bodhi*—the passage to the state of Buddha—of all celestial *Bodhisattvas*, such as Avalokiteshvara, Manjushri, Kshitigarbha, Akashagarbha; the nirvanic light that submerges, penetrates, transmutes, and devours the *Samsāra* is their Enlightenment saving the Universe, and in fact it is through the celestial Essences that this Light will act, before reabsorbing them in their turn in its infinite Silence.

In Buddhism, which is averse to speculations of a cerebral literalism, language seeks to communicate or provoke a state of "being" rather than of "thinking": understanding and being tend to merge as far as this is possible, whence the wide use of *upāyas*, "concepts as means", the justification of which is not so much a truth conceived in the abstract as an inward transformation and a kind of existential intuition, if such a paradox is permissible. Thus the idea of the *Bodhisattva* has for its aim above all to destroy egotism, and then the ego itself; perhaps the *Mahāyāna* at bottom reproaches its Southern opponents less with an imperfection of doctrine than with one of method, that is to say, it considers that the ideal of *Bodhi* is in practice unrealizable without the ideal of the *Bodhisattva*, who alone is capable of cutting the Gordian knot of egoity. Other views can assuredly be held on this point, but however that may be, if the *Bodhisattva* is supposed to save all sentient beings, this indicates above all a total gift of self, hence a perfect victory over the ego. Compassion then appears as the criterion of authenticity of Knowledge, as is the case with love in Christian *gnosis*,[35] for which wisdom without love is but "sounding brass, or a tinkling cymbal". Love is that which enables "understanding" to pass into "being", or that which attaches us ontologically to Truth and thus opens us to the transforming magic of the Symbol.

By way of conclusion, let us return to these fundamental ideas by specifying them further: the *Bodhisattva* could not accumulate innumerable merits and thereby an inexhaustible *karma* if he were not inwardly a Buddha, that is to say freed, as such, from transgression; it is because he can no longer fall into sin or passion that the *Bodhisattva* gains continuous merits and realizes sublime perfections; the sacrificial actions attributed to him symbolize both his perfections—the *Pāramitās*—and the sacrifice his very samsaric condition represents. What distinguishes the *Bodhisattva* from the Buddha is not necessarily an inferior knowledge—as we have said—but the fact of being in the *Samsāra*, or more precisely of finding himself there in a certain fashion and as a matter of principle; the terrestrial Buddha, for his part, is distinguished from the *Bodhisattva*s by the fact that a celestial Word has become "incarnate" in him and that he has thus obtained the function to found a religion—to speak in Western terms—and to exit transmigration thereafter; moreover, the one does not go without the other, for he who has effected an "exit" out of this world must henceforth

---

[35] We specify that here it is a question of *gnosis*, since for the way of love, which more often than not coincides with a relative exoterism, this is self-evident.

keep watch over this path and has no further function to exercise with regard to "sentient beings".[36]

There are, finally, four "realities" to be considered: *Samsāra*, *Nirvāna*, the *Bodhisattva*, and the Buddha; the latter is, in a certain sense and in his capacity of *Tathāgata*, "*Samsāra* having entered into *Nirvāna*", whereas the *Bodhisattva* is on the contrary and in principle "*Nirvāna* present in *Samsāra*"; it has also been said that the Buddha represents the contemplative aspect and the *Bodhisattva* the active aspect of *Nirvāna*, or that the former is turned towards the Absolute and the latter towards contingency. The Buddha is a ray emanating from the Center and returning to it, and the *Bodhisattva* is a circle projecting the Center into the periphery; the Buddha enlightens or saves by radiation, while the *Bodhisattva* saves by a spiraling movement. Or again: the Buddha transmits Light or Knowledge "vertically", whereas the *Bodhisattva* manifests "horizontally" Warmth, Compassion, Mercy.

The Buddha manifests the truth that "*Samsāra* is *Nirvāna*", and the *Bodhisattva* the truth that "*Nirvāna* is *Samsāra*"; but it could also be said that each manifests both truths in his own way, according to the aspect or function that predominates in each case. This amounts to saying that *Bodhisattva* and Buddha alike are manifestations at once free and necessary of the *Ādi-Buddha* or of Mahavairochana.

---

[36] The *Mahāyāna* is sometimes presented as being the doctrine, not of the earthly Buddha—hence in the *Nirmānakāya*—as is the case with the *Hīnayāna*, but of the "divine Buddha", in the *Dharmakāya*. What is absolutely certain is that in no case could the Mahayanic *sūtras* be of human origin and reflect an "evolution" of any kind, whatever their dialectical means may be.

Synthesis of the *Pāramitās*

When considering the most prominent thesis of the *Mahāyāna*, that which distinguishes it most characteristically from *Theravāda* Buddhism, one might be inclined to conclude that, in its general form, it is a way of love, analogous to the *bhakti* of India or of Christianity; it is important, however, not to isolate this appearance from its total context, and to know that the *Mahāyāna* comprises essentially two poles, the first being the thesis of the universal charity of the *Bodhisattva*, while the second is the metaphysical notion of the "Void", which corresponds strictly to *Advaita-Vedānta*, despite the differences in perspective that led to the opposition between Shankara and Nagarjuna. Far from appearing only in the guise of an implicit *gnosis*, and veiled by a language typical of a mysticism of love, this metaphysical notion is set forth plainly in numerous *sūtras* and makes itself known as the reason for being of the whole *Mahāyāna*; it determines its entire doctrinal corpus to such a degree that charity, which is its point of departure, finds itself infused by this notion. Indeed, the point of departure of the way—the *Bodhisattvayāna*—corresponds not merely to a moral option but to an awareness of the "voidness" of all things; the ego of the aspirant starts by identifying itself with the whole *Samsāra*; it is by understanding the nature of the *Samsāra* that the soul disengages itself from its error and starts with the undertaking leading to the realization of the universal Body of the Buddha.

Before proceeding further, however, we want to respond to a question concerning a phenomenon, paradoxical at first sight, which seems to lie at the root of *Mahayāna* alone: what is the meaning of the assertion, made by the Northern Buddhists, that in the early days of Buddhism the times were not yet "ripe" for the open preaching of the Mahayanist *sūtras* and that, until then—that is, until the epoch of Nagarjuna—these *sūtras* had remained either hidden or secret, and protected by the genii, the *nāgas*, against all profanation?[1] The key to the enigma lies in the fact that certain aspects of a Revelation require an appropriate field of resonance; this is to say that tradition has the

---

[1] The *nāgas* are represented as serpents; their symbolism—like that of dragons—as guardians of treasures or sacred precincts is well known.

role, not only of communicating vital truths, but also of creating a setting adapted to the manifestation of different modes of a particular character.

Such a phenomenon occurs to one degree or another within all religions. In every religion, several centuries after its foundation, one sees a new flowering or a kind of second youth, and this is due to the fact that the presence of a collective and material ambience, realized by the religion itself, creates conditions allowing, or requiring, the unfolding of an apparently new kind: in the West, the Middle Ages, with its great saints of a particular type, its chivalry, and its sacred art—fully developed and perfected, and thus definitive and irreplaceable—was the Christian epoch *par excellence*; and this was so in a manner different from the first centuries of Christianity which, in another respect, clearly retain the superiority of their original perfection; in Islam, likewise, the epoch of Ibn Arabi—who was the "pole" of his age—coincides with a world elaborated over several centuries of Islam and presents, on the plane of esoterism, a very ample and profound flowering, coming at times close to the initial prophetic atmosphere.

In Buddhism, this law or this possibility appears of an order of magnitude unknown elsewhere, and this is what makes for the originality of the *Mahāyāna*, not from the point of view of the content, but of the phenomenon: far from constituting merely a perplexing enigma, this second unfolding of the Buddhist Revelation is in fact a perfectly limpid possibility that was bound to manifest in its place and at its time in the fullest plenitude of its possibility. In speaking of the *Mahāyāna*, we are also speaking implicitly of the *Vajrayāna*—Buddhist Tantrism—which is sometimes presented as a "third setting in motion of the Law", and which repeats in its own fashion, within the framework of *Mahāyāna* itself, the second unfolding just mentioned; but whether it is the one or the other, or whether—in *Mahāyāna* terminology—it is the *Hīnayāna*, it is important to understand that there can be no effect without a cause: what we wish to say is that the sole possible cause of the values traditionally connected with the Buddha is the Buddha himself, and none other; the homage granted him by Brahmanists, including Shankara, is one more indication, among many other signs, of the avataric scope of his person.

In order better to characterize the profound intention or the meaning of the *Mahāyāna*, we would like to draw attention to the following factors: Buddhism, without ever abandoning its serenity, has something vertiginously quantitative in one of its aspects, something desperately riveted to "horizontal" causality, or to action and merit, and something, moreover, radically misogynist, if such an expression is permissible: one has the impression of getting lost in myriads of *kalpas* and in accumulations of seemingly limitless merits and demerits. This is how Buddhism wants to suggest the nature of the *Samsāra*, which is a bottomless abyss, a measurelessly endless system of concentric circles, and at the same time a spiraling motion without beginning or end,[2] or with no other beginning or end than that which limits it metaphysically, namely *Nirvāna*, which envelops all, absorbs all, extinguishes all. Now in esoterism, the despairing number of quantities is reduced to mere mirages, femininity is grasped in its universal essence, and Deliverance becomes a flash of lightning; what is thus affirmed is the eternal truth that our Deliverance was ever before us, and that within the seemingly insuperable difficulty there is a secret point where all becomes easy—mystery of intellection according to Zen, *Shingon*, and *Tendai*, and mystery of grace according to *Jōdo*. After countless efforts worth no more than a gesture, man is breathed in by the Heavens and falls so to speak, but ascentionally, into his own Deliverance; our merits have no positive value, they only eliminate—more symbolically than effectively—the obstacles that separate us from celestial attraction.

Every spiritual cycle, whatever its order of magnitude, comprises such alternations. On earth, Rigor is manifested before Mercy, be it only to prepare the advent of the latter; in the celestial regions, however, Mercy precedes Rigor and coincides in its substance with the beatific dimension of the Absolute itself.

"Charity" (*dāna*), which constitutes as it were the framework or the periphery of the *Mahāyāna*, is the first of the six *pāramitās* or virtues of the *Bodhisattva;* "wisdom" (*prajnā*) is the sixth and their completion. The four other *pāramitās* appear as intermediary virtues: these

---

[2] All of this is of course related to the extreme precariousness of the chances of entering the human state, which is to the other states what the center is to the periphery, or the point to extension.

are "renunciation" (*shīla*), "virility" (*vīrya*), "patience" (*kshānti*), and "contemplation" (*dhyāna*); these spiritual modes amount to so many paths, at once simultaneous and successive—a single one being able to determine a whole life, but without either needing, or being able to exclude, the daily practice of the others. Moreover, the first five *pāramitās* are not really separate from the virtue of *prajnā*, of which they are secondary aspects whose function is to contribute in their own way to the awakening of liberating Knowledge.

The essence of the *Mahāyāna* as a method is really the "transfer of our merits to others" (*parināmana*): "Enlightenment" as well as "Salvation" embrace, in the metaphysical scheme of things and in their moral intention, all the beings in the visible and invisible universe. If the *Bodhisattva* is supposed to "refuse to enter *Nirvāna* so long as a single blade of grass remains undelivered", this means two things: first—and this is the cosmic viewpoint—that the function of the *Bodhisattva* coincides with what in Western language would be termed the permanent "angelic presence" in the world, a presence that disappears only with the world itself, at the time of the final reintegration, which Western *gnosis* terms the "Apocatastasis"; and second—and this is the metaphysical viewpoint—that the *Bodhisattva*, in realizing the "voidness" of things, realizes thereby not only the "voidness" of the *Samsāra* as such but, by the same token, its nirvanic quality. For if on the one hand everything is "voidness", on the other hand everything is *Nirvāna*, the Buddhist notion of emptiness being both negative and positive as is expressed in the saying: "Form is void and Void is form". The *Samsāra*, which seems at first to be inexhaustible, so much so that the Bodhisattvic vow appears to have something excessive or even demented about it, is "instantly" reduced—in the timeless instantaneity of *prajnā*—to "universal Enlightenment" (*Sambodhi*); on this plane, all antinomy is transcended and as it were consumed. "Delivering the last blade of grass" amounts, in this respect, to seeing it in its nirvanic essence, or to seeing the unreality of its non-deliverance.

Since *prajnā* is the synthesis of the five other *pāramitās*, the *Mahāyāna* is reducible in principle to *prajnā*; in other words, the inward union with the transcendent "Void" could suffice in principle as a spiritual viaticum; however, because human nature is in fact contrary to unity and simplicity, the method of regeneration will therefore have to take account of all aspects of our samsaric imprisonment, whence the necessity for a path which, while presenting initially an element of unity and simplicity, proceeds from the multiple to the one and from the complex to the simple.[3]

It is not difficult to conceive how the first five virtues or spiritual methods are contained in the sixth: first of all, there is no possible *gnosis* without an element of renunciation or detachment; outwardly, *gnosis* of necessity comprises a factor of moral alternative upon which it can base itself and which enables it to unfold. Likewise, *gnosis* requires virility or "heroicalness": it comprises in fact an aspect of battle against samsaric seductions, both inward and outward; there is no spiritual victory without "the fight against the dragon". To these virtues of rigor are adjoined the virtues of mildness, namely, charity and patience; just as patience is, by its nature, the *shakti*—the complementary power—of renunciation, so charity is the *shakti* of virility. *Gnosis* requires, if one may so express it, an element of generosity and another of beauty: the "mathematical" and "masculine" aspect has need of a "musical" and "feminine" complement, the whole universe being moreover woven of this warp and this weft; without beauty, truth cannot manifest itself and still remain true to itself and yield its full message. Referring to the canonical image of the Buddha, we could express ourselves in the following manner: if the Buddha represents renunciation, the lotus supporting him will be patience; if he represents virility, the lotus will be charity; if he is supreme Knowledge, the lotus will be contemplation, with all the virtues this entails.

Amidism, which was taught in China by Tan-Luan, Tao-Cho, and Shan-Tao, then in Japan by Honen and Shinran, appears in some respects as a merciful synthesis of the six *pāramitās*: "universal Enlightenment" is latent in everything since each thing, being "void", "is none other than the Void"; now this Enlightenment can encompass and as it were sweep the individual upwards through the merciful *upāya* that is the remembrance of Amitabha as actualized by the formula *Namo'mitābhaya Buddhāya*. Given that spiritual realization

---

[3] This is what—be it said in passing—neither pseudo-Zenists nor pseudo-Vedantists want to understand, they who fancy that it is possible to make our nature magically disappear with mental reductions that are as pretentious as they are unavailing.

exists "prior" to man, the latter, who possesses no more reality of his own than foam does in relation to water, "falls" into his pre-existing *Nirvāna*, which takes the initiative, so to speak, in its capacity as *Bodhi*, "Enlightenment". Under these conditions—strange as it may seem—it is *Nirvāna* "in act" that takes on the role of the *pāramitās*; this is what tradition calls the "power of the Other", in contrast with the "power of Self", which is the spiritual principle of ordinary Buddhism, as also for those esoterisms that are independent of the cult of Amitabha, such as Zen or *Shingon*.

This celestial gift of *pāramitās* that are fulfilled in advance—or this salvific grace bestowed thanks to their prior realization by Amitabha, who himself is the projection of both the universal Buddha and the historical Buddha—is included in the Buddha's "Original Vow", which in reality is a cosmic or divine act upon which the whole doctrine of the "Pure Land" is erected.[4] Participation by devotees in the *pāramitās* is then reduced essentially to faith, of which three aspects, or three "mental states", can be distinguished: "truthful thought" or a "sincere spirit"; "profoundly believing thought"; the "desire to be reborn in the Pure Land".[5]

However, the *pāramitās* are not contained in these mental attitudes alone; they are above all inherent in the "remembrance of the

---

[4] There are forty-eight vows (*pranidhāna*s); only the eighteenth, which is by far the most important and which Honen described as the "king of vows", is the "Original Vow": "When I shall have attained the state of a Buddha, if the beings of the ten regions (of the universe) shall have believed in me with serene thoughts and shall have wished to be born in my Land and shall have thought of me be it only ten times—if these beings are not to be reborn there, then may I not obtain perfect Knowledge; none are excepted save those who shall have committed the five mortal sins and shall have blasphemed the Good Law" (The greater *Sukhāvatī Vyūha Sūtra* 8:18, according to the Chinese translation, the surviving Sanskrit texts being incomplete). The "ten times" of the text also has the meaning of "ten modes", such as thought, speech, vision, gesture.

[5] According to the *Amitāyur Dhyāna Sūtra*, 22. The first-named state excludes all dissimulation and all lukewarmness; the second state, according to Honen, implies an awareness on the one hand of our wretchedness and helplessness, and on the other hand of the saving power of Amitabha and his wish to save us if we invoke him with faith. The third mental state means that we offer all of our merits for the sole intention of being born in the "Pure Land", and that at the same time, within the scope of this intention itself, we take pleasure in the merits of others as if those others were ourselves, an attitude that confers on our path a secret radiance and a kind of impersonal amplitude.

Buddha" (*buddhānusmriti*) itself;[6] this is to say that this perpetual remembrance is at once renunciation or purity, virility or persevering activity, patience or peace, generosity or fervor, contemplation or discernment, wisdom or union. Indeed, to abide in this remembrance alone, or in the act that anchors it in duration by reducing time to an eternal instant, does not go without renunciation of the world and of oneself; this allows us, by the same token, to understand what role the *pāramitā* of virility plays here: if renunciation (*shīla*) is a participation in Eternity, virility (*vīrya*), for its part, will be situated under the sign of the Eternal Present, like the lightning bolt or the "third Eye". As for patience (*kshānti*), it consists, within this context of "remembrance", in abiding calmly in the Center, in the grace of Amitabha, whereas charity (*dāna*) is on the contrary a projecting of one's ego into the distance, or the extending of one's will beyond the individual shell: if patience is based on our awareness of possessing everything in grace, charity will be our awareness of living in all things, and of extending our spiritual activity to the whole of creation. The remembrance of Amitabha also implies, with all the more reason, contemplation (*dhyāna*) and Knowledge (*prajnā*); Knowledge corresponds in some respect to Plenitude and contemplation to the Void. We have already seen that the "Void" has both a negative and a positive meaning; it is its positive meaning that can be termed "Plenitude". The "Void" is "Plenitude" inasmuch as it is opposed to the samsaric "nothingness", not inasmuch as it constitutes its Quintessence, for in this respect all is Plenitude and all is Void.

These relationships could be described even more simply by specifying that the synthesis of the *pāramitā*s is realized most distinctly in the two conditions *sine qua non* of the *nembutsu*, namely "faith" and "action": action summarizes the active virtues and faith the contemplative virtues, although both comprise static and dynamic elements, such as abstention in the case of action and ardor in the case of faith. Moreover, these two categories bring us back to the twin pillars of all spirituality: "discernment" and "concentration", or doctrine and

---

[6] It should be pointed out here that, despite its divergent form, the Tibetan invocatory formula *Om Mani Padme Hum*, by virtue of its homage to the "Jewel" and the "Lotus", is equivalent to the Japanese *Namu Amida Butsu*; it is in effect addressed to the *Bodhisattva* Avalokiteshvara and for that reason also to the Buddha Amitabha, of whom this *Bodhisattva* is an extension.

method; in fact, all possible qualities, whether intellectual, psychic, or moral, are to be found under these two denominators for they derive either from the intelligence or from the will, and thus describe—by indicating what we should be—what we are in our innate and eternal "Buddhahood".

— .:. —

According to a spatial symbolism in use in the *Mahāyāna*, the universal Buddhas or the *Dhyāni-Buddhas*, also called *Jina*s, the "Victorious Ones", come forth by projection from the *Ādi-Buddha*: they are five in number and each rules over a cardinal point, with the most eminent of them, Vairochana, occupying the Center.[7] To Vairochana corresponds analogically the element ether; to Akshobhya, who is in the east, corresponds the element air; to Amitabha, the west and water; to Amoghasiddhi, the north and earth; and to Ratnasambhava, the south and fire. Now ether is everywhere, and everywhere it is central and immutable, like truth or contemplation; the sun rises in the east, invincible like a drawn sword, and invincible is air unleashed as a hurricane; the west indicates repose, as does water, which gathers calmly and endures all things; the north is cold like purity, and the earth is steadfast like renunciation; and the south possesses warmth and life, it is generous like charity. The *Ādi-Buddha*—or *Prajñāpāramitā*—is symbolically situated at the zenith or beyond space; with respect to the sensible elements, including ether, he rules over the supra-sensible element, namely consciousness, which means that he is identified, not with the cosmic principles or, to be more precise, with modes of relative knowledge as is the case with the *Dhyāni-Buddhas*,[8] but with Absolute Knowledge, which embraces all relativities while remaining outside them.

[7] Depending on the school, it is either Vairochana, or Vajradhara, or Amitabha, who is identified with the Supreme; many other fluctuations could be mentioned, especially where the quaternary is divided into two or is multiplied, each time with its attendant *Bodhisattva*s and *Shakti*s.

[8] Who correspond to the four archangels of Islam, Vairochana—at the Center—being the equivalent of *Ar-Rūh*.

116

In *Shingon* esoterism, the open fan of the five elements is closed again within "consciousness", which is the sixth and superior element: to be *Buddha* is to know totally the nature of what are seemingly external phenomena; it is therefore to know that they are not of a substance other than our own selves. To affirm that the *Bodhisattva* sees nothing but the "void" (*shūnya*) means that he perceives only the "voidness" (*shūnyatā*) of things, or that he beholds things in their suchness, which is identical with that of consciousness;[9] the elements are like the outward diversification, or like crystallized aspects, of this single consciousness; he who looks at the world sees himself, and he who realizes the depths of the heart contains the world. The synthesis of the five objective elements in the sixth, which is subjective, prefigures in its own way the spiritual synthesis of the *pāramitās*: in other words, earth, water, air, fire, ether—taken in their broadest meaning—are, finally, the outward and cosmic appearances of the first five *pāramitās*, the sixth element—*chitta* or consciousness—being by the same token the natural prefiguration of the sixth virtue, *prajñā*.[10] An analogous synthesis is achieved in Zen, where the path consists in discovering the infinite suchness of the heart and thereby in realizing, as in a lightning flash, "that which is".

But let us return to the synthesis enabled by the Vow of Amitabha: this synthesis presents a special relationship not only with the symbolism of the west, the setting of the sun, and the element water, but thereby also with the virtue of patience; at the same time, this perspective of bhaktic esoterism[11] identifies Amitabha with the *Ādi-Buddha*, in such fashion that the symbolism of the evening or of freshness, and also of patience, is granted a preponderant and as it were central significance; trusting self-abandonment to the "power of the Other" and to salvific grace pertains indeed to the nature of water and to "passive Perfection". For the man whose heart reposes in the

[9] This vision of the "voidness" of things is not unrelated to the fact that the noble man sees in every phenomenon the essential, whereas the base man sees the accidental; now the "essence" of things rejoins their "voidness" in that it is an opening toward the non-manifested, or a manifestation of an archetype.

[10] Esoterically, the lotus on which the Buddha is enthroned represents innate and latent knowledge, whereas the halo expresses the effective Knowledge realized by the *Tathāgata*.

[11] Hence of relative esoterism, which does not exclude, in its kernel, the most profound *gnosis* for whosoever has the calling to discover it.

supernatural certainty of salvific grace there remains finally nothing to await, humanly speaking, save the dissipation of all karmic effects; he is patient under the weight of the *Samsāra*, which he must still endure and which, for him, exhausts itself like his own earthly destiny. This perfection of trust or quietude cannot, obviously, be a matter purely and simply of passivity; in other words, it would amount to nothing if it did not comprise, essentially, the complementary aspects of activity and impassivity; each *pāramitā* is akin to a mirror that reflects objects without ceasing to be what it is; there is no spiritual patience without its concomitant renunciation and strength. This is the unmistakable meaning of Amidist texts, as seen in these words from the illustrious Honen:[12] "The man who longs for Paradise and who sets his whole mind on this single intention will behave like someone who hates or even abhors the world. . . . As for the passage (in the book of Shan-Tao) on a heart strong as a diamond, which allows nothing to either trouble or vanquish it . . . it means that we must not let our merits[13] be squandered in just any direction whatsoever. . . . Seeing that the diamond is an indestructible substance, may it serve then as an example to show us that neither should the heart allow itself to be broken in its resolve to attain the goal."

---

[12] *Honen the Buddhist Saint* (Kyoto, 1949), Vol. 3, Ch. 21, 8; 22, 10.

[13] That is, the benefic forces emanating from the accumulation of our past merits, or good *karma*.

A Note on the Feminine Element in *Mahāyāna*

"Transcendent Wisdom" (*prajnā*), the loftiest of the six spiritual disciplines (*pāramitās*), is personified in a divinity bearing the very name of Prajnaparamita; if man becomes wise, it is in fact owing to pre-existing Wisdom, whose function, at once virginal and maternal, is its inherent Beatitude and Mercy. This divinity is the "Mother of all the Buddhas" and thus she is not without analogy to the goddess Tara, or more precisely to the "White Tara" who, likewise, is associated with "Transcendent Wisdom" (*Prajnā*); the Mongols call her "Mother Tara" (*Dara Eke*) and designate her as "Mother of all the Buddhas and *Boddhisattvas*", whereas the Tibetans give her the name of "Savioress" (*Döl-Ma*). Seen from the point of view of the human support or of the "glorious body",[1] one can recognize Prajnaparamita or Tara in queen Maya, mother of the historical Buddha:[2] just as the Buddha can be said to be a manifestation of the Absolute Buddha—the *Ādi-Buddha* or Vajradhara, or Mahavairochana depending on the various terminologies—so does his august Mother manifest the complementary power

---

[1] This is the *sambhogakāya*, or beatific body, which is situated between the earthly body, *nirmānakāya*, and the divine Body, *dharmakāya*.

[2] "He (the king Shakya) had a queen called Maya, as if to say that she was free from all illusion (*māyā*); a splendor proceeding from his splendor, like the sun's magnificence when it is free from any obscuring influence; a queen supreme in the assembly of all queens. Like a mother for her subjects . . . she was the most eminent of goddesses for the whole world. But queen Maya, having beheld the great glory of her newborn child . . . could not sustain the joy he brought to her; and so as not to die of it, she ascended to Heaven" (*Buddhacharita* of Ashvagosha, 1:15, 16; 2:18). According to one *Jātaka*, "the mother of a Buddha . . . is a person who has realized perfections throughout a hundred thousand *kalpa*s and who has been faithful to the five precepts from the day of her birth." Guénon has remarked that "the mother of the Buddha is called *Māyā-Devī* and that, among the Greeks and Romans, Maia was also the mother of Hermes or Mercury." "The Annunciation takes the form of 'Mahā-Māyā's sacred dream', in which she sees a glorious white elephant descending from the skies to enter her womb. . . . It is not stated explicitly, but can be assumed, that the birth was 'virginal'; in any case, it is interesting that the story was already known to Saint Jerome, who mentions it in a dispute on Virginity and in connection with the miraculous births of Plato and Christ" (Ananda K. Coomaraswamy, *Hinduism and Buddhism*, "The Myth").

of the universal Buddha, or the saving grace inherent in *Nirvāna* and emanating therefrom.[3]

Since "extremes meet", it is significant that the most intellectual and most ascetic attitude, hence in a way the most "virile" possible, namely Knowledge (*prajñā-pāramitā*), coincides with a feminine principle, as if, at the very height or depth of abstraction or annihilation, there occurred a kind of compensatory reversal; in Vedantic terms, one would say that *Ātmā*, in being perfectly *Sat* and *Chit*, Being and Knowledge, comprises thereby, and necessarily so, *Ānanda*, Beatitude. Use of the symbolism of femininity may seem surprising in a Buddhist climate; though it is true that feminine symbols refer in the first instance, and quite evidently, to universal realities that have nothing human about them, the human concomitances of the symbol nonetheless remain what they are: in other words, the immediate human significance of the image retains all of its rights without there being any reason to fear irreducible antinomies or moral conflicts. Sages are the first to understand that femininity itself is independent of earthly accidentality or of the contingent, samsaric aspects of the carnal creature; if it is opportune to turn away from seductions and, in some respects, from the binding chain of attachments, regardless of the nature of their supports, it is however neither possible nor desirable to escape from femininity as principle, which is nirvanic in essence and thus divine. The in principle more or less asexual nature of the divinities of the *Mahāyāna* pertains only to privative contingencies and not to positive substance; thus the fluctuations found in Mahayanist imagery and in its eso-exoteric interpretations indicate in their own way the complexity of all these relationships and the human predicament in the face of this complexity. If a woman is supposed to "despise her femininity"[4] in the paradise of Amitabha, this means that she is entirely freed from the physiological and psychological servitude

---

[3] Analogous remarks could be made about Gopa Yashodhara, the spouse of Shakyamuni, and about their son Rahula. All the nobility of this wife shines forth in the fact that she grieved, not for the mere reason that Shakyamuni had left her, but because he had not taken her with him in his exile in order to share in his austerities; she understood the reason for this later and entered the Buddha's community.

[4] According to the greater *Sukhāvati Vyūha* which, together with the lesser *Sukhāvati Vyūha* and the *Amitāyur Dhyāna Sūtra*, is the chief scriptural authority for Amidism. Christian symbolism, according to which "one neither marries nor is given in marriage" in Heaven, refers to this aspect of things, whereas the Muslim symbolism of the houris derives from the same perspective as Tantrism.

of her earthly condition, but not from her celestial substance, otherwise the power of taking on a "feminine form" attributed to divinities described as either "masculine" or "asexual" would make no sense; the ostracism contained in the dogmatic formulation is proportioned to the sincerity of the renunciation. We have here two perspectives that intertwine and modulate each other: in the first, woman is considered as the principal factor of seduction binding one to the *Samsāra*, to the point of appearing to be the very genius of the latter; in the second perspective, which is so to speak the opposite side of the same circle, femininity reveals itself instead in its positive reality as maternity, virginity, beauty, and mercy;[5] this is the Christian opposition—or complementarity—between Eve and Mary. And this is important: in regard to Heaven, each creature is considered to have a "feminine" character—which is why it is said, in Hinduism, that each soul is a *gopī* in love with Krishna; however, from the point of view of participatory analogy—not of complementary opposition—each soul is considered on the contrary to have something "masculine", and this is what Buddhism has in mind when it seems to want to deny women access to Heaven. This, we must insist again, is independent of the question of the "glorious body", which belongs to an altogether different order, being a cosmic and not a spiritual question.

In certain sectors of Buddhism there exists, incontestably and even of necessity, a direct or indirect tendency to interiorize femininity and sexuality, and not simply to reject them—whence the occurrence of marriage, unthinkable at the origin, for some adepts in cer-

---

[5] It should be noted in the present context that the whole *Amitāyur Dhyāna Sūtra* is addressed by the Buddha to a woman, the Queen Vaidehi, just as the lesser *Sukhāvatī Vyūha* does not fail to specify that it is addressed to women as well as men, even though at first the admission of women into the fold of Buddhism did not take place without some difficulty. "Whatever son or daughter of a family shall hear the name of the blessed Amitayus (an aspect of Amitabha), the *Tathāgata* ('He who hath thus gone'), and having heard it shall keep it in mind . . . when that son or daughter of a family comes to the point of death, then that Amitayus, the *Tathāgata*, surrounded by an assembly of disciples and followed by a host of *Bodhisattva*s, will stand before them at their hour of death, and they will depart this life with tranquil minds. After their death they will be reborn in the *Sukhāvatī* world, in the Buddha Land of the same Amitayus, the *Tathāgata.* Therefore then, O Sariputra . . . every son and every daughter of a family ought with his whole mind to make fervent prayers in view of that Buddha Land. . . . Every son or daughter of a family who shall hear the name of that Enunciation of the Law and keep in memory the names of those blessed Buddhas will be favored by the Buddhas and will never again return, being once in possession of the transcendent Wisdom" (Lesser *Sukhāvatī Vyūha*, 10, 17).

tain branches of the *Mahāyāna*, especially in Tibet and in Japan; the example of Shinran, disciple of Honen, is particularly noteworthy.[6] Aside from the requirements of ascetic and disciplinary dogmatism, Buddhist asexualism is really but a means of affirming the idea of "voidness", or one might say that asexuality expresses an aspect of the "void";[7] thus it is said that the *Bodhisattva* sees nothing but the "void", which must be understood in a negative or samsaric sense as well as in a positive or nirvanic sense.[8]

An important aspect of the symbolism of femininity is, in the *Vajrayāna*, the couple *upāya-prajñā*, represented in Tibetan iconography by two embracing deities: it is well known that *upāya* is the "method"—or the "mirage"—which reveals the Truth in the most efficient way, whereas *prajñā* is the liberating knowledge that the *upāya* awakens; this sexual symbolism also applies, in principle, to the couple "void-form" (*shūnya-rūpa*) or *Nirvāna-Samsāra*, for the reciprocity is analogous or even fundamentally identical. Though such a symbolism may appear to be situated at the diametrically opposite point of Buddhist asexualism, in reality it coincides with it in the sense that all polarity is transcended in union and as if annihilated in a common infinitude, or in supreme non-duality.[9] In order to really grasp the relationship between this image and the concepts of *upāya* and *prajñā*, one must know that the second element is "ourselves", for it is our transpersonal essence, whereas the first element is the *Logos*, which, across the samsaric darkness, awakens and actualizes That which we are; each creature—*Shingon* emphatically asserts—is a Buddha unawares.

[6] We could mention here the visit Honen received on his deathbed from Queen Vaidehi, the famous woman disciple of the Buddha, a supernatural occurrence proving that celestial asexuality is manifested, not in the "glorious body", but in the absence of samsaric passion and in the beatitude of inward union.

[7] It is only too obvious that modern views about woman, due to a generalized egalitarianism, and then to a certain—strictly negative—feminization of man combined with an artificial virilization of woman, are here null and void. However, one must take into account a compensatory phenomenon at the end of times, which is that piety or spiritual gifts are more frequently found among women than men.

[8] "Where there is form"—the Buddha said—"there is void, and where there is void, there is form. Void and form are not distinct."

[9] It is said that the Buddha, before dying, ascended to Heaven to preach the *Dharma* to his mother Maya; and this meeting can well symbolize the supreme Union, for it is really the celestial complement—in a positively converse way—of the *Tathāgata's* earthly birth; this was the divine birth of Maya in Prajnaparamita.

Dharmakara's Vow

The notion of myth usually evokes a picture of traditional stories replete with a wealth of symbolism and more or less devoid of historical foundation; however, this second opinion should not be allowed to play too peremptory a role in the definition itself of myth, for it suffices to say that the particular function of myth renders the importance of its historicity basically irrelevant in the very measure that this function is properly understood. What guarantees the spiritual function of a sacred story is its symbolism, on the one hand, and its traditional character, on the other: in the case of stories belonging to the *Mahāyāna*, it is the Buddha who stands as guarantor for the reality and therefore the efficacy of the story; that is to say, his person guarantees, if not absolutely the historical truth of the facts, then certainly at least their spiritual truth, which takes precedence over the historicity,[1] and their salvific virtue, which is the reason for being of the myth's existence. That being said, in no way do we wish to cast the slightest doubt upon the earthly existence of a *Bodhisattva* called Dharmakara; our intention is merely to emphasize the fact that the story in question is above all a manifestation, by the Buddha Shakyamuni, of the principle of the salvific coincidence between Mercy and faith; moreover, we may accept that the Buddha Shakyamuni, in offering this story, was in truth speaking about himself and offered an aspect of himself: as a personification of the total *Logos* he was able to endow his own power of Mercy with the name *Amitābha*, "Infinite Light", and to describe by means of the story of Dharmakara and his Vow the mystery of the coincidence of which we have spoken. But this symbolic transfer to a previous Buddha of a power belonging to Shakyamuni cannot exclude, quite obviously, the possibility of the historical fact; in which case, it is in his capacity as "absolute Buddha" or *Ādi-Buddha* that Shakyamuni has the power, not only to define and self-actualize himself by means of a story-symbol, but also to refer himself concretely and salvifically

---

[1] If such were not the case it would be impossible to explain why the four Gospels can contradict one another on certain details, or why these facts did not worry the ancient Christians, or how it is that the visions of the saints can diverge. This same principle of the primacy of spiritual reality explains with all the more reason the existence of "mythical" differences between the religions.

to the work of a historically antecedent Buddha, one representing more particularly the aspect of Mercy.

This power could be said to be analogous to the power which, in the cosmic sector of Islam—and not outside it—is incumbent upon the Arabian Prophet in relation to the Semitic Prophets who preceded him. This then is how Shakyamuni can actualize, in his quality of *Logos*-Essence or *Logos*-Synthesis, the enlightening or salvific powers of the other Buddhas, when these are considered from the point of view of their various qualities and not of their single essence; whether it is a question of different Buddhas or of different qualities of the sole Buddha becomes for all practical purposes no more than a matter of perspective or even of dialectic.

An example has been taken here from Islam, not because it would be the only one possible, but because the analogy in this case is particularly direct; in Christianity, the use of the Psalms provides an example of the same order, in the sense that Christ, the "Son of David", projects himself, so to speak, into this anterior Revelation and makes it his own, with the result that the Psalter has become something like an authentic song of Christ, prophetically sensed moreover by David, for the relationship is reversible. However, the analogy with the case of Buddhism is less direct here because the emphasis remains focused on Christ, whereas in Buddhism it is placed on Amitabha, namely on the predecessor; yet in order to have access to the grace offered by Amitabha, one needs to take refuge in the historical Buddha, submit to his Law, and enter his Community.[2]

To approach the mystery of the *Bodhisattva*s, of their "refusal" to enter *Nirvāna*—or, what amounts to the same, the mystery of the Buddha Amitabha's "Original Vow" (*pranidhāna*)—one must start from the idea that there is within us as it were a "divine fragment" that wants to be delivered; it is this will of the "God within us" that Dharmakara—the future Amitabha—confronts with a series of conditions that, in short, culminate—or can be summarized—in the following: "O *Bhagavat*, if the beings of the innumerable and incom-

---

[2] This constitutes the "Triple Refuge": *Buddha*, *Dharma*, and *Sangha*, whereby one becomes a Buddhist.

mensurable Buddha-lands, who will have heard my name after I have attained Buddhahood, should turn their thoughts towards birth into my Buddha-land, and bring to maturity their merit with this goal in mind; if these beings were not to be born into my Buddha-land, even those who will have repeated this thought only ten times—always excepting those beings who obstructed the Good Law or abused it—then may I not attain to supreme Knowledge!" Now, without this will of the "Self" to be delivered "in us", the "pressure" expressed by this vow would be unintelligible; it could be said that God loves sanctity—or that He loves Himself in man—to the point of wishing to reward it on the outward plane as well, for whoso grants what is more, also grants what is less.

But the *Bodhisattva* can also be interpreted in another way, less far removed from the monotheistic conceptions or even in perfect agreement with them: the *Bodhisattva* is on the one hand the saint who has realized a particular angelic state, or in whom this state is "incarnated" in the most direct manner, and on the other hand he is this state itself, which in fact stops at the threshold of *Nirvāna* since the Angel as such cannot become God; the sufficient reason for the Angel is, indeed, to be what he is, namely a mirror of the Divine. Seen from this angle, the sacrificial and almost indefinite transmigration of the *Bodhisattva* is not so much a series of successive lives of a selfsame soul[3] as it is the individualization, repeated and multiplied—hence diverse in time and space—of an angelic state. Just as the Archangels crystallize divine Names in supraformal manifestation, at the summit of the macrocosm, so do the *Bodhisattva*s reflect the principial Buddhas:[4] thus the *Bodhisattva* Avalokiteshvara—"the Lord who gazes down in mercy"—is as an emanation of the metacosmic Buddha Amitabha, who is pure Mercy.[5]

---

[3] We know moreover how much Buddhism relativizes this composite termed the ego.

[4] Vairochana and the four other *Dhyāni-Buddha*s. Depending on how these things are envisaged, each Buddha can become central.

[5] It is moreover this aspect of luminous gentleness that explains the feminine—or, depending on the case, semi-feminine—form this *Bodhisattva* takes in the Far East (Kwan-Yin, Kwannon). The archangelic nature of Avalokiteshvara is evident, among other things, from his iconographical symbolism: he is sometimes represented with eleven heads and a thousand arms, which may be compared to the Semitic symbolism of the Archangels; we have spoken of this in *L'œil du cœur*, chap. "*An-Nūr*". But this nature appears above all in certain myths, such as the birth of Avalokiteshvara from a ray emanating from the right eye of Amitabha; here, the angelic aspect of the *Bodhisattva* erases all memory of a human destiny.

Let us recall here the doctrine of the three "hypostases" of the Blessed One: *Dharmakāya* (the "universal body") is the Essence, Beyond-Being; *Sambhogakāya* (the "body of bliss") is the "celestial Form", the "divine Personification"; *Nirmānakāya* (the "body of metamorphosis") is the human manifestation of the Buddha.

——— ·⋮· ———

The *Bodhisattva* Dharmakara, on the threshold of *Nirvāna*, made the Vow not to enter therein unless, once he had become Buddha, or "Enlightened", he would be able to offer a Paradise of Purity to all those who pronounced his Name—thenceforth nirvanic or divine— with an unmixed faith and with the conviction of being incapable of saving themselves by their own merits. Having become Buddha under the name of Amitabha, the celestial being keeps his word: through his Name he saves multitudes of believers, and the Buddha Shakyamuni participates in this work by bringing it to the knowledge of the men of this world or this cycle.

In this sacred story, first of all there is a contrast made between the *Bodhisattva* Dharmakara and *Nirvāna*; then we have their fusion in the person of the Buddha Amitabha. One may justifiably ask oneself what is the meaning of a Vow such as this, which exerts a kind of pressure on the nirvanic Reality: "If you do not grant me what I demand"—this in substance is what Dharmakara says to the infinite Reality and the supreme Bliss—"I refuse to enter into You"; what is the meaning of this refusal as a matter of principle and of the pressure it implies? For it seems that metaphysically there can be no common measure between man and the Absolute: the latter can determine everything, whereas man has no power over it. This is self-evident, but it does not exclude the fact that there is an aspect under which the relative itself is included in the Principle—for "each thing is *Ātmā*"— where it is seen now purely as a kind of internal dimension of the all-inclusive Absoluteness; however, this answer would be insufficient in the absence of a further argument, which moreover derives from the preceding one, namely that *Nirvāna* comprises—on the basis of what has just been said—a pole or mode that could be described as "feminine" or "receptive" and which is finally the divine *Prakriti*, the primordial Substance that is envisaged here according to the Buddhist perspective of the Void and Enlightenment. When things are viewed from this angle, that is to say on the basis of the "relative absoluteness" of manifestation and of the "femininity" of the already relative pole of the divine Principle, the way is open for understanding the meaning of the Vow.

There is a well-known Far-Eastern symbol that suggests the reciprocity in question in a particularly expressive manner: this is the *Yin-Yang* diagram, which shows firstly a white and a black field, and then a black dot in the white field and a white dot in the black field. Applying this symbol here, we may say that *Nirvāna* comprises a sector of relativity open to the cosmos whereas the *Bodhisattva* for his part possesses an element of absoluteness that integrates him in a certain respect in the absolute and metacosmic nature of *Nirvāna*.[6] *Nirvāna-Prakriti*, by virtue of its relativity—without which there would be no possible contact between Heaven and earth—"desires" man; to speak of the attractive power of Heaven is to imply the dimension of relativity that it comprises; now this dimension is none other than Goodness; and without a world, there is no Mercy. Man, who as such is relative, looks towards the Absolute; but *Nirvāna* under its relative aspect does not wish to absorb relative man, it desires man by virtue of his mystery of absoluteness; in other words it desires the *Bodhisattva* in order to give birth to the Buddha.

This reciprocity, where the higher desires the lower by virtue of an element of inferiority and the lower determines the higher by virtue of an element of superiority, enables us to understand, either directly or indirectly, why "there will be more joy in Heaven over one sinner that repenteth than over ninety-nine just persons who need no repentance", and also why it is that when a *Jīvan-Mukta*, one "delivered in this life", leaves this lower world "the Heavens resound with his glory". The saying that a *brāhmana* commands the *deva*s and other paradoxes of a similar kind share an analogous meaning; finally, the Buddha Amitabha would not come down with his two archangelic

---

[6] This is the "secret" (*sirr*) of the heart, in the language of the Sufis. If blasphemies against the "Father" and the "Son" can be forgiven, but not those uttered against the Holy Spirit, this is because the latter alone is concretely present in the soul since it inspires us, so that offence done to the Spirit cannot be due to ignorance or error. It may also be pointed out that the prostration of the Angels before Adam, related in the Koran, is not unrelated to the mystery of the element of absoluteness in the Heart-Intellect.

Bodhisattva acolytes and all his celestial court to meet his chosen one if there were not to be found in the latter a nirvanic and metacosmic element that the *Nirvāna* open to the cosmos might "desire".[7] This extrinsic *Nirvāna*, which attracts and which exercises Mercy, is "Virgin" and "Mother" or even—as the Song of Songs expresses it— "Sister" and "Spouse": it radiates and absorbs at one and the same time, it both enlightens and it desires; in relation to Heaven, which has become *Prakriti* in turning towards the cosmos, the latter becomes *Purusha*,[8] not of course by virtue of the cosmos, but by virtue of the divine *Purusha* with which the cosmos is identified through Grace and *Gnosis*. The feminine Divinity, who loves the masculine God, will likewise love the reflected image of God in the cosmos, and will seek to deliver that image by appropriating it to herself, thus absorbing it and rendering it divine.

The Vow of the *Bodhisattva* Dharmakara, the fulfillment of which belongs to the Buddha Amitabha, appears at first sight to be a very special and unusual favor, strangely remote in character; in fact, however, it does not mean anything else but the divine Principle of universal attraction, and thus of Mercy. In other words, if "remembrance of the Buddha Amitabha" grants access to the "Pure Land", this is because the name of this Buddha, which is a Name of the one Buddha,[9] really conveys the nirvanic Power.

The guarantee that this is so is the fact that this Name has been uttered by the historic *Avatāra*, and here we rejoin a principle already mentioned above, namely that it is the fact of the Revelation that guarantees both the truth and the effectiveness of the salvific means. Thus, if the Name of God is "holy", this is not because it is a word

---

[7] This global mystery has given rise to many ill-sounding assertions, the most common of which is that "God could not subsist without man"; this statement, admittedly, is not without its profound meaning, but the drawbacks of such a formulation greatly exceed its advantages.

[8] *Purusha* and *Prakriti*: the active and passive poles of Being.

[9] Whence the almost henotheist absoluteness attributed to Amitabha by his own adepts.

referring to God, but because it has been revealed by God Himself and through this very fact conveys something of the divine Power, and in principle even all the Power that the meaning of the Name suggests: the name *Allāh*, revealed at the origins of the Arabic language and confirmed by the Koranic Revelation, contains no limitation, whereas the Names of Mercy convey this mercy, but not the terrible aspects. Whether it is a question of Islam or Buddhism or another cosmic sector, to say of this saving Name that it is a divine gift and that it really saves means: first, that the Name contains the divine Absoluteness, which is exclusive; second, and more directly, that it contains the divine Infinitude, which is inclusive, and which inaugurates the third aspect, which the Name most directly conveys and transmits, namely Mercy that is attractive.

The Name of Amitabha, so it is said, contains both the Savior and the saved: for the latter has no power of his own, even his faith in Amitabha is conferred on him by this Name; it is enough for us to hear this Name and in hearing it to continue pronouncing it and in pronouncing it—or in hearing it—to avoid closing ourselves to the faith it contains and communicates to us. All this is said, not in order to absolve us from effort—without effort no life and *a fortiori* no spiritual path is possible—but in order that we may be thoroughly convinced that no merit belongs to us in our own right and in order that we not compromise our self-abandonment to the "Other" by any accentuation whatsoever of our egoity. In Christian language, one would say that we have to put Christ in place of our mind and the Virgin in place of our soul.

The salvific quality of Amitabha's Name derives from its holiness: to say that the Name is holy, as we have seen, means that it has been revealed and that it thereby proves its divineness under the double aspect of origin and substance, and hence also its qualities of Absoluteness, Infinitude, and Mercy. Now the holiness of the celestial gift demands on the part of man an initial sanctification that reflects this holiness in a certain manner; and this takes the form of a ritual consecration, on the one hand, and of a spiritual vow, on the other.

Purity of intention—as expressed and confirmed by such a vow—encompasses the fundamental virtues of the soul; obviously, it precludes the spiritual means from being employed for a purpose that is beneath its own content, such as the pursuit of extraordinary powers, or the wish to be famous and admired, or the secret satisfaction of a sense of superiority; purity of intention likewise precludes this means from being used for purposes of experimentation or for the sake of tangible results or other profanations of this sort. This is exactly what the vow is intended to avoid, as follows very clearly from the Islamic promise—made to the Prophet Muhammad by his Companions and mentioned several times in the Koran—to "fight in offering their goods and their lives" (*bi-amwālihim wa-anfūsihim*);[10] and this amounts to saying that there is no spiritual way properly so-called without a consecration and a vow.

The necessity for this vow casts light on what we have called, without the least intention of insinuating doubt, the "myth" of the Buddha Amitabha, since it is not hard to see that the earthly or human vow is like an answer to a celestial or divine vow: if man has to commit himself towards Heaven this is because Heaven has committed itself, through the very Revelation, towards man; one promise must answer the other. As for the pure intention that every spiritual vow implies, it has two essential components, one strictly human and the other purely spiritual, which are moreover far from excluding one another: in the first place the aim of the path is to save man's soul, in whatever manner this salvation may be understood; but it is also, for anyone capable of grasping it, simply "That which is": Truth in itself, or the omnipresent reality of the nirvanic Principle.[11]

---

[10] It will be noticed that the first term concerns attachment to the world and the second attachment to the ego: one must give oneself to God with all that one "possesses" and all that one "is". In Amidism, the human response to the celestial Gift consists in the "Triple Attitude": "sincere intention", "perfect faith", and the "wish to be born in the Pure Land", the latter being a cosmic anticipation of *Nirvāna*, or a liberating projection thereof.

[11] This is why Saint Bernard could say: "I love because I love" and not "because I wish to be saved"; obviously there is no incompatibility here, but the two attitudes are situated on different planes. The superior attitude is not unconnected with the theophany of the Burning Bush: "I am That I am." In the Evangelical counsels, the vow of "poverty" refers to separation from the world; the vow of "obedience", to separation from the ego; the vow of "chastity", to the choice of the heavenly Beatitude alone.

—— .:. ——

It is profoundly significant that the Buddha (in the *Amitāyur Dhyāna Sūtra*) related the story of Dharmakara-Amitabha to a woman in distress, Queen Vaidehi, indicating by this that the celestial gift is directed to pure receptivity and presupposes a consciousness of our samsaric distress; it is equally significant that the Buddha allowed Vaidehi to behold the Paradises of the Buddhas and that it is she who chose among them all the paradise of Amitabha, thus collaborating in her own manner in the subsequent Revelation. According to the traditional interpretation, Vaidehi represents the spiritual pilgrimage of man, which is regarded as leading into the Path of Amitabha, since the perspective of the "Pure Land" *sūtra*s is Amidist. Vaidehi's vision of other "Buddha-lands" and her own choice of Amitabha's land symbolizes, in this perspective, the actual process of Enlightenment or the degrees of the spiritual life.

There have been differences of opinion as to whether Queen Vaidehi, as co-revealer of the *Amitāyus Sūtra*,[12] was a *Bodhisattva* or an ordinary mortal, and whether the "Pure Land" doctrine is addressed to superior men or to the common run of people; each of the two opinions can be justified by some passage in the sacred texts. For our part, we would say that Vaidehi was a *Bodhisattva* destined to incarnate ordinary mortals in all the distress of their samsaric exile and that the "Pure Land" *sūtra*s address their message both to "pneumatics" and to simple "psychics" —to use the language of *gnosis*—for the one does not exclude the other: extremes meet, wisdom and holy child-likeness have their common ground.[13]

We are here in the presence of the mystery of simplicity: the nirvanic Void is simple and so is childhood; between the two extremes—

"Obedience" (*perinde ac si cadaver essent*) is founded on Christ's invitation: "Follow me", a fact which proves that this vow implies something very different from a simple moral discipline; Christ (who must be followed) is, in practice, "inwardness" (in view of the Kingdom of Heaven that is "within you"), together with "voidness" (for the sake of God: *vacare Deo*), these two attitudes, when combined, being the equivalent of "chastity".

[12] *Amitāyus*, "Eternal Life", is an aspect or complement of *Amitābha*, "Infinite Light".

[13] Otherwise one could not explain how minds like Shan-Tao, Honen, and Shinran could have chosen the "Pure Land" way and made themselves its champions.

if such a schematic treatment applies to the incommensurable—there lies all the complexity of universal possibilities, whether of good or evil, including the complexity of human ratiocinations. Simplicity is neither ignorance nor platitude: the decisive factors of our spiritual destiny are the discernment between the Real and the illusory, and permanent union with the Real; wisdom is simple, inasmuch as its expressions converge on That which alone is, and it has the gift of simplifying; but wisdom also comprises, for that very reason, all the sanctifying riches that the human soul, so diverse in its nature, may stand in need of during its pilgrimage towards the Immutable.

Absoluteness or exclusive Reality; Infinity or inclusive Reality; Goodness or liberating Substance; Revelation or obligating Manifestation; the whole of the Doctrine is to be found in these words. If our day-to-day experience confronts us with things that are real at their own level—that is to say, if in the world "such and such" realities exist—this is because before all else there is Reality "as such", which is not the world and by which the world is. And if the world exists, this is because Reality as such, or the Absolute, comprises Infinity or All-Possibility, whereof the world is a consequence and a content.

If the world is the world, this is because it is not God: unable to be either Absoluteness or Infinity, it is relative and finite; whence the presence of evil, which by its nature as privation proves *a contrario* that the cosmic Substance, and consequently and *a fortiori* the divine Nature, is essentially Goodness. And if in the world there is necessarily both good and evil, and if the good manifests by definition the divine Qualities and therefore Goodness, it follows that Goodness has also to manifest itself as such, and this it does through Revelation; and since it exists it obligates, because man cannot not choose the good. In Revelation and through it man rejoins the saving Goodness, the Infinite that includes all, the Absolute which is That which is, and which alone is.

The Absolute appears from the viewpoint of *Māyā* as a kind of contraction, which it cannot be intrinsically since no limiting determination can apply to it; one may say then, to speak as simply as possible, that Absoluteness in the sense of an extrinsically contractive Reality, necessarily comprises a compensating aspect expansive in nature, namely Infinity. Now Infinity, which includes everything, requires a seemingly negative dimension, namely creative Manifestation, which is positive insofar as it expresses the Absolute, but nonetheless privative by reason of the relativity of its nature and its productions. Creative Manifestation in its turn requires saving Manifestations, namely the Prophets or the Revelations; and those Manifestations demonstrate a new *Hypostasis*, namely the essential Goodness of the divine or nirvanic Reality. Infinity as a result of Absoluteness; creative Manifestation as a result of Infinity; saving Manifestation likewise as a result of Infinity but also, and by that very fact, as a result of the essential Goodness inherent in the Infinite: it is with liberating Mercy, which leads back to the Absolute, that the circle of divine Unfolding closes. The Universe is like a Revelation of the divine Nature, or like a divine play in which the nirvanic Reality reveals itself to itself and is mirrored in its own inexhaustible dimensions.

PART TWO

Buddhism's Ally in Japan: Shinto

Initial Remarks

That which chiefly warrants our including in this book a section on Shinto is the fact that the Japanese civilization can be said to stem, both structurally and in its particular genius, from the synthesis between Shinto and Buddhism. There has been assimilation of the two traditional influences at one level and maintenance of their separate characters at another; thus, whoever takes an interest in Japanese Buddhism should know something of Shinto and vice versa. Moreover, the Asiatic religions—Hinduism, Buddhism, Taoism—because of their spiritual transparency—absorb foreign traditional elements quite readily; so much so that a Shintoist divinity becomes a *Bodhisattva* without being altered in its essence, since the respective names cover universal realities.

We should also start by mentioning that if we intend to treat here of Shinto, the reason—or occasional cause—that prompted us was the "abolition" of the divine status of the Emperor of Japan; one thing leading to another, this patent manifestation of the anti-traditional spirit, and the characteristic absurdity it entails, brought us to study the traditional context of this imperial divinity, and what renders it directly intelligible. In the pages that follow, there is no question, needless to say, of going back to the Meijist falsification[1] of the semi-celestial dignity of the *Tennō*, but on the contrary of bringing the problem back to its "apolitical" and timeless serenity. May the reader forgive the character—at once too succinct and too dense—of the considerations we wish to present to him, and may he not lose sight of the fact that only an anti-metaphysical relativism has an interest in seeing insurmountable psychological barriers between the traditional worlds, whence its relentless insistence on the elements that divide and exclude. What, from our point of view, authorizes us to approach a subject seemingly so "foreign" as Shinto is that—to paraphrase a saying of Phillip Duke of Orléans[2]—"everything that is traditional is ours"; which is to say that Truth is one, as is humankind.

---

[1] Pertaining to the Meiji period, the one that inaugurated the modernization of Japan. That period, if it was more or less hostile to Buddhism, proved no more profitable to genuine Shinto.

[2] "Everything that is national is ours"—a word, namely, directed to the monarchists.

The Meaning of the Ancestors

The question of the spiritual meaning underlying myths is one that people like to relegate to the realm of feeling and imagination, and which "exact science" refuses to treat otherwise than through the medium of psychological and historical conjectures. However, for us, who do not believe in the efficacy of a knowledge cut off from total truth—unless it be a matter merely of knowing physical things that are actually palpable—the "science" in question readily substitutes exactness for intelligence, be it said without euphemism; it is indeed this very "exactness" that precludes the decisive operations of pure intelligence, since a meticulous and often arbitrary recording of facts that are possibly insignificant—or are rendered such thanks to the point of view adopted—replaces the intellectual perception of the nature of things. "Science" claims to be characterized by its refusal of all purely speculative premises (the *voraussetzungsloses Denken* of the German philosophers) and by a complete liberty of investigation, but this is an illusion since modern science, no more than any other, cannot avoid starting out in its turn from an idea: it is the dogma concerning the exclusively rational and more or less "democratic" nature of intelligence; in other words, it is assumed that there exists a unique and polyvalent intelligence, which in principle is true, and that everyone possesses it, which precisely would allow investigations to be entirely "free", but this is radically false. There are truths that can be attained only by intellection—which in fact does not lie within the capacity of every man of "sound mind"; and the Intellect, for its part, requires Revelation—serving as the occasional cause and as vehicle of the *philosophia perennis*—in order to actualize its own light in more than a fragmentary manner. Be that as it may, when people speak of "objective analysis" and, what is more, "based on facts" and "not on speculations" or "on abstractions", they always overlook the main interested party, namely the intelligence—or unintelligence—of the person who analyzes; they forget that, in many cases, the "analysis of facts" intended to "prove" such and such a thing whose existence or non-existence is nevertheless evident *a priori*,[1] only serves to make up

---

[1] For example, "facts" have been gathered to prove that woman is absolutely equal to man—as if, in a natural polarity, there could be absolute equality—or even that

for the absence—whether basic or accidental—of intellection, hence of an intelligence proportioned to the problem as posed.

When true myths are abolished, they inevitably come to be replaced by artificial myths, and in fact, the type of thinking intent on relying on its logic alone, while operating in a realm where this logic opens up no new horizons, turns out to be defenseless against the various scientistic "mythologies", rather as the abolition of religion leads finally not to a rational view of the Universe, but to a counter-religion that will not be long in devouring rationalism itself; for to set man absolutely free—he who is not absolute—is to set free all manner of evils in him, without there remaining any principle that would limit them. All this goes to show that basically it is a kind of abuse of language to give the name "science" to a knowledge that leads only to practical results while revealing nothing concerning the profound nature of phenomena; a science that by definition is devoid of transcendent principles can offer no guarantee as to the ultimate results of its own investigations.

Pure and simple logic is only a very indirect manner of knowing things; it is foremost the art of combining true or false information according to a given need for logical explanations and within the limits of a certain type of imagination, so much so that an apparently faultless reasoning can still be quite erroneous because of the falseness of its premises; and these premises normally depend not on reason or experience, but on pure intelligence, and this to the very extent that the thing to be known is of a lofty order. It is not the exactitude of science that we are blaming here, far from it, but the exclusive level of this exactitude, which renders this quality inadequate and inoperative; man can measure a distance by his strides, but this does not enable him to see with his feet, if one may so express it. Metaphysics and symbolism, which alone provide the decisive keys for the knowledge of supra-sensible realities, are in fact highly exact sciences—with an exactitude greatly exceeding that of physical facts—but these sciences

man is inferior to woman; one sees that the "scientific method" with its "objective" processes, "based on facts", lends itself to any kind of speculation whatsoever. Even in cases of a quite partial and outward polarity, such as natural symmetry, the parts are not absolutely equivalent: for example, the right eye is active and "penetrating", and the left eye passive and "receptive".

lie beyond the scope of mere *ratio* and the methods it inspires in a quasi-exclusive manner.

Some remarks first on the veneration of the dead: whenever one hears about Confucianism or Shinto, one immediately thinks of ancestor worship, guessing that it is Ancestors who take the place of God in these traditions or rather who fulfill the function of the Divinity, since one only replaces something that is absent; in reality, however, the Divinity itself is conceived in the Far East as a kind of Ancestor, and one's human ancestors are like a prolongation of the Divinity, or like a bridge between ourselves and it. God is the Heaven or Sun from which we are indirectly descended and of which the Emperor is the incarnation or direct descendant, depending on the case; as for the Sage, he is its incarnation by "force majeure", according to a spiritual and "vertical" lineage, and not a fleshly and "horizontal" one.

The innate conviction that our ancestors were "nearer the Gods" than ourselves, and that they incarnate something of an ideal, is to be found, implicitly or in practice, even among most of those professing a belief in evolutionism on all planes; one cannot help but feel that the ancients, even if they sometimes seem to have been naïve beings, possessed a wholeness of character and had none of that mixture of weakness and cleverness, of hypocrisy and cowardice, that characterizes average "latter day" men. Such a conviction derives from an intuition that is natural to normal man, it is therefore related to the religious instinct; like this instinct, it is infallible—"prelogical", if one prefers, but in a positive sense—that is to say, it arises from the very depth of our being; and by this is meant not the chaos of our "subconscious", but our ontological reality rooted in the universal Intellect, without which "was not any thing made that was made".

If the old traditions contain stories that now seem morally and psychologically almost incomprehensible, one must tell oneself that with the men of another age, the relationship of thought to act was much more direct than with us and also that the difference between the inward and outward worlds was not yet as sharply marked as happens with the distant descendants of those men that we are; ancient man was "more absolute" than we are in all he did: he was "more absolute" in good, but also more absolute in evil, or at least in certain forms of evil, for there are evils that belong only to the latter times.²

Many things with the ancients now strike us as rudimentary for the simple reason that we are unaware of what these things meant to them, so that we are judging only fragments or even mere appearances that are really quite deceptive; nor must it be forgotten that a certain kind of naivety was, after all, the expression of a still paradisial uprightness surviving amidst the ambiguities and paradoxes of man's earthly exile.³

Among the peoples of the Far East, the ancestor is at once the origin and the spiritual or moral norm; he is, for his descendants, the essential personality, that is to say the substance of which they are like the accidents; and piety consists precisely in viewing him thus and in

---

² It is not a question, for example, of believing that our Middle Ages was a "good era" in a total sense, for one can just as well admit that it was bad, on condition of drawing one's conclusion from spiritually valid criteria biased neither in favor of the modern world, nor of ancient paganism. All the saints have complained of their times, and the easy optimism that seems to be fashionable today regarding the times in which we live is but one more anomaly among many others. One can reproach the people of the Middle Ages with having profited but little from a climate as full of spirit and hope as theirs was and with having been too worldly and quarrelsome, and certainly there is no occasion to wonder at the great calamities that descended upon them; in fact, medieval worldliness contained all the seeds of present-day miseries. Jacques Maritain has observed (in his *Humanisme intégral*) that in the Middle Ages men were deficient with respect to "reflexive consciousness"—that is to say they were but "little preoccupied with their own psychic states and reactions"— and that, on the contrary, at the time when the Middle Ages were in decline (Ruysbroeck, Tauler), and still more after the Renaissance, this form of consciousness was much on the increase (Saint Teresa of Avila, Saint John of the Cross, Mary of the Incarnation). What, however, is not explained by the author of the above remarks is why this absence of reflexive consciousness was "missing" in the Middle Ages or why it made its appearance subsequently. Now what interests us most is precisely the cause of this change, namely: the crystallization of individualism—necessarily reflexive—and of the empiricism that results from it.

³ Among the nomads of the Biblical times there exists a wide scope comprising simultaneously the rude and the profound, without much of a transition from one to the other, which the man of our time—so prone to confusing rational training with intelligence—finds difficult to comprehend. The same kind of confusion is readily made with regard to the Apostles, who are taken to be "men of the people" in the most trivial sense of the word, and this simply because people today cannot imagine how men could be at once simple and noble, unlettered and contemplative; if the Apostles were capable, for instance, of arguing among themselves as to which of them would have the chief place in Paradise, they were but expressing freely and directly a feeling that present-day man would try to keep hidden in his inmost thoughts.

seeing in him but the bridge connecting them—his descendants—with the Divine.[4] The patriarch is something like the "Word made flesh"— let this be said without any abuse of language—and he is therefore what we ourselves ought to be, or what we must "become" because that is what we "are", and the perfection and glory of which it thus behooves us to perpetuate. The ancestors are the human imprints of angelic substances and, for that reason, also of divine Qualities; to be true to them is to be true to God; they oblige us to remain in conformity with the eternal "idea" whence we came forth, and which is the law of our existence and the goal of our life.

This connection between the ancestor and his angelic and divine prototypes appears moreover in the Japanese word *kami*, which denotes the ancestor and the literal meaning of which is "located above"; in sacred language, this word means "divine aspect", "cosmic principle", "spirit". The Shinto tradition is called *Kami-no-Michi*, or "Way of the Gods", which implies that it is also the way of the ancestors.

Shinto is possibly the most intact and hence the most complete form belonging to a traditional current that might be described as "Hyperborean Shamanism", which extends across Siberia and the adjoining Mongolian lands as far as North America; many mythological, cultural, and even vestimentary similarities support this idea; we could perhaps also highlight by way of parallelism that Mongols, Japanese, and American Indians all embody the heroic side of the yellow race, in the broadest sense of the word. For these peoples, it is above all Nature that is the sanctuary—which is emphasized in Japan by the *torii* placed in front of sacred landscapes—and this holiness of virgin Nature, this "transcendent immanence", is not unrelated to their thirst for freedom, their contempt for luxury, their taciturnity, and other

[4] Chinese tradition gives very paradoxical examples of this, such as a prince who, having blamed an ill deed on his Empress mother, was in turn blamed by all the sages. One must see the essence through the accident and in spite of it. There is something analogous in totemism, in which the totemic animal, while being infra-human on account of its animality, assumes the role of archetype, of source, and consequently of a norm in virtue of its symbolism, which links it, in an indirect and passive way, with the supra-human essences.

similar characteristics.[5] There is nevertheless in Shinto civilization—not to mention the Chinese and Buddhist influences—an element that partially separates it from the shamanic world of the North and this is the Malayan, or Malayo-Polynesian element; additional causes of originality are its insular situation, with all the psychological consequences this entails, and then the extreme plasticity of the *yamato* race, which has made Japan like a reservoir of the main spiritual and artistic currents of Asia. All these factors, and others still, create that incomparable and fascinating polyphony that might be called the "Japanese miracle".

To return to the analogies pointed out above, it can be said that Shinto, like the North American tradition, knows the cult of the great phenomena of Nature: sun, moon, rain-bearing hurricane, wind, thunder, lightning, fire, animals, rocks, trees, without forgetting the sky and earth that are their containers; above them all, as "Great Spirit", is Ame-no-Minakanushi-no-Kami, the "Lord of the true

---

[5] The analogy between the ancient Shinto songs and those of the American Indians is striking: "*Ho*, now is the time! *Ho*, now is the time! *Ho*! *Ha*! *Psha*! Come on, my children! Come on, my children!" (The most ancient Japanese *uta*, having come down from the warriors of Jimmu Tenno). "They shall appear, May you behold them! They shall appear, May you behold them! A horse-people are appearing. A thunder-people are appearing. They shall appear, behold! They shall appear, behold!" (Sioux). "Now the rising sun—has sent his rays towards the earth—coming from afar—coming from afar—coming from afar—a great number (of warriors) coming from afar, *he yo*!" (Pawnee). "Make us see, is it real? Make us see, is it real—this life I am leading? You, divine Beings, who abide everywhere—make us see, is it real—this life I am leading?" (Pawnee). A Sioux of the heroic times describes the Indian mentality as follows: "All who have lived much outdoors know that there is a magnetic force that increases in solitude and that is quickly dissipated by life among people; and even his enemies have recognized the fact that for a certain innate power and self-poise, remaining impassive in all circumstances, the American Indian is unsurpassed among men. . . . It is simple truth that the Indian did not, as long as his native philosophy held sway over his mind, either envy or desire to imitate the splendid achievements of the white man. . . . He scorned them, even as a lofty spirit absorbed in a stern task rejects too soft a bed, the enjoyment of delicate dishes, and the superficial entertainments of a rich neighbor. He possessed the conviction that virtue and happiness are independent of these things, and perhaps even incompatible with them. . . . To him, it appeared shocking and almost inconceivable that there were among these people who claimed superiority many unbelievers. . . . The historians of the white race have to admit that the Indian was never the first to break his oath. . . . The ancient Indian joined to a proud demeanor a singular humility. Spiritual arrogance was foreign to his nature and teaching. . . . In the life of the Indian, there was only one inevitable duty, . . . the daily recognition of the Unseen and Eternal" (Charles A. Eastman, *The Soul of the Indian*).

Center of Heaven". We shall have the opportunity to comment again on this cosmology.

——— ·:· ———

It may come as a surprise to some that the eschatological element apparently plays so minimal a role in early Shinto, but aside from the fact that this element is affirmed in the cult of emperors and heroes, or of ancestors in general, there is a perspective here whose equivalent is to be found among the American Indians who, likewise, emphasize present virtues rather than their future fruits; these fruits are in fact included in the virtues themselves and guaranteed by them, for the afterlife is strictly the effect of our earthly worth; to control the cause is to control the effect. This perspective is no doubt related to the warrior tradition, wherein words matter little and the act, as a decisive affirmation of the immortal person, appears almost as sufficing unto itself; in a certain sense, the act is character and character is salvation. We could express the same thing as follows: Shintoists can ignore the hereafter, as the case may be, provided they do not ignore either God or their own redemptive duties, exactly as monotheists can ignore the multitude of universes and therefore also the entire "extent" of the "Round of Existence" and the entire "duration" of a "Life of Brahmā"—that is to say the existence of extra-human worlds and the pre-Adamic and post-apocalyptic cycles—provided they know all that which concerns human eschatology; if the reproach leveled by Monotheists at the Shinto-Shamanists is justified, the reproach leveled by Hindus at the Monotheists will be so likewise, and if this latter reproach is unjustified, then the former one will not be any the less so—due consideration being granted in each case to the positive factors compensating for the respective ignorance shown.

In a comparable vein of thought, note was made above regarding the scarcity of moral precepts; in this connection we will quote the commentator Motoori Norinaga: "To know that there is no way to be followed is to know and follow the Way of the Gods",[6] namely Shinto.

[6] "The way that can be followed is not the true Way", says the *Tao Te Ching*, which is to say that action cannot lead to Non-Action (*Wu-Wei*), nor thought alone to Knowledge. According to the *Philokalia*, "the soul is righteous when its knowledge abides in the state that is natural to it. . . . When we remain as we were created, we are in a state of virtue".

The foundation of the virtues here is a consciousness of purity and impurity, of sincerity and insincerity,[7] a consciousness that is readily related to "honor"; moreover, it should be added that life consists, in large measure, of a series of always identical situations, and that the ideas and practices found in Shinto engender ways of acting that are practically speaking the equivalent of moral precepts, all the more so given that these ways of acting have become ingrained in the customs of the collectivity. Be that as it may, rather than having to submit himself to a set of precepts, man ought to remain anchored in original perfection, and this brings us back to the cult of ancestors: man should see in his forebears and even in his immediate relatives only what is perfect; to say of a deceased person that he has become *kami* means that he has rejoined his celestial prototype, of which—here below in this world—he had been the no doubt precarious but nevertheless real manifestation.[8]

It is also worth stressing the point that Shinto sees in man *a priori* the overall personality, the innate virtue, of which his actions are possible and often approximate manifestations by reason of the gap between an act and its intention. The personal substance is supposed to have the power to neutralize imperfect or erroneous actions; now it will be argued that bad actions, obviously, compromise the personality, which is equally true; both views are legitimate, but each is more opportune for the mentality it reflects and to which it is addressed. In a certain sense, Shinto morality has two poles: the "caste", which has

---

[7] According to the *Shintō Gobusho*, a compilation of the thirteenth century, "to do good is to be pure; to do evil is to be impure. The gods have an aversion to evil actions because such actions are impure". Similarly, according to the commentator Tomobe-no-Yasutaka, the ritual ablution "is not merely the washing of the body with lustral water; it means that one is following the good path. Impurity signifies evil or vice. Even though a man might wash away the uncleanness of his corporal body, he nevertheless would not be pleasing to the gods if he did not surmount his evil desires". The role played in Shinto by the color white and by green branches is related to the spirit of primordial purity characteristic of this tradition; it makes one think of India and also, may it be said again, of North America.

[8] Another aspect of the cult of ancestors is the following: venerable men after their death bequeath to us a psychic element that is able to fix itself in a specific place, most often in connection with their bodily remains; the survivors offer worship, not only to the immortal and deified ancestor, but also to that tangible *barakah* that subsists here below among them for their enlightenment and possibly for their protection. The cult of relics has no other meaning.

to be maintained, and the purificatory and other prescriptions, which have to be obeyed; now the "caste"—the divine origin—essentially implies a "solar" perfection, comparable to the sacred Mirror, which is the very image of Shinto.

There are ways of acting, feeling, and thinking that are shared by all Japanese—at least insofar as they remain true to themselves—and which perhaps derive as much from the warrior code of *Bushidō* and from a Confucianist inspiration as from pure Shinto; viewed from outside, this is a matter of a complex and subtle civility, but in a more inward sense this unwritten Law can go further and channel the soul after the manner of a *karma-yoga* or an *islām*. The Shinto ethic, which claims for the *yamato* race the attribute "divine", is perhaps essentially a style of action; it is in fact possible to conceive of a perspective in which style would take precedence over contents by largely neutralizing the imperfections of the latter, for a noble form is necessarily opposed to base actions;[9] but all of this is approximate. Moreover, it is likely that the contribution of Confucianist and Buddhist influences in the shaping of the Japanese soul makes it almost impossible to differentiate with exactitude the role of the purely Shinto influence.

[9] The archaic notion of salvation reserved for a caste can be explained thereby. Under the rather special conditions being considered here it is not the caste, properly speaking, that constitutes an elite, but rather the elite that constitutes the caste, that is to say, emphasis is laid on the quality itself rather than on its framework; quality, for its part, is guaranteed and controlled by discipline and the manner of living; heredity is only a providential factor.

Mythology of Shinto

The *Tennō*[1] is like the incarnation of Shinto; he is descended through his ancestor Jimmu Tenno from Amaterasu-Omikami, the solar Goddess, she herself being the issue of the divine Couple Izanagi and Izanami. Amaterasu-Omikami, the "Great Divinity of the Shining Sky", is also called Ohiru-memuchi-no-Kami, "She Who Possesses the Great Sun";[2] she corresponds to the universal and creative Intellect, to the luminous and merciful Center of the cosmos, therefore to what the Hindu doctrine denotes by *Buddhi* and the Islamic doctrine by *Ar-Rūh*; these comparisons are unmistakable, even though the concepts no doubt differ, depending on which aspect or relationship is emphasized. As for the divine Couple, this is none other than the equivalent pairing of *Purusha-Prakriti* in Hindu cosmology;[3] and just as *Buddhi* under its aspect of Vishnu incarnates itself in human *Avatāra*s such as Rama and Krishna, so also does Amaterasu engender Jimmu Tenno, founder and first Emperor of Japan.[4]

It is known that in Hinduism *Purusha* and *Prakriti* are the creative polarizations—"masculine" and "feminine"—of Being, *Īshvara*, who himself is the self-determination of Beyond-Being, *Brahma*; in Shinto, the supreme Principle is Ame-no-Minakanushi-no-Kami, the "Divine Lord of the Center of the Heavens", of whom it is said that He "hath engendered Himself" and that He "hath neither parents nor spouse nor children"; His "non-acting" is reminiscent of the *wu-wei* of Taoism. Sometimes He is replaced in appearance by Kuni-Toko-tachi-no-Mikoto, "Eternal Divine Earthly Being", which doubtless

---

[1] *Tennō* ("celestial Monarch") is the official title of the Emperor; *Mikado* ("sublime Gate") seems to be used, by the Japanese, only in poetical language.

[2] See Genchi Kato, *Le Shintô, religion nationale du Japon*, Paris, 1931, and *What Is Shinto?*, Tokyo, 1935. Also: Michel Revon, *Le Shintoïsme*, Paris, 1907. One also finds some instructive information in *Le Shintoisme, religion nationale*, by J.-M. Martin although, regrettably, this work is not free from some hostile prejudice.

[3] The "seven divine generations" that "preceded" the divine Couple—in principial and therefore "simultaneous" mode—represent possibilities that remain in Being without being called into manifestation.

[4] Jimmu Tenno founded the Empire in 660 B.C., that is to say, about the time of the Buddha, Lao-Tzu, and Confucius.

refers to Being properly so-called and which thus would correspond to the Hindu *Īshvara;*[5] here the word "earthly" seems to be a reference to Existence or productive Power.[6]

Just as the Couple *Purusha-Prakriti,* in Hindu symbolism, engender Brahmā, Vishnu, Shiva, Saraswati, Lakshmi, Parvati, and by extension or subdivision to other celestial aspects or angelic functions and then to the whole world, so also Izanami gives birth to several refractions of the cosmic Light, namely Earth—represented by the Japanese

[5] There is one group of Shintoists, known as the *Konkō* school, who worship Tenchi-Kame-no-Kami, the "Divinity who Embraces Heaven and Earth", that is to say *Ātmā,* the Divine Self, which contains all things. For the *Kurozumi* school, God is "Sincerity" or more accurately, He is the infinite Light of which this virtue is the human projection.

[6] In mythological languages, the word "earthly" is often used as a synonym of "manifestation", in the Guénonian sense of the word. Two subordinate aspects of the creative Principle are: Takamimusubi-no-Kami and Kamumimusubi-no-Kami—the "august Producer" and the "divine Producer"—who form a trinity with Ame-no-Minaka-nushi-no-Kami; the first is considered "male" and the second "female", which brings us back to the Couple *Purusha-Prakriti.* Given that mythologies are at opposite poles from all systematization, one should not be surprised at encountering "redundancies" and other inconsistencies of this kind. "At the time Heaven and Earth began, divinities came forth in the Plain of the high Heavens, whose names were: the god Ame-no-Minakanushi ('Master of the august Center of Heaven'), then the god Taka-mi-musubi ("High august Producer") and finally the god Kamumi-musubi ("divine Producer"). These three divinities came forth spontaneously (not having existed previously, according to Motoori), then hid themselves. Afterwards, when the earth—young and like floating oil—moved like a jelly fish, the god Izanagi and his young sister Izanami were born (after several divine generations, including Kuni-Tokotachi-no-Mikoto) from something shooting up like a reed. . ." (Beginning of the *Kojiki,* a sacred book of Shinto, quoted from Michel Revon, *Le Shintoïsme,* Paris, 1907). "Formerly, Heaven and Earth having not yet been separated, the female and male principles (*in* and *yō,* the Chinese *yin-yang*) having not yet been divided, they formed a chaos similar to an egg, and in this indiscriminate mass was a seed. The purest and clearest part diffused itself lightly and formed Heaven; the heaviest and grossest part became compact and formed Earth. The more subtle element easily became a unified body; but the heavier and grosser element became solidified with greater difficulty. Heaven was thus made first, and then Earth. Then, between them, divine beings were produced. Thence it is said that at the beginning of the world's creation, the soil of the land floated like a fish playing in the water. Then there was produced, between Heaven and Earth, something that in its form resembled the shoot of a reed. And this thing transformed itself into a god . . ." (Then follows the appearance of a creative Trinity, then the enumeration of other versions of the cosmogonic process.) (Beginning of the *Nihongi,* a Shinto book, quoted from Michel Revon, *Le Shintoïsme*).

islands—and the Gods of Nature; as for Izanagi, he alone engenders the "Three Noble Children": the solar Amaterasu-Omikami, who is gentle and loving and who reigns over the high celestial spheres; Tsukuyomi-no-Mikoto, Divinity of the Moon, who reigns over the kingdom of night; and Susano-wo-no-Mikoto, Divinity of the Tempest, who reigns over the sea and earth; these correspond respectively to the principles designated in the Hindu doctrine as *Sattva, Rajas, Tamas*, which they represent but in principial, thus "archangelic" mode, on the model of the Hindu *Trimūrti*.[7]

If the abovementioned Divinities[8] corresponding to the *Trimūrti* are taken as emanating from Izanagi alone—in Hindu parlance from *Purusha* alone—this is by reason of the eminent distinction that exists, in the Cosmos, between its quasi-divine—or "archangelic"—Center and the periphery, whose extreme limit for our world will be matter; thus also, in the human being, the Intellect is distinguished from the periphery "body and soul" constituting the ego. In other words, the cosmic Center, which is supra-formal, is attributed to Izanagi (= *Purusha*) and the world of form to Izanami (= *Prakriti*) conjointly with Izanagi; like the relationship "Principle-manifestation", the relationship "Center-periphery"—on the very plane of manifestation—is equivalent to the complementary opposition "virility-femininity", which explains the intention behind the Shintoist symbolism under consideration.

We have seen that the divine Couple engenders the Japanese isles, which constitute a reduced image of the Universe; all nature, with its mountains, waters, fauna, and flora, and then humanity—represented by the Japanese people—are the work of the divine Couple. The divine origin of Japan coincides thus, symbolically speaking, with

---

[7] According to other sources, these divinities are procreated by the Couple Izanagi-Izanami. Sometimes a "male Sun", Hiruko, is mentioned next to Amaterasu, but without assigning any importance to him, so it seems.

[8] We regret the excess recourse to capital letters as well as to quotation marks, but we are compelled to use them due to the habits, inconsistencies, or abuses found in other books; or we do so to correct the verbal imprecision of a language that, depending on the case, can be somewhat outworn. For instance, if it is correct to write "the gods" in lower case letters, this is because the "gods"—in its plural form—are always assumed to be false; but, leaving aside the fact that some authors go so far as to write "the Saints" in capitals, we see no reason why we should write "the Gods" in lower case letters when we believe them to be real.

that of the world, somewhat like the end of Jerusalem, in Christ's prophecies, coincides with the end of the world; what Jimmu Tenno, "superhuman man", brought to the Japanese is not of course a new divine origin, but the consciousness of their divine origin, an origin that is proper to all men and the forgetfulness of which entails the loss of all human virtues and rights; it is perfectly natural that Japan, being the "place" of the Shinto Revelation, should be for this tradition the center of the world, for such is *mutatis mutandis* the viewpoint of every traditional perspective: that "place" is "center" where God has manifested Himself. Hence it will be easy to understand that an objection based on the fact that the population of Japan—with the exception of the Ainus—arrived in the times called prehistoric from Korea, Southern China, and the Malay Archipelago, and therefore must have been in existence prior to Jimmu Tenno, is without importance in this context; if before the founding of the Empire, the population of the Japanese islands was undergoing a process of chaotic elaboration, Jimmu Tenno united the tribes and, by "divine mandate", made of this human *materia*—providentially assembled within the same country—a "mirror" of humanity and of the Universe; he was, in a direct sense "son of the Solar Goddess" because, being "born of the Spirit", he was "without origin and without end".[9]

Like all mythologies, that of Shinto includes features that at first sight may seem disconcerting but which are full of meaning: thus it is a bird—a wagtail—that taught copulation to the divine Pair; here the bird stands for the demiurgic and deifugal tendency and retraces, in the cosmogonic order and without moral intention, the Biblical mystery of the serpent.[10] Tradition also relates that Izanami, after having

[9] This celestial ancestry might indicate, moreover, that the birth of Jimmu Tenno took place under supernatural conditions.

[10] Concerning the features associated with the Shintoist cosmogony, Motoori Norinaga said: "Who would have invented so ridiculous, so unbelievable a story, were it not true?" And he adds that human intelligence, being narrow-minded, is unable to understand the actions of the Gods. "For as long as men still understood the true nature of their myths they were not shocked by their 'immorality'. The myths are never, in fact, immoral but, like every other form of theory (vision), amoral. . . . The content

given birth to her last son Homusubi, God of Fire, succumbed to her burns and had to go down into hell, of which she became the Goddess: cosmic Substance does indeed have a darksome aspect of chaos and unintelligibility, which appears as soon as one considers the rupture of equilibrium brought about by the actualization and differentiation of the cosmic tendencies, but solely at their own level; to speak in Hindu terms, although *Prakriti* always remains virginal on her own principial plane, she appears to be modified on the—relatively illusory plane—of her productions, where the appearance of the fire-light principle carries with it the principles of passion and obscurity—passion by "individuation" and obscurity by "inversion"—which amounts to the distinction between Lucifer and Satan; the farthermost bounds of existential totality seem to be submerged in a kind of nothingness that is never reached. The same truth is also expressed by the myth of the descent of Izanagi into hell: Izanami, who has already tasted the infernal food, is unwilling to accompany her spouse back to the upper world;[11] however, she consents to submit the question to the subterranean gods, on the condition that Izanagi not look inside her house; yet, after a long wait, he loses patience, looks through the window, and catches sight of the festering corpse of Izanami who, feeling she has been "humiliated", rushes out in pursuit of Izanagi, together with the denizens of hell;[12] but he escapes from the world of darkness and blocks up the entrance with a huge boulder and thus the two partners

of the myths is intellectual rather than moral . . . and whosoever deprecates the hero's 'morals' has already misinterpreted the genus" (Ananda K. Coomaraswamy, "On the Loathly Bride", *Speculum*, Oct. 1945). According to Saint Denis the Areopagite, "it is not inappropriate to disguise celestial things beneath the veil of the most contemptible symbols. . . . On the other hand, heavenly realities shine through negative formulas that respect the truth, and through comparisons whose correctness is hidden behind the appearance of an ignoble object. . ." (*On the Celestial Hierarchy*). The point of view is slightly different here, since it is a question of symbolism as such and of the inaptitude of created things for representing uncreated Reality, but these considerations apply *a fortiori* to myths, where formal imperfection appears more directly than with static symbols.

[11] This myth is not unrelated to that of the fall of Lucifer, providential agent of the progressive "materialization"—and "darkening"—of the world.

[12] Matter, though "divine" inasmuch as it fashions bodily creatures, nonetheless includes an aspect of hostility to the Spirit. The material world, multiple and impure by reason of life itself, is none other than the "subterranean" and "humiliated" body of Izanami, that body whose celestial "protoform" ever remains in incorruptible virginity.

are separated; then Izanagi, after making his ablutions in a river, gives in this manner birth to Amaterasu, Tsukuyomi, and Susano-wo. This descent into hell is reminiscent not only of the myth of Orpheus and Eurydice but also of the medieval legend of Raimondin and Melusine and even, in certain of its details, of the Biblical account of the fall of Adam and Eve; in all these myths, we see *natura naturans* being transmuted into *natura naturata*, or revealing herself under the latter aspect; the Spouse of the creative Spirit loses her divine nature, is recognized by the Spirit as non-divine, and thus becomes separated from him. But as this drama is played out on the ambiguous plane of Existence alone, the Spouse remains intact *in divinis*, whence the union of Eurydice and Orpheus in the Elysian fields and the final reuniting of the lovers of Lusignan.[13]

Mention should also be made of the fact that the divine Couple of Shinto gave birth to two miscarriages—a "leech" and an "islet of foam"—because Izanami, upon meeting Izanagi, was the first to speak; on the occasion of a second meeting it was Izanagi who spoke first, and then they gave birth to Japan, that is to say the terrestrial world. Here again a parallel with the sin of Adam and Eve can be seen; what the Japanese myth wishes to emphasize is that the initiative towards evil—the deifugal tendency—comes from the "feminine" element, which "seduces", whereas creation as such—the positive content of existence and not the existential separation—emanates from the "masculine" element. Eve, who is of the earth, makes Adam believe that she is formed of heavenly substance, which she is in her essence but not in her accidentality; here there is a confusion of planes, not an error affecting the essential reality.

Izanami dies in giving birth to Kagutsuchi, the "Radiant One", also called Homusubi, "He Who Engenders the Fire": the reason for this, it seems to us, is that the devouring Fire reveals the mortal character of the Substance it feeds on, and thus it is by Fire that the contrast between *natura naturans* and *natura naturata* is as if unveiled; in the Fire, the divine Spirit incarnates itself inasmuch as it is opposed to

---

[13] In ancient Egyptian mythology, Osiris, slain by Seth and then cut into pieces to fertilize the earth, pertains to the same symbolism: in both cases, the immolated Divinities prefigure death, through which all living beings must pass. In Islam it is said that after sinning, Eve lost her beauty and was parted from Adam for five centuries; Adam forgot Eve and did penance, but, as in the myths described above, the two primordial parents finally met again; they were reunited on Mount Arafat.

Substance or matter, so that there is analogy between the birth of Fire—mortal for the Mother—and the impatience of the Husband, whose glance provokes the separation. Plainly we have here a question of cosmic principles and not of the perceptible elements that manifest them "outwardly"; it is true, however, that earth, in all her impotence and impurity, corresponds in a certain sense to the infernal body of Izanami and that the glance of Izanagi is like the discernment between cosmic Substance and this outermost coagulation. There is also here an analogy with the first glance of Adam and Eve following their sin, whereby their nakedness was revealed to them;[14] it marks the passage from a perspective that is "inward", principial, synthetic, and unitive to one that is "outward", contingent, analytical, and separative; what is seen is no longer the unity of essence, the immutable Principle, but the existential plane, contingent manifestation. In other words: the divine Wife died because the Fire was born that burns up the cosmic veils, those that conceal the existential planes or the contingent degrees—the reflections in contingency—from the eyes of the divine Husband; as for him, thinking to see universal Substance ever-beautiful and ever-virgin, he suddenly perceives earthly matter, which is its most inferior reflection and "end point". Fire indeed causes a passage—at least symbolically—from one degree of reality to another; that which *a priori* appears as a heavenly thing is revealed, once Fire has consumed it, as a wretched substance: a certain tree that one might have regarded as paradisial and immortal is reduced to a base heap of ashes; instead of being a divine aspect, it is but dust. Let us add that the "vertical" perspective of the mythologies—as also the mentality of the more or less primordial men to whom they are addressed— quite obviously distinguishes the Fire-principle from physical fire, but it does not make an "essential" distinction between the two; this is a most important point to be noted concerning all phenomena of a *kami* nature. On the other hand, whenever dealing with stories of this kind, one must never forget that what in the story is presented as a sequence of events really represents a principial situation, therefore one pertaining to the Immutable.

---

[14] In the Shinto myth the humiliated Izanami in effect says to her husband: "You have beheld my state; now I shall behold yours in my turn." Whereupon Izanagi is likewise humiliated—the text (of the *Nihongi*) does not mention how—and answers: "Our kinship is broken."

— .:. —

Highly significant too is the myth of the captivity of the Sun in the Cave: the opposition on the cosmic scale between Knowledge and Passion is presented as a struggle between the Sun and the Tempest, Amaterasu-Omikami and her brother Susano-wo-no-Mikoto; in order to avoid the violence of her brother, the solar Goddess hides herself in the celestial Cave, casting all the regions of the Universe into total darkness; then the "eight hundred myriads of Gods"—refractions of the intelligible Light, but now cut off from their divine Source and so to speak deprived of life—cause Amaterasu to come forth by the play of a "mirror" symbolizing the solar disc.[15] This mirror, which is none other than the Intelligence governing the sensible world (the *Virāj* of Hindu cosmology),[16] "inhales" the Light towards the cosmic labyrinth,

[15] As an additional lure there was the cock's crow, the dancing of a nude Goddess, and the laughter of the Gods; now there is an evident symbolical connection between the cock-crow and dawn, then between the unveiling of a beautiful body and the sun's emergence from the darkness, and lastly between liberating laughter and the sudden flashing of the newborn day. Some have thought they recognized in the above mentioned dance a symbol of fertility; let us not forget to mention that one ascribes to the dancing Goddess—Uzume—a kind of mischievous obscenity, which adds to the myth a popular or peasant note in keeping with its agrarian symbolism. While dancing Uzume was struck by a "divine possession"; this is the prototype of the *kagura*, the sacred dance of the great festivals.

[16] If the "solar Mirror" corresponds to *Virāj*, Amaterasu Omikami will in her turn correspond to *Hiranyagarbha*, the "golden Embryo" whence the world proceeds; Jimmu Tenno will then be—still speaking in Hindu terms—equivalent to Manu, at least on the scale of the Japanese Universe. In the temple of Ise, the Holy of Holies of Shinto, is kept a replica of, or substitute for, the octagonal mirror that made Amaterasu come out of the Cave; this earthly mirror—which is not necessarily the work of human hands—is the seat of the "real Presence" of the Divinity, which thus attends the rites and listens to the prayers. "According to the ancient tradition, when Ninigi-no-Mikoto descended from the 'Plain of Heaven' (Takama-ga-Hara) to the summit of mount Takachiho in the province of Hiuga, in order to establish his rule over the lower world (Japan), his grandmother the Sun Goddess presented him with a sacred mirror with instruction to keep it always at his side, in the main hall of his palace; and whenever he looked into it, he was to remember he was looking at the Goddess herself as ever present in the mirror. It is said that this custom was solemnly observed by all the succeeding Emperors down to the time of the Emperor Sujin at the beginning of the first century B.C., but that Sujin, overawed at the thought of such close proximity to so sacred an object, and fearing that some calamity might befall him and his realm, had

whose arteries—receptacles of light like the mirror—are identified precisely with the "myriads of Gods"; as in the case of the mirror, it is necessary to distinguish here between an aspect of "recipient" and an aspect of "luminosity", according to whether one is looking "downwards" or "upwards": in relation to the initial Light—Amaterasu—the "solar Mirror" and the "Gods" are receptacles, but in relation to the respective spheres that they illuminate, they themselves are light. In the same myth, Susano-wo is banished to the earth, which indicates the final victory of the "Sun" over the "Tempest" or, more precisely, of Knowledge over the passional element; but this passional element, in its capacity of "productive energy", is necessary for the cosmic economy, and this is why Susano-wo, without losing his celestial dignity, had earthly descendants.[17]

An important aspect of the mytho-cosmology of Shinto is the following: plants sprang from the manifold hairs of Susano-wo-no-Mikoto; or again, living creatures issued from the corpse of the Goddess who Possesses Food, Ukemochi. One cannot help being reminded here of analogous myths in the *Rig-Veda* and the *Mundaka Upanishad*: the world springs from the sacrifice of *Purusha*,[18] whose immolated portions become the creatures in their diversity as well as the castes as such; however—and this is metaphysically crucial—it is only "one quarter" of *Purusha* that is thus fragmented, while the other "three quarters" remain unaffected in the immutability of the Principle.

In the "divine age", earth was still joined to Heaven by the bridge *Ama-no-Hashidate*; this bridge collapsed while the Gods were asleep. This sleep marks a kind of divine "absence", therefore a deprivation of graces for the earth, and this absence could only be a "concordant reaction" or response to an "absence" on the part of men in relation to Heaven.

a shrine built for it in the village of Kasanui in the province of Yamato and assigned the care of it to his virgin daughter, Toyosuki Irihime. This then was the beginning of the times when the human and the divine became separated. About the beginning of the Christian era, the sacred emblem was transferred to the province of Ise, where the great shrine has remained ever since" (*Honen, the Buddhist Saint*, chap. "Historical Introduction by the Translators" [Ringaku Ishizuka and Harper Havelock Coates], Kyoto, 1949).

[17] He was nonetheless, in a certain sense, the first "sinner".

[18] Let us also recall the sacrifice of Osiris, which we alluded to in a previous note.

———— .:. ————

The complexity of mythologies, their enigmas and apparent incoher-encies, are explainable not only by differences of perspective found in every science—and *scientia sacra* most of all—but also by a diversity in levels of reality: the same principle can be considered at one and the same time in different modes and at different degrees, so that a certain fluctuation is unavoidable between viewpoints and aspects;[19] it is as if "vertical" realities, intersected by "horizontal" planes, were oscillating between Heaven and earth, and it is not without good reason that it has been said of ancient Japan that "the notions of god and priest were interchangeable". If the Gods do not seem to be omniscient, if—for example—they put questions to human diviners, this is for the same reason that, according to the Koran, the Angels had to learn the names of all things from Adam: it is that man, as a "central" being, is situated at the foot of the "vertical axis" uniting earth to Heaven, whereas the Angels, though superior to man as regards their existential level, are nevertheless situated in the "spiroidal periphery" of the cosmos, with the exception of the Archangels, who occupy the degree of the universal Intellect, yet whose secondary personifications are precisely what constitute the ordinary Angels; from this it follows that a "God" can be envisaged at three degrees: angelic, archangelic, and divine. This type of complexity makes it understandable why a mythology appears under a form that is more or less discontinuous or disparate, in the manner of a mosaic, and not under the form of a homogeneous enunciation, and why it is necessarily accompanied by an oral or written commentary; thus the inspired commentators—legitimate by reason of their orthodoxy—intervene not in order to add some conjectural interpretations of their own contriving to the sacred sym-bolism, but quite the contrary, in order to draw from those symbols the lights enshrined therein from the beginning. In the tradition that it is the commentators' mission to preserve—by rendering it intelligible according to the needs of the times—what at first sight might appear abstruse is in reality the sign of the inexhaustible nature of Revelation.

One must avoid, in this realm, the convenient but useless hypoth-esis of "borrowings" ; for example, the fact that the left eye of Izanagi gave birth to the Sun and the right eye to the Moon—to Amaterasu

---

[19] Thus it is that differences in local tradition coincide with differences of perspective.

and Tsukuyomi respectively—by no means obliges one to think that this myth has been copied from some Chinese myth that happens to resemble it, for the analogy between the eyes and heavenly bodies is deeply rooted in the nature of things and is to be found in the most diverse traditions. If in the Japanese myth it is the left eye, contrary to expectation,[20] that gives birth to the Sun, this is because here the Sun is envisaged—as is moreover the case in the Germanic languages—under an aspect of femininity, of which it will then represent, not its passive and fragmentary side, but on the contrary its active and maternal side: the Sun possesses fecundity, it is active in "creating" children, whereas the Moon—male according to a matriarchal perspective —is "sterile" in the sense that it knows not maternity, which alone is a "radiation"; the lunar male wanes in its fruitless solitude, obtaining fullness only thanks to woman, who in giving him pleasure confers upon him, as it were, a life-giving "light". In this manner of viewing things, it is the past that appears "real" or "better", exactly as happens in ancestor worship or in the idea of "tradition" generally and for the same reasons: the future is unreality, or uncertainty, that which— humanly speaking—has not been and might not be and which in any case can exist only as a result of the past; the past is identified with the origin, hence also with the timeless; and the future, inasmuch as it is beatitude or deliverance, is like the return to the origin, and therefore also to Eternity.

Another version of the myth of Izanagi and Izanami[21] represents the three Divinities—Amaterasu, Tsukuyomi, and Susano-wo—as being born before Homusubi, therefore prior to the descent of Izanami into the "Land of Darkness" (*Yomotsukuni*);[22] in that case, the three

---

[20] Physiognomists know that the right eye expresses the future and the left eye the past. The relation of the sun to the future and of the moon to the past is perfectly plausible; thus it is not without reason that the moon has been likened to "cosmic memory".

[21] These two names mean, respectively, the "male who invites" and the "female who invites", presumably in view of creative union.

[22] See Masaharu Anesaki, *Japanese Mythology*, in *The Mythology of All Races*, Vol. VIII, Boston, 1937.

Divinities do not spring from Izanagi alone, but are the product of the divine Couple; the two perspectives are separated only by a matter of emphasis or specification, the one considering the common act of the ontological poles and the other stressing the special relationship between the male Principle and the cosmic Center—constituted by the three Divinities—as explained above.

On the other hand, we have also seen that the death of Izanami prefigures the death of every creature; it is said that it is Izanami who causes beings to die in order to avenge herself for the "humiliation" inflicted on her by Izanagi,[23] while he, for his part, is ceaselessly recreating life in order to re-establish the balance. The rupture—although relative and "illusory"—between the divine Spouses manifests itself consequently as a war between life and death, death coming from *natura naturata* or *materia secunda*, that is to say from the material coagulation of the macrocosmic Substance, while life is always arising afresh from the creative Principle, or rather from its male and "vertical" aspect. And this again leads us back to the Biblical myth according to which it is through woman that death has come into the world; the Holy Virgin, who overcomes death, is like the personification of the celestial and non-materialized aspect of universal Substance, which always remains virginal with respect to her productions.

At the time of the rupture between the divine Couple, the Wife said to the Husband: "Each day I shall cause a thousand of your people to die in your kingdom"; to which Izanagi replied: "And I shall give birth every day to one thousand five hundred people", which expresses symbolically the proportion between death and life. Be that as it may, it is not only death and life that arise from this rupture, but also darkness and light, war and peace, and all the other contrasts of the cosmos; it is also said that at the moment when Izanagi returned from hell and washed off his defilements, the infernal mud produced Yaso-Maga-Tsu-Hi, the genius of multiple calamities[24] who was followed immediately by Kamu-Nahobi, the genius of restoration.

---

[23] According to an ancient custom, flowers were formerly offered in Arima, at the tomb-sanctuary of Izanami, as if to cast a celestial veil over her sacrificial "humiliation".

[24] The Sinhalese recognize a similar genius, by the name of Maha-Kola-Sanni-Yaksaya, the demon of great diseases, whose every head stands for a different evil. In Greek mythology, Pandora plays at the same time the part of Yaso-Maga-Tsu-Hi and Izanami, therefore also the part of Eve.

Another divergence of perspective worth pointing out is as follows: we mentioned above that the supreme Principle is Ame-no-Minakanushi-no-Kami, "The Divine Lord of the Center of the Heavens",[25] and that this divine Name is sometimes supplanted by that of Kuni-Tokotachi-no-Mikoto, "Eternal Divine Terrestrial Being" or "He Who Eternally Stands Above the World";[26] now other interpretations see but one divinity in these two; or again, they add to them other Divinities, calling this whole ensemble *Daigenshin*, the "Great Divine Origin"; which in its turn is identified with Amaterasu-Omikami, the solar Goddess, who thus assumes—as in the case of Amida in Pure Land Buddhism—the part of supreme Divinity.[27] This example can provide an idea of the complexity of mythologies in general and of Shinto in particular.

Finally, it is well to consider yet another aspect of the cosmogonic myth: it is said that the divine Couple, standing on the "floating bridge of the Sky"[28] stirred the sea with their celestial lance, enriched with precious stones; a drop of sea water fell from the lance and became the island Onokoro, meaning "Self-Coagulated"; it was there that the Pair established themselves before proceeding to the creation of beings. Now this lance makes one think of phallic symbolism under its many forms, as for example the "Reed-pen" and "Ink" of the Islamic doctrine, and above all of the "vertical dimension" of *Purusha* in Hindu doctrine, which in its "intersection" with the "horizontal dimension" of *Prakriti* gives rise to the creative effusion. The sea, in the Shinto myth, is none other than the sum total of the possibilities of manifestation and thus it is identified with the "Lower Waters" of the Hebraic doctrine; the "Upper Waters" indicate then the prototype of those possibilities *in divinis*, the infinite Beatitude;[29] if it is Susano-wo, God

[25] Who is doubtless identified with Ame-no-Tokotachi-no-Misoko, "The August One Who Stands on the Floor of the Sky".

[26] Sometimes called Tsuchi-Tokotachi-no-Mikoto, "The August One Who Stands on the Floor of the Earth." It is from him that Amaterasu received Shinto.

[27] Such syntheses, far from being unusual or excessive, are on the contrary altogether characteristic of metaphysical symbolism and the non-formalistic mentality that corresponds to it. The "Great Spirit" of the American Indians is another particularly controversial example of this mentality.

[28] This bridge is often identified with the rainbow. It is known that the latter symbolizes the joining of Heaven and Earth.

[29] See *L'homme et son devenir selon le Védânta*, by René Guénon, note p. 72.

of the Tempest, who governs the "sea", this is precisely because of the "passional" character of the demiurgic movement;[30] on the other hand, if the primordial chaos is compared, in Shinto, to an "ocean of oil", this is because of the "weight" and "heat" of that substance, "weight" being a reference to existential "solidification" and "heat" to the "passional" element to which we have just alluded.[31]

---

[30] On the subject of the Tempest-God, let it be added that, exiled on earth, he engendered "evil spirits"; his sister Amaterasu dispatched against them and their allies celestial armies—or armies helped by Heaven—and after the victory she established the imperial dynasty still reigning over Japan. The descendants of Susano-wo are purely passional creatures, thus violent and maleficent, but necessary for the cosmic equilibrium, and, in this sense, they are of "divine" origin; they correspond, not to demons strictly speaking, but to the "giants" and "titans" of the Western mythologies, as also to the inhabitants of the *Asura-Loka* in the Buddhist diagram of the "Round of Existence" (*Saṃsāra*). The demonic order is "subterranean" and not "marine" like that of the Tempest-God.

[31] Further precisions on this cosmogony are the following: "The two primordial ancestors are (in the *Kojiki* book) entirely humanized (instead of being symbolized by snakes), but the remembrance of the cosmic caduceus is no less transparent in this myth (of the primordial marriage). Izanagi and Izanami—having received from the Gods the command to create the earth—stood upon the celestial bridge (suspended in the air) and thrust the bejeweled lance (the solstitial axis) into the sea and stirred it (which calls to mind the churning of the ocean in Hindu mythology). After having thus stirred it, they withdrew the lance, and the salt water that dripped from it became the island Onogoro. It is then that the two beings descended from Heaven onto earth and established the celestial pillar; after which, they built a hall measuring eight arm-lengths (which is to say the hall of the solstitial axis and the zodiac, the latter having eight sectors in Japan). Izanagi and Izanami then became aware of their sexual difference and decided to unite in order to create other islands and other lands. They solemnly walked around the pillar—the sister on the right side and the brother on the left—and having met, performed the conjugal act (the author sees in these two circular movements in opposite directions a remembrance of the intertwined serpents of the caduceus); this is the Japanese version of the Biblical 'Fall', but interpreted as a sacred marriage and without the shadow of 'sin'. . . . They engendered a son, Hiru-ko 'leech-child', so named—it is said—because he was soft and boneless like a leech; but actually there seems to be an allusion here to the primitive—and serpentine—form of the parents" (Julius Schwabe, *Archetyp und Tierkreis*, Basle, 1951, from Karl Florenz, *Die historischen Quellen der Shinto-Religion*, Göttingen, 1919). In these notes, it is added that the steeply arched bridges found in front of Shinto shrines imitate the celestial bridge, which coincides with the arc of the zodiac, and also that the pillar is none other than the bejeweled lance, and that such pillars—called the "majestic pillar of the center"—were the objects of worship in ancient Japan; the Yoshida temple in Kyoto still has such a pillar.

Virtues and Symbols of Shinto

We mentioned earlier that the *Tennō* is like an incarnation of Shinto by the fact that he is descended, through Jimmu Tenno, founder of the empire, from the solar Goddess Amaterasu Omikami; we should now also mention the spiritual prerogatives implied in this origin and function. One can, by analogy, form an idea of these prerogatives by referring to the rather similar case of the *sharīfs* in Islam—the descendants of the Prophet—who enjoy a privileged situation in a human and even an eschatological sense: God has pardoned them in advance thanks to the *barakah* attaching to the blood of Muhammad; one has to accept their possible shortcomings as one accepts divine decrees, with patience and if possible even with gratitude; their blessing is beneficial, their anger brings ill luck; if they are pious, they have every chance of attaining sainthood. Such privileges, however surprising they may seem at first sight, are far from arbitrary; they adhere to every line that is of "avataric" origin, therefore also to the line of Jimmu Tenno who, for his part, incontestably had the quality of a "Prophet";[1] but since "noblesse oblige", the quality of *sharīf* or *Tennō* requires the virtues that were as if incarnated by their respective ancestors.

From what has just been said it is plausible that the divine character of the *Tennō* cannot be "abolished" either by a decree or even by the Emperor himself, whose personal views have no power over the imperial quality or the virtualities that this quality comprises.

The great virtues in Shinto are essentially represented by the "Three Treasures"—which were originally ten in number—namely: the Mirror, the Sword, and the Jewel; respectively, these stand for

---

[1] Other such examples are, in the Far East, the "living Buddhas" (*tülku*) and the descendants of Confucius. The case of the Chinese Emperors, however, seems to have been altogether different—no doubt excepting the primordial dynasty; their function was exercised in virtue of a "heavenly mandate", rather as was the case with the pre-Christian and Christian Roman Emperors and Caliphs of Islam. There are cases where it is the throne or the emblems that temporarily confer a divine character, such as the "Lion Throne" of Mysore or, in a more general way, the divine emblems with which the Hindus clothe little children—or sometimes adults also—in order to worship the Divinity through the human receptacles. The conditional infallibility of the pontiffs— *ex cathedra* or "on the Chair of Moses"—falls into the same category.

truth, courage, and compassion, or wisdom, strength,[2] and charity. According to tradition, the ten sacred Treasures—among which are the "Mirror of the open sea", the "Mirror of the shore", the "Sword of eight spans", the "life-giving Jewel", the "Jewel of health and strength", the "Jewel that raises the dead", the "Jewel that keeps evil from the pathways", and the "Scarves of diverse powers"[3]—were transferred by Nigi-hayahi-no-Mikoto from Heaven to earth; in the course of history, many miracles have taken place thanks to the supernatural virtues of these Treasures; thus it is not without reason that they have been compared to the Ark of the Covenant of the Hebrews.[4]

[2] "The samurai was cold, like his weapon, but he never forgot the fire in which it was forged. His impetuosity was tempered by his code of honor. In the feudal days, Zen had taught him stoicism and made of courteousness the mark of bravery. Confucianism had in the Tokugawa period intensified that sense of duty which made him disregard all obstacles. He did not court pointless danger, for his courage was never in question. He marched to certain death not with the blind fury of fanaticism but with a set resolution of doing whatever was demanded of him" (Kakuzo Okakura, *The Awakening of Japan*, chap. "The Voice from Within"). Here too we would like to mention a certain parallelism with the spirit of the American Indians, but without wishing to underestimate the clear divergences between the two cultural climates: "It is impossible not to recognize that these primitive people knew how to cultivate precious virtues that our materialist and lax civilization has let slip away. A certain scorn for the body, a voluntary training in enduring suffering, which for the Indian is the prelude to mystical visions, lends these simple men a dignity, a courage, and a self-control that compel admiration; and this indifference towards earthly goods, this disdain of material values, of property, confers on them a generosity and an elegance also in the manner of giving, rarely found in our world despite the fact that charity had been taught to us" (Regina Wineza, "La danse du Soleil", *Ecclesia*, June 1957).

[3] These are classified into four categories: the Mirrors, the Sword, the Jewels, the Scarves; the first three constitute the divine emblems of the Empire, and therefore of the *Tennō*.

[4] ". . . During the murderous naval battle . . . between the Genji and Heike clans, some Genji soldiers attacked the enemy vessels and were so audacious as to try (what sacrilege!) to pick the lock of a sacred tabernacle where there was a replica of the Divine Mirror (set in the temple of Ise) as an emblem of the Sun Goddess. The Goddess revealed herself in a dazzling light and the attackers lost their sanity" (Genchi Kato, *Le Shintô, religion nationale du Japon*). Such facts, far from being mythological—for the absence of miracles would be more astonishing than the miracles themselves—corroborate in their way the divine origin and metaphysical truth of the myths, thus the whole tradition. Tradition conveys and transmits not only truths, but also celestial forces that no human ingenuity could replace.

The Mirror is the most important symbol of Shinto, so much so that it serves all in all as an image of God; and likewise it is sincerity— related to the element "truth"— that here ranks as the cardinal virtue. One could also speak of "purity" in the same sense; at the origins, physical cleanliness—which has become a characteristic feature of the Japanese people—coincided with mental and moral purity, as we remarked above; lustral water had a quasi-sacramental quality, as it has as well in other religions where ritual ablutions play a part. As for sincerity, it is far from being no more than a relatively "outward" moral rectitude; its connection with truth on the one hand, and with the symbolism of the mirror on the other, indicates that its scope is much greater, that it brings the whole being back to the ontological Source of man's sense of the real; the human soul is meant to identify itself with the divine Mirror, which is at once radiant and implacable like the sun.

The Mirror, as we have said, serves as an image of God; thus Shinto has a somewhat "iconophobic" side that relates it, in this one respect, to the Jewish and Islamic religions; however, the absence of images has other motives in Shinto than in Semitic monotheism, for it is in point of fact nearer to the perspective of the American Indians, who likewise do not depict the Great Spirit; in other words, the Shinto perspective is centered on Nature considered in her virginity and divinity, and this has nothing to do with the Semitic fear of idolatry, as in fact is proven by the introduction into Japan of Buddhist images, and also and especially by the unsurpassable quality of Buddhist art in that country; as is the case for the American Indians, the phenomena of nature, including the animals, manifest the Divinity and thus render the use of sacred images superfluous.[5] Needless to say, the absence of images with the Semites can coincide, in the consciousness of certain

---

[5] Shinto shrines are virtually empty; they contain, in a Holy of Holies inaccessible to visitors, only the Mirror and the Sword. Popular portrayals of Shinto divinities do not derive from sacred art, although being obviously traditional in style. On the other hand, the influence of Buddhist iconography has given rise to Shinto images whose sacred character is undeniable, but which are "Shinto-Buddhist" rather than Shinto as far as their spiritual origin and their validity are concerned.

individuals and especially in esoterism, with the Shinto and "calumetic" perspective.

The foregoing remarks warrant a digression: Jews and Muslims usually believe that the Biblical—or Koranic—prohibition of images of God concerns Christian, Hindu, and Buddhist sacred images; however, such is not the case, for God said to Moses, "Thou shalt not make images"; He did not say, "I shall make no images"; indeed, sacred images that are revealed are made by God, not by man. For the monotheistic Semites, man himself is the only image of God made by God;[6] whereas Christians, Hindus, and Buddhists received images that, far from having been invented by humans, assumed a concrete form thanks to celestial inspirations of which it can be said that their prototypes are in Heaven; Asian artists—and those of medieval Europe— are like the "mediums" of the divine Artist, especially during the epochs in which the canonical types were set.

In the West, some people see idolatry not only in Buddhism but even in Shinto, and in the latter case they will speak of lytholatry, hydrolatry, and zoolatry and so on, not forgetting the misunderstood cult of the Mirror; now idolatry consists essentially in the reduction of the content to the symbol, outside of any metaphysical background; consequently, idolatry by definition excludes all consciousness of symbolism. What characterizes Buddhism—and also Hinduism *a fortiori*—is precisely that it is fond of expressing, notably in its theory of the *upāyas*, its awareness of the "mythological" character of all formal data; and that is why it has little concern in giving any semblance of historicity to its symbols, quite the contrary: it wants to intimate what the great rending of the veil is, and to suggest from the outset that facts themselves are but "emptiness".

— ·:· —

[6] However, Greco-Roman images of the "classical" period as also the naturalistic Christian images of modern times—beginning with the Renaissance up to the present—plainly fall under the divine prohibition, for they are the work of human minds and hands and nothing else. It is "humanism" and, in the last analysis, "art for art's sake".

Some people believe they can reconcile Shinto with modernism by insisting on its character as a "natural religion"; if what they mean by this is that Shinto is anchored in the symbolism—and metaphysical transparency—of Nature, they would be right; but as their intention is to oppose it to "supernatural" religions, they obviously empty it of all its content and reason for being. To speak of a "natural religion" is a contradiction in terms, just as it is superfluous to speak of a "supernatural religion"; a religion either is or is not; to say that it is purely "natural" or "human" amounts to saying that it is nothing, that it is devoid of authority or of any real efficacy. And since religion is superhuman by definition, it cannot comprise any evolution, but only an "unfolding" that does not however add to it any new quality; it is true, humanly speaking, that in order to become civilizations, Revelations need to take progressive hold of the ideas and modes of behavior of a collectivity, just as traditions having to separate themselves from pre-existing civilizations—as in the case of Buddhism and Christianity—need to undergo some trials and errors and a period of elaboration in order to become altogether "themselves"; but this concerns traditions only as formal and collective phenomena and not as spiritual realities ruling souls.

It is highly probable that the properly esoteric "dimension" of Shinto must have been furnished by the *Mahāyāna*, which would give the symbiosis of these two traditions all its meaning; what we want to say is that Shinto corresponds approximately to the "Lesser Mysteries" of Western Antiquity,[7] whereas the *Mahāyāna* represents the "Greater Mysteries", those that lead beyond the "current of forms". It would be surprising if Shinto did not also include in principle an esoterism of its own; yet it seems that the arrival of Buddhist esoterism was in fact providential, which is to say that it answered a profound need of the Japanese soul, as is proven moreover by the emergence in Japan of a number of esoteric *Mahāyāna* schools, not to mention the depth of Buddhist art in that country.

Now, if Shinto is expressly the tradition of the Japanese, this does not mean that it has nothing to teach the rest of mankind, for every religion possesses, by definition and in principle, a kind of universal

---

[7] Shinto, apart from its chivalrous character, is moreover an agricultural tradition, as is the Chinese tradition viewed under its most common aspect. This explains the affinity between Shinto and Confucianism.

radiation, rather in the way a flower is there for all to see. Shinto strikes us first of all by its perceptible manifestations, by the truly fascinating quality of its art and its rites or, in a more general sense, by that pure, fresh, and primordial quality emanating from it; Japanese craftsmanship—independently from its Chinese and Buddhist inheritance—is distinguished by an exquisite simplicity and a kind of sober refinement allowing one to divine all that is precious in the Japanese soul, namely an innate feeling for nature and the natural—a feeling that allows a Japanese craftsman to create a masterpiece from a blade of grass[8]—then the love of beauty,[9] self-domination, courtesy, and heroism.[10] These qualities at once spiritual, moral, and artistic found a particularly favorable ground in Zen, and it is doubtless within the

[8] These traits can also be found in Malay arts or crafts, notably in architecture. There is among the Japanese an undeniable Malay element.

[9] To the question of how it was possible for the most artistic people on earth to have adopted with eagerness the errors and hideousness of the industrialized West, we shall answer by posing another question, namely how it was possible for the Middle Ages, although in possession of a perfect art, to have committed a similar betrayal at the time of the Renaissance, and in spite of the Christian morality with which this neo-paganism was colliding, and how could "Holy Russia", glittering with Byzantine splendors, have succumbed to that same influence, at least to a certain extent and despite its rooted dislike of the Latin West? The only possible explanation is that sacred art comes from Heaven and that its corruption comes from men. The tremendous success, in Japan as elsewhere, of the male attire of the West—a manner of dress at once puritan, revolutionary, and industrialist—can be explained by the fact that it expresses and suggests, with the insistence of a profession of faith, the illusory cosmic and eschatological "extraterritoriality" of modern man, whereas traditional garments are geared towards our final human ends, whence their compatibility with the sacred.

[10] Much praise has been given, and rightly so, to the qualities of the Japanese woman; but what is forgotten by those who advocate her "emancipation" are the traditional conditions of existence that formed her. The sexes are not two races, the one tyrannical and the other tyrannized; every woman has a father just as every man has a mother; the Japanese woman would not be what she is had she not inherited the qualities of strength, authority, and discipline from innumerable fathers, just as the Japanese man has benefited from the gentleness, patience, and self-sacrifice accumulated over centuries by his mothers. In quite a general way and outside the problem of metaphysical and physiological inequalities, when people speak of "freedom", they too easily lose sight of the fact that freedom has value only insofar as it allows us to realize our spiritual destiny, in conformity with our nature.

spirit and activities of Zen that Japanese Buddhism has most intimately absorbed the pre-existing genius of Shinto.[11]

---

[11] The other branches of Japanese Buddhism—we have in mind here above all of
Jōdo-Shinshū—also necessarily bear the imprint of the Japanese genius. At the beginning of this century, Kakuzo Okakura very judiciously observed that "the task of Asia
today, then, becomes that of protecting and restoring Asiatic modes. But to do this
she must herself first recognize and develop consciousness of those modes. For the
shadows of the past are the promise of the future. . . . But it must be from Asia herself,
along the ancient roadways of the race, that the great voice shall be heard. Victory
from within, or a mighty death without" (Kakuzo Okakura, *The Ideals of the East*,
chapter "The Vista", London, John Murray, 1905); "The ideal monk is the child of
freedom, who, dying to the mundane, is reborn to the realm of the spirit. He is like
the lotus which rises in purity above the mire. He is silent, like the forest in which
he meditates; untrammeled, like the wind that blows his gown around him. . . . The
highest desire of an Indian or Japanese householder was to reach the age at which,
leaving worldly cares to his children, he might learn that higher life of a recluse known
as *Banaprasta* or *Inkyo*. . . . But the social and the supra-social worlds never clashed, for
each was the counterpart of the other. . . . Asia is nothing if not spiritual, but the man
of the spirit is not one of names or forms" (*The Awakening of Japan*, chapter "Buddhism and Confucianism"); "The venerable East still distinguishes between means and
ends. The West is for progress, but progress toward what? When material efficiency
is complete, what end, asks Asia, will have been accomplished? When the passion
of fraternity has culminated in universal cooperation, what purpose is it to serve? If
mere self-interest, where do we find the boasted advance? The picture of Western
glory unfortunately has a reverse. Size alone does not constitute true greatness, and the
enjoyment of luxury does not always result in refinement. The individuals who go to
the making up of the great machine of so-called modern civilization become the slaves
of mechanical habit and are ruthlessly dominated by the monster they have created.
In spite of the vaunted freedom of the West, true individuality is destroyed in the
competition for wealth, and happiness and contentment are sacrificed to an incessant
craving for more" (Ibid., chapter "The White Disaster").

APPENDIX

Selections from Letters and Other Writings

1

Figure 1

The Chinese *yin-yang*, symbol of the universal polarity.

Figure 2

A more dynamic form of the *yin-yang*, suggesting the cosmogonic process.

Figure 3

Family emblem, a Japanese stylization of the *yin-yang*.

Figure 4

The *tomoye*, Shinto symbol—a type of triple *yin-yang*—painted on ritual drums that are played to accompany the *bugaku* dance; it evokes the motion of waves and represents the ternary of the divine aspects and cosmic tendencies (Hindu doctrine: *Sat-Chit-Ānanda, Trimūrti,* three *gunas*), and also the current of forms. The rhythm of the drum punctuates the cyclical unfolding of the form-bound coagulations. It is comparable to Hokusai's famous print of the "Wave".

Figure 5

Another version of the same symbol, in tricolor form: ocher, red, green. It is found, for example, on fans, which thereby assume a kind of "magical" function.

2

If Hindus and Buddhists believe in reincarnation, this is because they interpret sacred texts literally, exactly as Monotheists do who believe, in following the literal meaning of certain texts, that Heaven is "above" and hell "below"; in other words, assuming that hell is beneath the earth, and so on and so forth. For a Hindu, to believe that man is reincarnated is no more wrong than, for a Monotheist, to believe that God dwells behind the clouds, and that the souls of the elect "ascend" to Heaven; what is wrong, however, is to consider these two interpretations as dogmas.

At all events, it must not be forgotten that, according to Hindu and Buddhist texts, "human birth is difficult to obtain"!

3

You allude, in your letter, to the silence of Hinduism and Buddhism about the resurrection. I shall say that the silence of the transmigrationists on resurrection is answered by the silence of the resurrectionists on transmigration. But there must be, in Hinduism, at least some trace of the monotheistic dogma, just as conversely the monotheistic doctrines must contain some trace of the Hindu and Buddhist dogma, in the notion of "limbo" notably; "limbo", being neither heaven nor hell, implicitly suggests transmigration. Moreover, the concrete difference between eschatologies is one of the greatest of mysteries—what I mean is the differences one finds between posthumous states depending on the traditional systems.

4

The Prophet, being the founder of a religion, is a *Samyaksam-Buddha*; Ali and Abu Bakr, being apostles, are *Bodhisattvas*; neither of them could be a *Pratyeka-Buddha*. One can see a *Pratyeka-Buddha* in Uways al-Qarani—or in our times and in India, in Sri Ramana Maharshi—but not in an apostle who would have had to have some disciples. Furthermore, not every spiritual man can represent everything; it is not a question here of capacity, but of providential manifestation. Christ embodied supreme wisdom—it could not be otherwise—but he addressed sinners and did not manifest the spiritual mode of a Badarayana, author of the *Brahma Sūtra*. And God knows best.

5

Limitations that are existential should never be expressed in individual terms, by speaking for example of the ego "which sat so heavily on my shoulders". Every metaphysician ought to know that transcending the ego is not—and cannot be—the annihilation of it, contrary to a certain literalist interpretation that misunderstands the elliptical dialectic of the East; there is no common measure between Deliverance and individuality, so that the latter could never oppose the former. The difference between the non-delivered and the delivered is not that the second has no more individuality, which would be a contradiction in terms since he is a man; the difference consists simply in that the non-delivered is locked in his individuality whereas the delivered is detached from it; he "possesses" individuality but "is" not that individuality. Without question, the *Avatāras* are people, not only on earth but also in Heaven; this does not exclude in any way the fact of their Supreme Identity, for, once again, there is no common measure here. This is what the *Mahāyāna* teaches by means of the doctrine of the "simultaneous bodies" of the Buddhas: *nirmānakāya*, *sambhogakāya*, and *Dharmakāya*; now the third body is nirvanic or divine. If such were not the case, the delivered could not appear, after their death, in visions or in beatific dreams; and Heaven never deceives anyone.

Thus, individuality subsists as a dimension—until the *Apocatastasis*—in the manner of a house into which one can enter and exit; during terrestrial life it is subject to vicissitudes, whatever the spiritual degree of a given man. A spiritual truth can address itself to a man because he "is" an individual, but it can also concern him because he "possesses" an individuality, and "inasmuch" as he possesses one.

6

Some might object that only Christ manifests in a direct mode the eternal "Incarnation" and that, as a result, the manner of manifesting it is indirect in the other Revelations; we could answer by saying that only the Buddha manifests the eternal *Bodhi* in a direct manner, and therefore that the *Bodhi* appears in an indirect manner in Christ, and so on and so forth. This is due to the fact that we speak of "Incarnation" because of Christ, and of "Enlightenment" because of the Buddha; the possible designations of the prototype of Revelation and of Deliverance are indefinite in number. There is in manifestation an unfolding of symbols, and each symbol refers to a real aspect of the divine Model, or of the universal models deriving therefrom; but since it is a matter here of the same principial and primordial reality, namely the entry of the Absolute into relativity—whatever the degree considered may be—the modes or symbols are not mutually exclusive: the entry of the Koranic Revelation into the body of the Prophet can be termed an "incarnation" of the Word, just as the entry of the Holy Spirit—bearer of the Word—into the body of the Virgin is a "descent" of the Divine Book; and likewise, these two modes are within the *Bodhi*, and the *Bodhi* is within them.

7

As to the question "Why invoke?" the profoundest response would no doubt be: "because I exist", for Existence is in a certain way the Word of God, by which He names Himself. God pronounces his Name to manifest Himself—to "create"—in the direction of "nothingness", and the relative being pronounces this Name to "be", in other words to "become once again what he is" in the direction of Reality.

The idea of "duty" is very useful, humanly speaking, for the world needs the invocation. What matters is not our personal worth, nor the graces God makes apparent to us, but the fact of the manifestation of the Name. Moreover, we have no worth except thanks to this Name. We are incapable of doing any good by ourselves; everything that we do is conjectural, except the Name, the agent of which, precisely, is God; we thus lend ourselves to the divine act.

Japanese Buddhists have rightly stressed the fact that the invocation is not meant to produce joy; this lack of joy is ourselves; so much the better if grace pierces this wall; but this is something independent from the immediate efficacy and the final validity of our prayer. You are right to say that the ego wishes to seize everything, even grace. I think that books on Japanese *Jōdo-Shinshū* would provide you with insights on this subject.

8

The immeasurable merit of Amida—or the merciful quality of the Absolute, in a more real or less unreal sense—can have the effect of instantaneously burning away the karmic layer of ignorance separating man from *Nirvāna*; it is not that *Nirvāna* is "given", but that ignorance is "removed".

At a lesser level, *Shinshū* declares the existence of a bhaktic Paradise located in the West, something that the simple faithful interpret literally.

In *Les Sectes bouddhiques japonaises* by Steinilber-Oberlin, one can read: "At the end of our earthly life, we cast off the last traces of this corrupted existence, and reborn in the Land of Purity and Happiness we obtain the Buddha's Enlightenment."

Christian *gnosis* is directly analogous in a certain sense to *Shinshū* in that Redemption, namely the inexhaustible merit of Christ, is a manifestation—or the manifestation—of the merciful Power of the Infinite; Redemption does not "bestow" *gnosis*, but it removes what separates us from it if we know how to place ourselves into the requisite conditions. As in *Jōdo-Shinshū*, there is in Christianity a literal and bhaktic application and a metaphysical and jnanic application.

Shinshū is an ontological way, all things considered; what must be found—among a thousand possibilities—is the thread linking us to the Absolute; this thread appears to be infinitesimal, but it suffices because it is what it is.

9

You tell me that you are interested in Buddhism, which is all very well, and that you meditate according to the method of Zen, which is impossible in your case; because in order to practice a spiritual method, one must adhere first of all to the religion to which it belongs—for Zen one must validly be a Buddhist—and then one must be validly accepted by an orthodox spiritual master. This amounts to saying that, in practical terms, one needs to go to Japan and enter a Zen monastery; although one must still make sure that the abbot is not a heretic, because the modern influence has penetrated everywhere.

It makes no sense to practice a spiritual method outside of the indispensable conditions and traditional rules; there is even every chance that this would be detrimental. First of all, one must be sure that such a path is "willed by God" for us; next, one must realize a psychological, moral, and mental atmosphere that renders the path possible; this is not something that can be done on one's own.

Every religion and every form of spirituality has essentially a two-fold basis: the distinction between the Absolute and the contingent, between the Real and the illusory, the Permanent and the impermanent, *Ātmā* and *Māyā*, the Sovereign Good and the world; and then the anchoring of the soul in this Sovereign Good. And this is done within the framework of a traditional form, on the one hand, and on the other, of personal virtue.

10

Eastern masters almost never understand the situation of the Westerners they initiate; they almost always lose sight of two factors, even though they are fundamental—because in the East this question never really arises—namely the psychological conditions and the conditions of the ambience, which are difficult to meet in an abnormal world such as ours; I could almost say: the moral and aesthetic conditions of the path. That is why the practices of Zen, for instance, grafted onto the mental trivialities engendered by modern life, are in general more harmful than useful; for one must be deeply imbued with the sense of the sacred, and also by a kind of holy childlikeness, to be able to benefit from initiatic graces, or spiritual graces as such.

The question for you is that of knowing whether, for God, you are Christian or Buddhist; assuming that your sense of the sacred and your intuition of spiritual forms have enabled you to assimilate the specific atmosphere of *Mahāyāna* to a sufficient degree, I will tell you that the situation in that case is strictly analogous to what it is in Christianity, the central spiritual means being the *mantra*, the jaculatory orison in other words, all the more as you have received the initiation referring to Amitabha Buddha, who corresponds metaphysically to Christ. And I would not recommend a Western Buddhist any other path than that of the invocation of Amitabha—be it in its Japanese form or in its Tibetan form—assuming, of course, that one have in the eyes of God a valid reason for being Buddhist and for entering a path that is so foreign to our traditional climate in the West. I suppose that this question is not entirely resolved for you.

If I understand correctly, it can happen that you take "metaphysical" communion in the church; now if you are validly affiliated with Buddhism and if you practice a Buddhist method, all Christian rites are excluded. Moreover, one does not take communion "metaphysically"; one concentrates on God, the Absolute, the Real, or on the radiation of His Mercy, and one lets God act as He will. What you are doing, according to your letter, is doubly dangerous, first because it is a heterogeneous mixture of sacred forms and then because we have no right to impose a doctrinal program on Grace; Grace acts as it wills. Tibetans, not knowing Western religions, confuse them with secondary cults and are not competent in these matters. And you most certainly have not "gotten beyond infidelity and religion"!

11

One of the part-human, part-divine phenomena that has fascinated me the most ever since my childhood is the *mudrā*; the one in which the hand is vertical, the thumb holding the middle finger so that they form a circle, the ring finger being half inclined, the other two fingers remaining nearly vertical; in short, this *mudrā*-synthesis which seems to present a pearl, a jewel, a *cintamāni*, an elixir; a *mudrā* that teaches and communicates, not by means of a word, obviously, but through a divine or nirvanic gesture, precisely. A gesture that seems to extract—or to have extracted—what is the most precious, the most directly salvific, from a complex Message; which brings to mind that other *mudrā*, which the "flower sermon" represented for the Buddha.

12

Buddhism sees the world only as a chaos of irreducible substances (*dharmas*), of which the innumerable combinations produce subjective and objective appearances; like Christianity it does not have a cosmology, strictly speaking, which means that both of these two great perspectives regard the world not in its reality or unreality but solely with reference to the means of leaving it. For the Buddhist even more than for the Christian, to seek to know the nature of the world is a distraction; for the Hindu, however, knowledge of the cosmos is an aspect of knowledge of the Absolute since it is nothing other than *Ātmā* as *Māyā*, or the "universal Soul" as "creative Illusion". This perspective, which begins with the Absolute, is truly metaphysical whereas the Buddhist and Christian perspectives, which begin with man, are initiatic, that is, centered above all on spiritual realization; since they are intrinsically true, however, they also contain the Hindu perspective, and conversely.

The Shankarian refutation of Buddhism does not show why Buddhism is false but why Hinduism cannot admit it without nullifying itself.

13

You allude in your letter to the painful invectives of Shankara against the Buddha. What is at stake in this case is not the intrinsic reality of the Buddha but an extrinsic aspect, that of the destroyer of Brahmanism; in fact Buddhism threatened to completely overrun the world of the *Veda* and the castes. Hindus readily grasped the *distinguo* I have just mentioned well before our time, and I have reason to believe that in our day all Hindus venerate the Buddha without thereby disavowing Shankara, who was in his time the medium of a reviving Hinduism; it is as if the Brahmanic gods had armed him with a sword.

As for a spiritually positive reality becoming the symbol of a negative and hostile reality in another spiritual and traditional perspective, there is more than one instance of this phenomenon, but it does not concern intrinsic truth. Such a phenomenon can be repeated even within one and the same tradition; Shiism is an extreme example of this. In our western world, I could mention the demonization of the gods of antiquity by Christianity and within Christianity itself the antagonistic interpretations of Saint Thomas Aquinas and Saint Gregory Palamas, each of whom is regarded as orthodox or heretic, good or bad, depending on denominational prejudice.

14

There is a certain complementary relationship between the Buddhist and Shankarian reactions: Buddhism reacted against a Brahmanism that had become somewhat sophisticated and Pharisaical, and Shankara reacted against the doctrinal simplifications of Buddhism—simplifications that were certainly not incorrect in themselves but contrary to the traditional metaphysics of India. If Brahmanic spirituality had not suffered a measure of obscuration, the peaceful expansion of Buddhism would not have been possible; likewise, if the Buddhist point of view had not been centered on man and his final ends, Shankara would not have had to reject it in the name of a doctrine centered on the Self.

Therein lies the great difference: the Buddha delivers by eliminating what is human after first defining it as suffering; Shankara delivers solely by the knowledge of what is real, what is pure Subject, pure Self. But to eliminate everything human is not possible without metaphysics, and to know the Self is not possible without eliminating what is human: Buddhism is a spiritual therapy, which as such requires metaphysics,[1] whereas Hinduism is a metaphysics, which by the same token requires a spiritual therapy.

15

Some scholars have quite improperly concluded that the Shankarian advaitism—"non-dualism"—stems in the final analysis from Nagarjuna, hence from Mahayanic Buddhism, which Shankara condemns most implacably. The reason for this false association is that there is a certain parallelism between advaitism and the Nagarjunan perspective in the sense that both represent a metatheistic immanentism, although the starting points are totally different. No doubt, the Buddhist *Nirvāna* is nothing other than the Self: *Ātmā;* but whereas for the Hindus the starting point is that reflection of the Self which is the "I", for the Buddhists on the contrary the starting point is entirely negative and moreover purely empirical: it is the *Samsāra* as the world of suffering, and this world is merely a "void", *shūnya*, which it is not worth the trouble of trying to make sense of. Buddhists deny the concrete existence of the soul and consequently that also of the Self—they conceive in negative mode what the Hindus conceive in positive mode—Hindus, for their part, reject no less categorically this negativism of the Buddhists, which appears to them like a negation of the Real itself.

16

In order really to understand Nagarjuna, or the *Mahāyāna* in general, one must before everything else take account of two facts, first that Buddhism presents itself essentially as a spiritual method and there-

---

[1] "According to the teaching of the Buddha there are two orders of truth: supreme truth and the truth of appearances. Those who have not yet discovered the difference between these two truths have not understood the deepest meaning of the doctrine" (Nagarjuna in the *Mādhyamika Shāstra*).

fore subordinates everything to what is methodical and, secondly, that this method is essentially one of negation. From this it follows, on the one hand, that metaphysical reality is considered with reference to method, that is as "state" and not as "principle", and, on the other hand, that it is conceived in negative terms: *Nirvāna*, "Extinction", or *Shūnya*, the "Void". "Affirmation", in Buddhist wisdom, has the same meaning and function as "ignorance" in Hindu wisdom. To describe *Nirvāna* or *Shūnya* in positive terms would amount, in Vedantic language, to wishing to know the pure Subject, the "Divine Consciousness", *Ātmā*, on the plane of objectivation itself, hence on the plane of ignorance.

17

It is difficult to deny, if one is still sensitive to true norms, that the machine tends to make man into its own counterpart; that it renders him violent, brutal, vulgar, quantitative, and stupid like itself, and that all modern "culture" is affected thereby. This is what partly explains the cult of "sincerity" and the mystique of "engagement": one must be "sincere" because the machine is devoid of mystery and is as incapable of prudence as of generosity; one must be "engaged" because the machine possesses no value apart from its productions, or because it demands ceaseless oversight and even complete "self-surrender"[2] and thus devours mankind and all that is human; one must refrain from complacency in literature and art because the machine does not behave in this manner and because in the minds of its slaves and creatures its ugliness, noise, and implacability are mistaken for "reality." Above all, one must not have a God, since the machine has none or even usurps this role itself.

We would stress that in speaking of "God" we have in mind, not a concept that would be contrary—or inasmuch as it would be contrary—to Buddhism, but the "nirvanic" Reality that underlies all traditional concepts of the Absolute, which is expressed in the

---

[2] If it be objected that the same was true of the crafts of old, we would reply that there is a notable difference, in that these occupations displayed a properly human and thus contemplative character, and on that account entailed neither the agitation nor the oppression characteristic of the machine age.

Mahāyāna by the universal *Dharmakāya*, or in other words, by the *Ādi-Buddha*: Amitabha (Amida) or Vairochana (Dainichi), according to the respective schools.

18

If Buddhism denies the outward, objective, and transcendent God, this is because it puts all the emphasis on the inward, subjective, and immanent Divinity—whether it is called *Nirvāna*, *Ādi-Buddha*, or by some other name—which moreover makes it impermissible to describe Buddhism as atheistic. In the Amidist sector, Amitabha is the immanent Mercy that our faith can and must actualize in our favor; all beauty and all love are concentrated in this personification of Mercy. If it happens that some Buddhists assert that Amithaba does not exist outside ourselves or that he would not exist without us—analogous formulations are to be found in Eckhart and Silesius—they mean that his immanence and his saving efficacy entail our existence and our subjectivity, for one cannot speak of a content without a container; in brief, if Buddhists seem to put man in the place of God transcendent, this is because man as a concrete subjectivity is the container of immanent liberating Substance.

19

If Christianity appears as something new, we are told, it could be argued that the same is true of every other religion; but the issue here is obviously not the simple fact that every beginning is new, for in this case we would never think of attributing novelty to Christianity alone. Sinai clearly marks a new stage in Judaism, and yet there was no intention of abolishing the religion of the Patriarchs; its spirit is such that it neither invites nor encourages innovation in any way; the orthodox Messianism of the Jews—it should be emphasized—is opposed to the idea of progress. The same is true of Islam: far from presenting itself as something new, Islam wishes only to restore—not "reform"—what existed from the beginning; the Prophet is simply the last in a succession of Prophets, known and unknown, and he brings nothing that was not brought by his predecessors in one form or another; according to the Koran "there is no change in the words of God". The situation is just the same in Hinduism and Buddhism: each cosmic cycle has its *Avatāra* or *Buddha*; even the historical Buddha had no intention of innovating; he manifested *Bodhi*, Enlightenment, just as countless Buddhas did before him and will do after him; his Enlightenment is not in itself something new but the actualization of an eternal reality, that of *Nirvāna*, which bursts forth whenever the human cycles permit or demand it.

20

Intrinsically "orthodox" dogmas, that is, those established in view of salvation, differ from one religion to another; consequently they cannot all be objectively true. However, all dogmas are symbolically true and subjectively efficacious, which is to say that their purpose is to create human attitudes that contribute in their way to the divine miracle of salvation. This, in practice, is the meaning of the Buddhist term *upāya*, "skillful means" or "spiritual stratagem", and it is thanks to this efficient intention—or this virtually liberating "truth"—that all dogmas are justified and are in the final analysis compatible despite their antagonisms.

21

In Northern Buddhism, the shaktic principle is manifested by the goddess Kwan-Yin as well as by Tara.[3] Kwan-Yin—the Kwannon of Japanese Buddhism—stems from the *Bodhisattva* Avalokiteshvara, supreme genius of Mercy; this quality or function explains the feminization of the *hypostasis*. As for Tara, she is derived from *Prajnāpāramitā*, "Transcendent Wisdom"; she is "Mother of all the Buddhas" and "Savioress", hence *Shakti*. In the same way, Mary has been qualified as the

---

[3] We are using here the word "goddess" in a symbolic and approximative or, if one wishes, practical fashion, given that Buddhism excludes the idea of a personal divinity. As for the *Bodhisattvas*, they correspond on the one hand to the archangels and on the other—more ordinarily and *a priori*—to the great saints who save souls and afterwards enter into the celestial "iconostasis".

"Mother of all the Prophets" and as "Co-Redemptress"; not to mention the appellation—actually highly elliptical—of "Mother of God".

This last example shows us that the *Shakti* can be a human person, an earthly and *a posteriori* heavenly woman; other examples, belonging to the Hindu world, are Sita and Radha, who are sometimes invoked together with Rama and Krishna, whence the names Sitaram and Radhakrishna. In Buddhism one has to mention, aside from the *Bodhisattvas*, the great figure of Maya, the mother of the Buddha who, like the Mother of Christ, has a double message: her own nature and her child; the two miracles being powers of ascension and of liberation. The first of these messages is multiple and perpetual, it is an inexhaustible rain of blessings; the second is unique and historical, it is the divine maternity.[4]

22

Quite clearly, deiformity essentially entails femininity, despite the opinion of certain ancient moralists who had difficulty reconciling the two; the one entails the other for simply logical as well as metaphysical reasons; even without knowing that femininity derives from an "Eternal Feminine" of a transcendent order, one is obliged to take account of the fact that woman, being situated like the male in the human state, is deiform because this state is deiform. Thus it is not surprising that as "misogynist" a tradition as Buddhism consented finally—within the *Mahāyāna* at least—to make use of the symbolism of the feminine body, which would be meaningless and even harmful if this body, or if femininity in itself, did not comprise a spiritual message of paramount importance; the Buddhas (and *Bodhisattvas*) do not save solely through doctrine, but also through their suprahuman beauty, according to the Tradition; now to speak of beauty is to speak implicitly of femininity; the beauty of the Buddha is necessarily that of *Māyā* or of Tara.

The "misogyny" of Buddhism is explained by the fact that its method, at its origin and in general at least, appeals essentially to the

---

[4] In Mahayanic Buddhism, we encounter also the "white Tara" and the "green Tara", both princesses married to the Tibetan king who introduced Buddhism into his country; they incarnate two different and complementary modes of celestial favors.

characteristics of masculine psychology, which is to say that it operates basically with intellection, abstraction, negation, strength, and with what Amidism calls "power of self"; the same observation applies, if not to Hinduism as such, at least to certain of its schools and doubtless to its average perspective, which culminates, as in Buddhism, in the excessive and, to say the least, schematic idea that woman as such cannot attain Deliverance, that she must first be reborn in a masculine body and follow the methods of men. Ancient discussions on the question of knowing whether or not woman possesses a "soul" have a similar import: at issue was not the immortal soul, but the intellect in its most specifically masculine aspect. Be that as it may, the decisive point is not that woman has the concrete capacity to make use of such methods, it is simply that, being human, she clearly has the capacity for sanctity.

23

Unquestionably, Judaism and Islam accentuate transcendence, whereas Christianity is founded upon theophany; Buddhism takes its point of departure in the mystery of immanence. Each of these standpoints negates or limits *a priori* the others, but realizes them *a posteriori* in a way appropriate to its perspective.

Compared to Judaism, Christianity moreover comprises a certain accentuation of the element of immanence, whence its quasi-rejection of outer prescriptions and its insistence upon inner qualities. And Buddhism necessarily combines its initial immanentism—its cult of *Nirvāna*, "inward" by definition—with a theophanism that is both exclusive and inclusive: in principle there is only a single Buddha, but his mystery is nonetheless manifested in a profusion of divine personifications.

24

The Muslim "loves him who loves God and hates him who hates God" (*hadīth*) and who, therefore, is hated by God, since divine hatred leads to damnation. The Christian, for his part, must love his enemies, inasmuch as they are loved by God, and they are so loved because every man has the possibility of salvation, and God "sendeth rain on the just and on the unjust". The Christian loves that which, in man, is capable of loving God, and that is why his charity does not extend expressly to animals, and still less to the damned, contrary to what happens in Buddhism. Buddhist charity is a participation in the divine—or more exactly the "nirvanic"—Charity, and is founded, as regards its object, on the capacity of beings to suffer; the normal nourishment of the Buddhist is vegetal, since plants do not suffer; nevertheless, charity extends even to plants in the sense that a man of goodwill would not think of causing them to perish without necessity, any more than he would make an animal suffer needlessly, and this applies to all men, whatever their traditional perspective may be.

25

If one were to love and admire everything, as for example certain dreamers of a more or less Buddhist cast of mind would have it, the fulminations of the *Magnificat* or of the Sermon on the Mount would be inexplicable. Charity or "compassion" is not flabbiness, apart from the fact that charity may require harshness.

26

If Buddhism, which only possesses a morality designed for contemplatives, has to a certain extent been able to pacify formerly warlike peoples, this may be connected to the fact that the law of "karmic" causality and the successive advents of the Buddhas appear in this case as the sole expressions of divine will; man must therefore take upon himself—from the point of view of "concordant actions and reactions"—all the risks involved in such equivocal acts as the elimination of a life or the destruction or taking of someone else's property.

27

The marvels of the basilicas and the cathedrals, of the iconostases and the altarpieces, as well as the splendors of Buddhist Tibeto-Mongol and Japanese art or, prior to it, those of Hindu art, not forgetting the summits of the corresponding literatures—all this did not exist in the primitive epochs of these various traditions, epochs that were precisely the "golden ages" of these spiritual universes. Thus the marvels of traditional culture seem like the swan songs of the celestial messages: in other words, to the extent that the message runs the risk of being lost, or is effectively lost, a need is felt—and Heaven itself feels this need—to exteriorize gloriously all that which men are no longer capable of perceiving within themselves. Thenceforth it was outward things that had to remind men where their center lies; it is true that this is in principle the role of virgin nature, but in fact its language is only grasped where it traditionally takes on the role of a sanctuary.[5] Moreover, the two perspectives—sacred art and virgin nature—are not mutually exclusive, as is shown notably by Zen Buddhism; this proves that neither can altogether replace the other.

28

The Buddhist conception of art is, at least in certain respects, not remote from the Christian: like Christian art, Buddhist art is centered on the image of the Superman, bearer of the Revelation, though it differs from the Christian perspective in its non-theism, which brings everything back to the impersonal; if man is logically at the center of the cosmos, that is, for Buddhism, "by accident" and not from theological necessity as in the case of Christianity; human beings are "ideas" rather than individuals. Buddhist art revolves around the sacramental image of the Buddha, which was given moreover, according to one tradition, in the lifetime of the Blessed One in different forms, both sculptural and pictorial. Contrary to what happens in Christian art, statuary takes precedence over painting, although the latter is nonetheless strictly canonical; it is not "discretionary" like Christian statuary. In the realm of architecture, we may mention the *stūpa* of Piprahwa built immediately after the death of Shakyamuni; moreover, elements of Hindu and Chinese art were transmuted into a new art

---

[5] Among the ancient Aryans, from India to Ireland—except, more or less, the Mediterraneans in historic times—and in our day still among the shamanist peoples, Asiatic and American.

of which there were a number of variants both in the *Theravāda* and the *Mahāyāna* schools. From a doctrinal point of view the art in this case is founded on the idea of the saving virtue emanating from the superhuman beauty of the Buddhas: the images of the Blessed One, of other Buddhas, and of *Bodhisattva*s are sacramental crystallizations of this virtue, which is also manifested in religious objects, "abstract" as to their form but "concrete" in their nature. This principle furnishes a conclusive argument against profane religious art as practiced in the West, for the celestial beauty of the God-Man extends to the whole of traditional art, whatever the particular style required by a given collectivity; to deny traditional art—and here we have Christianity chiefly in mind—is to deny the saving beauty of the Word made flesh; it is to be ignorant of the fact that in true Christian art there is something of Christ and something of the Virgin. Profane art replaces the soul of the God-Man, or of the deified man, by that of the artist and of his human model.

29

The symbol is an "exteriorization in view of an interiorization", and this is shown in a particularly striking way in Buddhist art where the images express, sometimes with unsurpassable power, all the transcendent serenity of the Blessed One.

30

One may wonder why the Hindus, and still more so the Buddhists, did not fear to provide occasions for a fall in their sacred art, given that beauty—sexual beauty above all—invites to "let go of the prey for its shadow", that is, to forget the transcendent content through being attached to the earthly husk. Now it is not for nothing that Buddhist art, more than any other, has given voice to the fearsome aspects of cosmic manifestation; at the very least this constitutes a "reestablishing of the balance": the spectator is forewarned never to lose sight of the menace of the pitiless *Samsāra* everywhere present, nor that of the Guardians of the Sanctuary. *Darshan*—the contemplation of the Divine in nature or in art—quite clearly presupposes a contemplative temperament; now it is this very temperament that comprises a sufficient guarantee against the attitude of casualness and of profanation.

31

The fundamental idea of the way of Amitabha (Amida in Japanese) coincides in substance with this saying of Christ: "With men it is impossible, but not with God: for with God all things are possible" (Mark 10:27). This is the Buddhist perspective of the "power of the Other" (*tariki* in Japanese), not of "power of self" (*jiriki*); it means that man adopts an attitude of faith "that moves mountains", combined with a divine and sacramental support which, for its part, is what in reality brings about salvation; there is something analogous in the case of Christian communion, which in fact imparts an incommensurable grace without man having any part in it, except as regards receptivity, which clearly has its requirements.

But the sharp alternative between a "way of merit" and a "way of grace"—for that is what the *distinguo* between the principles *jiriki* and *tariki* means in Japanese Buddhism—this alternative is, we think, more theoretical than practical; in concrete reality, there is really more of an equilibrium between the two procedures, so that the distinction evokes the Far-Eastern symbol of the *Yin-Yang*, composed, as is known, by a white half containing a black dot, and a black half containing a white dot, this being the very image of harmonious complementarity.[6] Shinran, the disciple of Honen, wished to place the accent solely on the "power of the Other", which from a certain mystical point of view is defensible, on condition of not reproaching Honen for stopping half-way and of having wrongly maintained an element of "power of self"; for, since initiative and activity are natural to man, we do not see what advantage there would be in depriving him of them. Faith, it seems to us, is much easier to realize if one allows man the joy of collaborating with it; there is in fact a criterion of concrete reality in our personal activity and a guarantee of efficacy, whereas faith

---

[6] For example, man bears in his soul a feminine element, and woman a masculine element; and it is necessarily thus, not only because every person has two parents, but also because each sex belongs to one and the same human species.

alone—as a condition of salvation—rests on nothing that is ours and that we could control. Honen knew as well as Shinran that the cause of salvation is not in our work but in the grace of Amida; but we must somehow open ourselves in some fashion to this grace, otherwise it would suffice to exist in order to be saved.

32

Without wishing to formulate a reproach on a plane pertaining to intrinsic orthodoxy—though this plane belongs nonetheless to the relativity of the *upāya*—one cannot help feeling that there is something excessive in the totalitarianism of a Zen, on the one hand, that sets out to dispense with all trace of *tariki* and of a *Jōdo*, on the other, that aims to pass over *jiriki* entirely. It is certain that man can, in principle, save himself "by his own means", but it is necessary that such an effort be blessed by a celestial Power, hence a "power of the Other"; and it is likewise certain that man can, in principle, be saved by simply abandoning himself to Mercy, but such an abandonment must contain an element of initiative, for the absence of any "power of Self" is contrary to the nature of man. The followers of Shinran, a protagonist of extreme *tariki*, sometimes reproach Honen, who was Shinran's spiritual master, for maintaining that the act of invocation combined with faith is the cause of salvation, which appears to them as an inconsistency and a lack of faith; for them faith alone saves, and the activity of prayer is no more than a token of gratitude. Now the more Shinran seeks to make the path easier, the harder he makes it for us to trust, because if everything depends on faith and not on deeds, the validity—or the psychological substance—of faith becomes all the more tenuous; formulated differently, it is humanly difficult to believe in a Mercy that requires absolutely nothing on our part. With Honen, on the contrary, deeds contain an objective guarantee of authenticity with respect to faith since they facilitate and strengthen it, thus favoring the essential condition for rebirth in the "Pure Land"; this way of seeing things, far from compromising our trust in Mercy, contains furthermore an active element of happiness. Besides, it is not so much Shinran's intrinsic thesis that we are criticizing here as the partisanship displayed by his followers in criticizing Honen's thesis, which is sufficient and irreproachable, though doubtless less striking from the point of view of a certain totalitarianism that is both logical and emotional.[7]

Buddhism presents itself *a priori*, that is, in its formal framework, as a way of the "power of Self", hence one based on the element Truth as an immanent power of enlightenment and liberation; but it gives rise *a posteriori*, with perfect logic and without straying from its initial design, to a path according to the "power of the Other", hence one based on the element Presence as a transcendent power of mercy and salvation. Buddhist revelation offers in actuality two principles, one general and the other particular—the second being inset within the first: first the principle of salvation through one's own effort, of which the young Gautama seated under the *Bodhi* tree is the paradigm, and then a principle of salvation by virtue of the saving power inherent in the state of *Buddha* obtained by Gautama. First, Gautama shows us the path by his example; and then, having become Buddha, he preaches this same path while at the same time giving himself—his Buddhahood[8]—as a sacrament; and he does so in the form of the "Pure Land" *Sūtras* or, to be more precise, in the form of the saving Name of Amitabha Buddha, of which he himself, Gautama Buddha, is in some way the present earthly personification. Amitabha Buddha thus appears as the *Logos* as such, whereas the historical Buddha is a given Prophet manifesting the *Logos* by right of identification. Gautama or Shakyamuni is the individual become Buddha and showing how to become one, and Amitabha is eternal and hence pre-existent Buddhahood, which attracts by its all-powerful Mercy.

In other words: the path according to the element Truth participates actively in the enlightening realization of the Buddha, and the

---

[7] The question that matters here is less one of knowing who is right than of knowing to whom the messages are addressed. Be that as it may, Shinran did not bring any improvement; he simply shifted the doctrinal emphasis of Amidism—which in itself is acceptable, but not to the detriment of the previous position; to think otherwise is to fall into the illusion of "theological progress". All told, there are three possible paths: predominance of the "power of Self"; predominance of the "power of the Other"; and a balance between the two.

[8] This Buddhahood is also presented as "Body of the Law", *Dharmakāya*; the absolute Buddha is identified with the *Dharma*-Principle, whereas the personality of the earthly Buddha is the Law as theophanic Presence. Analogously, the soul of the Prophet—according to Aishah—is identified with the Koran, or more precisely with the "human substance" of the Koran, that is, with its Arab character.

path according to the element Presence participates receptively in the immeasurable merit of this same realization. On the one hand, the follower imitates the example of the *Bodhisattva* Shakyamuni, and this is the way of the Theravadins and also, within *Mahāyāna* itself, that of the adherents of Zen, the disciples of Bodhidharma; and, on the other hand, the follower avails himself of the avataric and sacramental power of the Buddha—or of the saving power of Buddhahood—and this is the way of Amidists, from Vasubandhu to Shinran.

The question of knowing why a man can, and sometimes must, follow the path of the "power of Self" when he could follow that of the "power of the Other" need not be asked, for human nature is diverse—as is also, before all else, the Divine Possibility that creates it; furthermore, the two paths are most often combined,[9] so that their opposition in the form of Zen and Amidism is merely a phenomenon of extreme polarization.

33

The famous "tea ceremony" in Japanese Buddhism is an example that has become liturgical of this interiorizing manifestation—or of this "manifestation of the Void"—of what even ordinary actions of men penetrated of God can be. The "tea ceremony" is great, not because of a moral sublimity, but by virtue of a "being" or a *gnosis* made manifest in an otherwise inconspicuous activity, thus highlighting the contrast between the profundity of "being" and the humbleness of the action. An example, of a different order, is provided in the life of Abd al-Qadir al-Jilani: the saint relates a little story about cats, and the whole audience begins to weep from spiritual emotion, after having listened with boredom to the brilliant sermon of a great theologian.

34

Buddhism does not begin with the notion of the ego, as do the religions of Semitic origin, but with the wholly empirical reality of suffering; its

---

[9] The *Tendai, Shingon,* and *Kegon* schools accept in principle or in fact the combination of the two methods, namely, the cult of Amida and intellective meditation.

EDITOR'S NOTES

Numbers in bold indicate pages in the text for which the following citations and explanations are provided.

Treasures of Buddhism

3: *Amitabha* (Sanskrit) or *Amida* (*Japanese*) is the Buddha of "infinite light", who, as a *bodhisattva* named Dharmakara, vowed not to enter *Nirvāna* until he had brought all who invoked his Name into the paradise of his Pure Land, also known as *Sukhāvatī* ("place of bliss") or the Western Paradise.

"The faith that saves": "For by grace are ye saved through faith; and that not of yourselves: it is the gift of God" (Eph. 2:8).

4: Note 3: *Asanga* (c. 300-c. 370) was an Indian sage and major exponent of the *Yogācāra* school within *Mahāyāna* Buddhism.

Nagarjunian "Void": Nagarjuna (c. 150-250), founder of the *Mādhyamika* or "middle way" school of Buddhism and widely regarded in the *Mahāyāna* tradition as a "second Buddha", is best known for his doctrine of *shūnyatā*, "voidness" or "emptiness", and for the correlative teaching that *Nirvāna* and *samsāra* are essentially identical.

5: Note 4: Katsushika *Hokusai* (1760-1849) was a Japanese painter and print-maker of the Edo period.

Kitagawa *Utamaro* (c. 1753-1806) was a Japanese designer, painter, and printmaker.

Note 6: The *Lankāvatāra Sūtra* ("*Sūtra* on the Descent to Sri Lanka") is one of the principal *Mahāyāna* texts and greatly influenced the development of Buddhism in Tibet, China, and Japan.

6: *Shakyamuni*, meaning "sage of the Shakya clan", is one of the titles of Siddhartha Gautama, the historical Buddha (c. 563-c. 483).

Shankara (788-820) was one of the most influential sages in the history of India and the pre-eminent exponent of *Advaita Vedānta*, the Hindu perspective of "non-dualism". The author regarded him as the greatest of Hindu metaphysicians.

The *life of the Buddha* refers here to the historical facts concerning Siddhartha Gautama.

Note 7: *King Prasenajit* (sixth century B.C.), sometimes known as Pasenadi, belonged to the Aiksvaka dynasty and ruled Kosala (modern-day Oudh), the capital of which was *Shravasti.*

King Udayana of Kaushambi was the ruler of Vatsa and a contemporary of Gautama Buddha.

7: *Vishnu* is the second God of the Hindu trinity (*Trimūrti*), Brahmā being the first and Shiva the third. Vishnu is the maintainer, preserver, and protector of the created order.

Kwannon (Japanese), *Kwan-Yin* (*Chinese*), or *Avalokiteshvara* (*Sanskrit*) is the Buddhist goddess or *bodhisattva* of Mercy.

Gaius Julius *Caesar* (100-44 B.C.) was Roman Emperor from 49 B.C. until his death.

"Veni, vidi, victus sum" is Latin for "I came, I saw, I was conquered"; a variation on *Veni, vidi, vici* ("I came, I saw, I conquered"), an utterance attributed to Julius Caesar after his victory over Pharnaces II of Pontus.

Note 9: The *ethnographical museum* in question was the Museum of Ethnology in Basle, Switzerland, visited by the author when he was twelve.

Nothing could be more arbitrary than art criticism: for the author's exposition of traditional art and his critique of modern theories of art, see "Principles and Criteria of Art", in *Language of the Self* (Bloomington, Indiana: World Wisdom, 1999), pp. 79-112.

10: *Amidism* refers to the Buddhist *Jōdo* or Pure Land sect, whose central spiritual practice is the invocation of Amida, or Amitabha, the Buddha of "infinite light". In Japan, Amidism is comprised of the *Jōdo-shū*, or "pure land school", founded by Honen, and the *Jōdo-Shinshū*, or "true pure land school", founded by his leading disciple, Shinran (see editor's notes for note 20 below).

Nichiren (1222-82) was a Japanese Buddhist monk who taught that enlightenment is available to all human beings through simple faith in the compassion and saving power of the Buddha as described in the *Lotus Sūtra*, a faith one expresses by invoking the *mantra*, "I take refuge in the Lotus of the wonderful law *Sūtra.*"

Kegon is a school of Japanese Buddhism, derived from the teachings of the Chinese monk Shinsho, who visited Japan in the eighth century.

Tendai is a school of Japanese Buddhism founded by the eighth century monk Saicho (767-822), posthumously known as Dengyo Daishi.

Shingon is an esoteric school of Buddhism brought from China to Japan by the Japanese monk and scholar Kukai (774-835), later referred to as Kobo Daishi, meaning "great teacher Kobo".

Note 20: *Shinran* (1173-1262), a disciple of Honen and founder of the *Jōdo-Shinshū* or "true pure land school" of Japanese Buddhism, rejected all "ways of effort" and advocated complete reliance on the "power of the other" as manifest in the Name of the Buddha Amida, a single pronunciation of which is sufficient for rebirth in the Buddha's paradise, *Sukhāvatī*.

Honen Shonin (1133-1212), founder of the *Jōdo-shū* or Pure Land school in Japan, taught that everyone without exception can be reborn into Amida's paradise simply by faithful repetition of his Name.

11: *"All things are* Ātmā": "*Ātmā* was indeed *Brahma* in the beginning. It knew only that 'I am *Brahma*'. Therefore It became all. And whoever among the gods knew It also became That; and the same with sages and men. . . . And to this day whoever in like manner knows 'I am *Brahma*' becomes all this universe. Even the gods cannot prevail against him, for he becomes their *Ātmā*" (*Brihadāranyaka Upanishad*, 1.4.10).

The *eremitic ideal*, or hermetic ideal, calls for the seclusion of the monk or religious aspirant from the social order.

12: Jesus said unto him, "Thou shalt love the Lord thy God with all thy heart, and with all thy soul, and with all thy mind. This is the first and great commandment. And the second is like unto it, Thou shalt *love thy neighbor as thyself*" (Matt. 22:37-39).

Ramana Maharshi (1879-1950) was a teacher of *Advaita Vedānta* and a sage of the modern era. Elsewhere the author has written, "In Sri Ramana Maharshi one meets ancient and eternal India again. Vedantic truth—that of the *Upanishads*—is reduced to its simplest expression. . . . In these latter days Sri Ramana was as it were the incarnation of what is primordial and incorruptible in India" (*Spiritual Perspectives and Human Facts: A New Translation with Selected Letters*, ed. James S. Cutsinger [Bloomington, Indiana: World Wisdom, 2007], p. 129).

13: *Shotoku Taishi* (574-622) was a Japanese *Prince Regent* in the Asuka period who is considered the father of Japanese Buddhism.

Hojo Tokimune (1251-1284) was a regent of the Kamakura Shogunate who repelled the *Mongol invasion* and spread *Zen* Buddhism in Japan.

Note 32: *Charlemagne* (c. 742-814) was the first Emperor of the Holy Roman Empire.

Louis IX (1214-70) was the King of France from 1226 and one of the leading Crusaders.

Joan of Arc (1412-31), the "Maid of Orléans", led the French army to victory over the English during the Hundred Years War before being captured, tried, and burnt at the stake by Anglo-Burgundian forces. She was canonized by the Roman Catholic Church in 1920.

Vincent de Paul (1581-1660) was a French priest devoted to the care of the poor. He was canonized in 1737.

The *Saddharmapundarīka Sūtra* (*"Lotus of the Good Law" Sūtra*) is one of the most influential *Mahāyāna* texts, probably composed in the first century B.C., and provides the philosophical basis for many Japanese schools of Buddhism.

For *the decadence of the "last days"* see editor's note for "The Question of Illusion", pp. 38-39.

14: The *Ādi-Buddha* is the primordial, supra-historical Buddha, sometimes identified with Vairochana.

Note 33: The *Bhagavad Gītā*, the best known of all Hindu sacred texts and part of the much longer epic *Mahābhārata*, consists of a dialogue between the prince Arjuna and his charioteer, the *avatāra* Krishna, concerning the different paths to God.

Note 34: The *Tao Te Ching*, traditionally ascribed to the ancient Chinese sage Lao-Tzu, is the fundamental sacred text of Taoism.

Originality of Buddhism

15: "The *letter* killeth, but the spirit giveth life" (2 Cor. 3:6).

16: For *Amidism* see editor's note for "Treasures of Buddhism", p. 10.

Note 1: *Tsongkhapa* (1357-1419) was an influential Tibetan monk whose teachings formed the basis for the *Gelug* school within Tibetan Buddhism.

John of the Cross (1542-91), whose mystical works include the *Ascent of Mount Carmel* and the *Dark Night of the Soul*, was a Spanish priest and co-founder, with Teresa of Avila, of the Discalced Carmelites.

Teresa of Avila (1515-82), whose most important work on the spiritual life is the *Interior Castle*, was a Carmelite nun and co-founder, with John of the Cross, of the Discalced Carmelites.

Girolamo *Savonarola* (1452-98), a Dominican friar and apocalyptic preacher, was known for his prophetic condemnations of corruption among the clergy and for his denunciation of Pope Alexander VI and his court.

17: Note 3: The *Hellenistic aberration of Gandhara* refers to the Greco-Buddhist cultural syncretism evidenced by statues of the Buddha found at Gandhara (Peshawar in present-day Pakistan) and elsewhere in the sub-continent (see below the chap. "Christianity and Buddhism", author's note 14). Many misconceptions about the purported Greek origins of the Buddha image were decisively dispelled by the great art historian, Ananda K. Coomaraswamy (1887-1947) (see editor's note for "A Note on the Feminine Element in the *Mahāyāna*", p. 119) in his essay "The Origin of the Buddha Image", *The Art Bulletin* 9:4 (1927):287-329, and in other writings.

For *King Prasenajit of Shravasti* and *Udayana of Kaushambi* see editor's notes for "Treasures of Buddhism", p. 6.

18: The principle of *karma* or "*concordant actions and reactions*", most immediately concerning the equilibrium of natural forces and energies, is found everywhere in the East but particularly in the Taoist tradition. As the French metaphysician René Guénon (1886-1951) remarked, it is "a principle that does not concern the corporeal world alone, but indeed the totality of manifestation in all its modes and states" (*Miscellanea* [Hillsdale, New York: Sophia Perennis, 2003], "On Mathematical Notation", p. 79).

19: "Behold, *the kingdom of heaven is within you*" (Luke 17:21).

20: In his famous *Rule*, one of the foundation stones of Christian monasticism, *Benedict* of Nursia (480-547) says: "Just as there is a wicked *zeal of bitterness* which separates from God and *leads to hell*, so there is a good zeal which separates from evil and leads to God and everlasting life" (72:1-2).

"*Each thing is* Ātmā": "*Ātmā* was indeed *Brahma* in the beginning. It knew only that 'I am *Brahma*'. Therefore It became all. And whoever among the gods knew It also became That; and the same with sages and men. . . . And to this day whoever in like manner knows 'I am *Brahma*' becomes all this universe. Even the gods cannot prevail against him, for he becomes their *Ātmā*" (*Brihadāranyaka Upanishad*, 1.4.10).

Note 6: In the *Samdhinirmocana Sūtra* and the *Aggivacchagotta Sūtra*, the Buddha says of his teaching that it is "*profound, difficult to realize, difficult to understand, ungraspable by reason*".

21: Note 7: *Henri de Lubac* (1896-1991) was a French Jesuit priest, cardinal of the Catholic Church, and prolific theological writer.

Meister *Eckhart* (c. 1260-1327) was a German Dominican writer, regarded by the author as the greatest of Christian metaphysicians and esoterists.

Angelus *Silesius*, the "Silesian Angel", was the pen-name of Johannes Scheffler (1624-77), a Catholic priest and mystical poet greatly influenced by the teachings of Meister Eckhart.

Omar Khayyam (1048-1125) was a Persian astronomer, mathematician, and poet, best known for his mystical *Rubā'iyyāt* ("quatrains").

24: Note 8: The *French Revolution* of 1789-1799 destroyed the *Ancien Régime*.

The *Renaissance* was a European cultural movement of the fourteenth to seventeenth centuries which affirmed a humanistic philosophy and heralded in the modern age.

Message and Messenger

25: "*It is expedient for you that I go away*" (John 16:7).

Note 1: The *Gītā Govinda* ("Song of Govinda"), written by the Sanskrit poet *Jayadeva* (b.c. 1200), is a twelfth century work concerning the love of Krishna, an *avatāra* or incarnation of Vishnu, for his consort Radha (see editor's note for "Selections from Letters and Other Writings", p. 187).

The prophet *Abraham* is a patriarchal Biblical figure in the monotheistic traditions of Judaism, Christianity, and Islam who is considered the father of both the Jews and the Arabs through his sons Isaac and Ishmael.

26: *It is he* [the Buddha] *alone who "has broken his existence like a breastplate"* (*Dīgha Nikāya*, II.106).

For *Nagarjuna* see editor's note for "Treasures of Buddhism", p. 4.

Note 2: "*God alone is good*" (Luke 18:19, Mark 10:18).

Did he [Christ] not pray, like a mere mortal, despite his divinity?: "And it came to pass, that, as he [Christ] was praying in a certain place, when he ceased, one of his disciples said unto him, Lord, teach us to pray, as John also taught his disciples. And he said unto them, When ye pray, say, Our Father which art in heaven, Hallowed be thy name. Thy kingdom come. Thy will be done, as in heaven, so in earth. Give us day by day our daily bread. And forgive us our sins; for we also forgive every one that is indebted to us. And lead us not into temptation; but deliver us from evil" (Luke 11:1-4; cf. Matt. 6:5-15).

Did he [Christ] not at first restrict his Message just to the people of Israel?: "These twelve [apostles] Jesus sent forth, and commanded them, saying, Go not into the way of the Gentiles, and into any city of the Samaritans enter ye not: But go rather to the lost sheep of the house of Israel" (Matt. 10:5-6; cf. Mark 6:7-13, Luke 9:1-6, 10:1-12).

27: *Bodhidharma* (c. 470-543) was a monk from south India who crossed the Himalayas and brought Ch'an or *Zen* Buddhism to China in the late fifth or early sixth century. He is regarded as the twenty-eighth patriarch of Zen Buddhism.

The "*Flower Sermon*" was a wordless teaching in which the Buddha held up a white flower to signify the ineffable nature of *tathatā* ("suchness"). Zen Buddhism attributes its origin to this teaching.

Blaise *Pascal* (1623-62) was a French philosopher, mathematician, and scientist.

The expression "*an infinite sphere whose center is everywhere and its circumference nowhere*" can be found in the *Liber XXIV Philosophorum*, a thirteenth century booklet by an anonymous author; some scholars have also attributed the expression to the fourth century Roman philosopher and grammarian Gauis Marius Victorinus.

"*All is* Ātmā": "*Ātmā* was indeed *Brahma* in the beginning. It knew only that 'I am *Brahma*'. Therefore It became all. And whoever among the gods knew It also became That; and the same with sages and men. . . . And to this day whoever in like manner knows 'I am *Brahma*' becomes all this universe. Even the gods cannot prevail against him, for he becomes their *Ātmā*" (*Brihadāranyaka Upanishad*, 1.4.10).

Vairochana, whose *Sanskrit name* means, "he who is like the sun", is referred to as the "*solar Buddha*" and is the expression or "personification" of *Shūnya*, the "*Void*".

Note 5: For *Kobo Daishi* see editor's note for "Treasures of Buddhism", p. 10.

For *Dengyo Daishi* see editor's note for "Treasures of Buddhism", p. 10.

The Question of Illusion

32: "My kingdom is not *of this world*" (John 18:36).

Note 1: The *Gulshan i Raz*, or "Mystic Rose Garden", by *Mahmud Shabistari* (c. 1250-1320) is one of the greatest works of Persian Sufism.

34: Note 3: Johann Wolfgang von *Goethe* (1749-1832) was a German poet, novelist, and playwright.

35: "*There are more things in heaven and earth than are dreamt of in your philosophy*" comes from the play *Hamlet* (I.v.167-168), written by William *Shakespeare* (1564-1616), the playwright, poet, and actor widely regarded as the greatest writer in the English language.

36: The *forbidden tree of Genesis* is the Tree of the Knowledge of Good and Evil from which Adam and Eve ate the forbidden fruit, thus committing the "original sin" (see Gen. 2-3). For a detailed commentary by the author see "The Primordial Tree", in *Esoterism as Principle and as Way* (London: Perennial Books, 1981), pp. 79-89, and "Delineations of Original Sin", in *The Play of Masks* (Bloomington, Indiana: World Wisdom, 1992), pp. 55-60.

37: The author's most detailed critique of *the nihilistic and anguished philosophies so prevalent in our epoch* can be found in *Logic and Transcendence: A New Translation with Selected Letters*, ed. James S. Cutsinger (Bloomington, Indiana: World Wisdom, 2009).

38: "*One thing needful*": "One thing is needful: and Mary hath chosen that good part, which shall not be taken away from her" (Luke 10:42).

"Woe unto the world because of offences! for *it must needs be that offences come*; but woe to that man by whom the offence cometh" (Matt. 18:7).

38-39: Buddhism distinguishes three ages after the passing of Shakyamuni Buddha: a first age when the "*Law of the Buddha*" is fulfilled; a second age when it is merely "*imitated*"; and a third age—the current "*latter times*"—

Editor's Notes

when it is *"forgotten"*.

39: The *Dark Age* is the *Kali Yuga* of Hindu chronology, the last and most corrupt of the ages.

Cosmological and Eschatological Viewpoints

43: Note 6: The doctrine of *Apocatastasis*, universal salvation, was expounded by Origen (185-252), the most prolific and influential of the early Church Fathers. Esoterically the doctrine is linked with the recovery, through sleepless attention, of man's primordial unity in God.

45: "Woe unto the world because of offences! for *it must needs be that offences come;* but *woe unto that man by whom the offence cometh"* (Matt. 18:7).

47: It *"is not I who created the world"* answers to Isaiah 45:12 where the Lord says, "I have made the earth, and created man upon it".

For *"concordant reactions"* see editor's note for "Originality of Buddhism", p. 18.

Voltaire (1694-1778), the pseudonym of François-Marie Arouet, was a deist, the best known of the Enlightenment *philosophes*, and an implacable critic of the Roman Catholic Church.

Plato (c. 427-c. 347 B.C.) was a student of Socrates, teacher of Aristotle, and the greatest of the ancient Greek philosophers.

The Roman poet *Virgil* (70-19 B.C.) was the author of the *Aeneid,* the *Eclogues,* and the *Georgics.*

Augustine (354-430), Bishop of the North African city of Hippo, was preeminent amongst the Western Church Fathers.

Note 11: *Thomism* is the school of theological thought arising out of the teachings of Thomas Aquinas (c. 1225-74), the Italian Dominican priest and scholastic theologian, known in Catholic tradition as the "Angelic Doctor".

48: *Lucifer,* literally the "shining one", is the Angel of the Morning Star who fell from heaven (Is. 14:12-15); in Christian tradition Lucifer is identified with Satan.

Note 12: *The Fall* refers to the eating of the forbidden fruit by Adam and Eve in the Garden of Eden, the "original sin" (Gen. 2-3) (see editor's note for

205

"The Question of Illusion", p. 36).

49: *Mara* was a personification of *evil*, sin, and death *who tempted* Gautama *Buddha* during his meditation under the Bodhi Tree.

The synoptic Gospels relate how *Satan tempted Christ* during the forty days in the wilderness (see Matt. 4:1-11, Mark 1:12-13, and Luke 4:1-13).

50: Note 13: *Le règne de la quantité et les signs des temps* was published in 1945; the first English edition was published as *The Reign of Quantity and the Signs of the Times*, translated by Lord Northbourne (London: Luzac, 1953).

René *Guénon* (1886-1951) was a French metaphysician and prolific scholar of religions, one of the formative authorities of the perennialist school, and a frequent contributor to the journal *Études Traditionnelles* ("Traditional Studies").

52: "For we that are in this tabernacle do groan, being burdened: not for that would be unclothed, but clothed upon, that *death* might be *swallowed up in life*" (2 Cor. 5:4).

53: Note 20: The *Agganna Sutta*, a text in the *Pali Tipitaka*, contains the Buddha's discourse about the universality of the *Dharma* and includes passages about caste and morality; in the second part of the *Sutta* the Buddha explains man's origins and the way in which humankind came to inhabit the earth.

Insights into Zen

55: "It is written, Man shall not live by bread alone, but by *every word that proceedeth out of the mouth of God*" (Matt. 4:4; cf. Deut. 8:3).

56: Note 2: Carl G. *Jung* (1875-1961) was a one-time colleague of Sigmund Freud, the founder of psychoanalysis. Jung became an influential psychologist who theorized the process he called "individuation", whereby the personal and "*collective unconscious*" are brought into consciousness as part of the integration of the psyche.

57: Note 3: Immanuel *Kant* (1724-1804), a German philosopher influenced by Enlightenment thinkers such as Rousseau (see note immediately following), sought a rational basis for morality in the principle of "the categorical imperative".

Jean-Jacques *Rousseau* (1712-78) was a French philosopher and writer, associated with ideas about "natural goodness" and the "Noble Savage".

58: "*A very deep meaning*": this phrase occurs in English in the author's original French.

58-59: Note 5: *Kakuzo Okakura* (1862-1913) was a scholar who affirmed Asian cultural identity against the depredations of Western modernization. Today he is best known as the author of *The Book of Tea*.

59: For René *Guénon* see editor's note for "Cosmological and Eschatological Viewpoints", p. 50.

Note 5: *Der Blumenweg* by *Gusty L. Herrigel* appeared in English translation in 1958 as *Zen in the Art of Flower Arrangement*. Gusty Herrigel's husband, Eugen Herrigel (1884-1955), was the author of the widely-read *Zen in the Art of Archery*, first published in 1948 and appearing in English translation in 1953.

60: Note 8: The *Scholastics* belonged to a school and method of critical thought based on dialectical reasoning which prevailed in many universities and theological institutions during the Middle Ages; it was closely associated with Thomas Aquinas (see editor's note for "Cosmological and Eschatological Viewpoints", p. 47).

61: The *Prajñā Pāramitā Hridaya Sūtra* ("Heart of the Perfection of Wisdom *Sūtra*"), or "Heart Sutra", is a short Sanskrit work and one of the most popular of *Mahāyāna* Buddhist texts.

Elementary Remarks on the Enigma of the *Kōan*

66: *Aristotle* (384-322 B.C.) was an ancient Greek philosopher whose works had a profound influence on the intellectual tradition of the three Semitic monotheisms.

Note 4: *Ta-Hui* (1089-1163) was a twelfth century Zen master.

Mahaprajnaparamita, "great transcendent wisdom", is the *shakti* or consort of the supreme *Ādi-Buddha*.

In the *Vajrayāna* tradition, *Vajradhara* ("diamond holder") is identified with the primordial or *Ādi-Buddha* and also with the *Dharmakāya* or "nirvanic" body of the Buddha.

Note 5: For *Jung* see editor's note for "Insights into Zen", p. 56.

Jiddu *Krishnamurti* (1895-1986) was proclaimed by the Theosophical Society as the "New World Teacher" of the "Order of the Star of the East", a role which he disavowed. He later became an iconoclastic teacher and speaker on "spiritual" themes who was popular in the West in the two decades before his death.

Psychologism may be defined as the assumption that man's nature and behavior can be explained by psychological factors alone, which can be laid bare by a scientific and empirical psychology. Elsewhere the author speaks of psychologism as "the prejudice of wishing to bring everything back to psychological causes, which can only be individual and profane. Everything then becomes the fruit of a contingent elaboration: Revelation becomes poetry, religions are inventions, sages are 'thinkers' and 'researchers', that is, mere logicians, if indeed they are still such; infallibility and inspiration no longer exist; error becomes an 'interesting' and quantitative 'contribution' to 'culture', and so on; if every mental phenomenon is not reduced to material causes, there is at least the denial of any supernatural or even simply supra-sensory cause and, by the same token, the negation of any principial truth. According to this way of seeing things, man is doubtless more than just his body, but he is nonetheless reduced to being a human animal, which means that he is no longer anything; for man limited to himself is no longer truly human" (*Form and Substance in the Religions* [Bloomington, Indiana: World Wisdom, 2002], "The Five Divine Presences", p. 64).

Nirvāna

67: *Macarius of Egypt* (c. 300-c. 390), or Macarius the Great, a Desert Father renowned for his sanctity and miracles, founded an ascetic community which became one of the chief centers of early Egyptian monasticism.

Palamite theology is the doctrine of Gregory Palamas (c. 1296-1359), an Athonite monk and later Archbishop of Thessalonica, best known for his defence of the contemplative techniques used by the Hesychast Fathers and for his distinction *in divinis* between the Divine Essence and the "Energies".

Areopagitic theology stems from Dionysius the Areopagite (dated c. 500 by many scholars), the author of several important mystical works, including *The Divine Names*, *The Mystical Theology*, and *The Celestial Hierarchy*.

Patristics or *Patristic theology* refers to the religious writings of the early Church Fathers.

68: Note 4: "*Why callest thou me good? God alone is good*" (Mark 10:18, Luke 18:19).

69: "For *in Heaven there is no marrying or giving in marriage*" (Matt. 22:30).

71: Abu Zakariya Yahya *Muadh Ar-Razi* (830-871) was a Sufi teacher and writer in central Asia.

Christ could say that He is the "Life": "Jesus saith unto him, I am the way, the truth, and the life: no man cometh unto the Father, but by me" (John 14:6).

72: "Brahman *is not in the world*": Elsewhere the author writes: "It is useless to seek to realize that 'I am *Brahma*' before understanding that 'I am not *Brahma*'; it is useless to seek to realize that '*Brahma* is my true Self' before understanding that '*Brahma* is outside me'; it is useless to seek to realize that '*Brahma* is pure Consciousness' before understanding that '*Brahma* is the almighty Creator'. It is not possible to understand that the statement 'I am not *Brahma*' is false before having understood that it is true. Likewise it is not possible to understand that the statement '*Brahma* is outside me' is not precise before having understood that it is; and likewise again it is not possible to understand that the statement '*Brahma* is the almighty Creator' contains an error before having understood that it expresses a truth" (*Spiritual Perspectives and Human Facts: A New Translation with Selected Letters*, ed. James S. Cutsinger [Bloomington, Indiana: World Wisdom, 2007], p. 116).

73: Paramahamsa *Ramakrishna* (1834-86), a *bhakta* of the Hindu Goddess Kali, was one of the great Hindu saints of modern times. See the author's "*Vedānta*", in *Spiritual Perspectives and Human Facts: A New Translation with Selected Letters*, ed. James S. Cutsinger (Bloomington, Indiana: World Wisdom, 2007), pp. 124-126.

For further reflections on *the Holy Virgin* see the author's "Christic and Virginal Mysteries", in *Gnosis: Divine Wisdom: A New Translation with Selected Letters*, ed. James S. Cutsinger (Bloomington, Indiana: World Wisdom, 2006), pp. 119-124.

74: *Kabbalah* is a mystical stream of esoteric teachings within the Judaic tradition.

Lakshmi, regarded in most Hindu traditions as the wife of Vishnu, is the Goddess of good fortune and the embodiment of beauty.

Although never defined as dogma, popular recognition of the Blessed *Virgin* as "*Co-Redemptress*" dates from ancient times and can be found in both the Eastern and the Western Churches.

The third of the Ecumenical Councils, meeting in Ephesus (431), declared that the *Virgin* Mary is rightly called *Mater Dei* or *"Mother of God"*.

Christian tradition refers to the *Virgin* Mary as *"Spouse of the Holy Spirit"* since it was the Holy Spirit, and not her husband Joseph, who brought about the conception of Jesus in her womb (see Matt. 1:18, 20, Luke 1:34).

Note 13: In Judaism, the *Shekhinah* is the dwelling-place or presence of God in the world; traditionally it was thought to dwell in the Holies of Holies in the Temple of Jerusalem.

Durga, "the unfathomable one", is one of the most widely used names in Hinduism for the Divine *Mother*. The consort of Shiva, she destroys the demon of ignorance and confers blessings of knowledge and love on spiritual devotees.

For *Kwan-Yin* see editor's note for "Treasures of Buddhism", p. 7.

In Tibetan Buddhism, *Tara*, the "Mother of all the Buddhas" or "Mother of Compassion", is the female counterpart of the *Bodhisattva Avalokiteshvara* (see editor's note for "Treasures of Buddhism", p. 7).

Pté-San-Win is the heavenly White Buffalo Cow Woman who brought the *Sacred Pipe* to the Plains Indians of North America. For an explication of this ritual instrument's symbolism and religious significance, see the author's "The Sacred Pipe", in *The Feathered Sun* (Bloomington, Indiana: World Wisdom, 1990), pp. 44-70.

Krishna is the eighth *avatāra* of the Hindu God Vishnu.

Christianity and Buddhism

77: *The "kingdom" of the Buddha, like that of Christ, "is not of this world"*: "My kingdom is not of this world; if my kingdom were of this world, then would my servants fight, that I should not be delivered to the Jews: but now is my kingdom not from thence" (John 18:36).

Note 1: *Rama* is the seventh *avatāra* or incarnation of the Hindu God Vishnu and the hero of the *Rāmāyana*, the oldest of the Hindu epics.

For *Abraham* see editor's note for "Message and Messenger", p. 25.

Moses is a prophet, religious leader, and law-giver within the Abrahamic monotheisms, renowned for leading the Israelites out of Egypt and receiving the Ten Commandments on Mt. Sinai.

Muhammad (570-632), the prophet and founder of Islam, received a series of divine revelations from 610-632 which comprise the book of the Koran.

78: *"Dead letter"*: "The letter killeth, but the spirit giveth life" (2 Cor. 3:6).

The *Mosaic Law* refers to the *Torah* or first five books of the Hebrew Bible, traditionally attributed to Moses.

Note 2: For *Shankara* see editor's note for "Treasures of Buddhism", p. 6.

Note 3: *Apophatic theology* or the "way of negation" (*via negativa*), is a means of approaching God by stating what He is not.

79: "Give not that which is holy unto the *dogs*, neither cast ye your pearls before *swine*, lest they trample under their feet, and turn again and rend you" (Matt. 7:6).

"Wisdom according to the flesh": "For our rejoicing is this, the testimony of our conscience, that in simplicity and godly sincerity, not with fleshly wisdom, but by the grace of God, we have had our conversation in the world" (2 Cor. 1:12).

Wisdom "according the Spirit": "For those who live according to the flesh set their minds on the things of the flesh, but those who live *according to the spirit* set their minds on the things of the spirit" (Rom. 8:5).

80: The author provides a masterly account of the principles informing the widely-misunderstood Hindu *caste system* in his essay "The Meaning of Caste", in *Language of the Self* (Bloomington, Indiana: World Wisdom, 1999), pp. 113-146.

Note 6: "For he is not a Jew, which is one outwardly; neither is that *circumcision* which is outward *in the flesh*: But he is a Jew which is one inwardly; and *circumcision* is that of the heart, *in the spirit*, and not in the letter; whose praise is not of men, but of God" (Rom. 2:28-29).

81: For *psychologism* see editor's note for "Elementary Remarks on the Enigma of the *Kōan*", p. 66.

Know how to tell a wolf from a lamb: "Beware of false prophets, which come to you in sheep's clothing, but inwardly they are ravening wolves" (Matt. 7:15).

For *concordant actions and reactions* see editor's note for "Originality of Buddhism", p. 18.

Christ's Law—requiring that one love one's enemy and turn the other cheek: "But I say unto you, That ye resist not evil: but whosoever shall smite thee on thy right cheek, turn to him the other also. . . . Love your enemies, bless them that curse you, do good to them that hate you . . ." (Matt. 5:39, 44).

"*For the love of God*": "Thou shalt *love* the Lord thy *God* with all thy heart, and with all thy soul, and with all thy strength, and with all thy mind" (Luke 10:27; cf. Matt. 22:37, Mark 12:30, Deut. 6:5).

82: The "*letter killeth, but the spirit giveth life*" (2 Cor. 3:6).

83: A *categorical imperative* refers to an absolute or unconditional require-ment. The phrase is most commonly associated with the German philoso-pher, Immanuel Kant (see editor's note for "Insights into Zen", p. 57) and his *Groundwork for the Metaphysics of Morals* (1785).

84: Note 14: The apostle *Luke* was one of the four evangelists, or ascribed authors of the canonical Gospels, as well as the author of the Acts of the Apostles in the New Testament.

For *King Prasenajit of Shravasti* (*or Udayana of Kaushambi*) see editor's note for "Treasures of Buddhism", p. 6.

Note 15: "And he took bread, and when he had given thanks, he brake it, and gave to them, saying, This is my body which is given for you: *this* do *in remembrance of me*" (Luke 22:19).

85: The "*gift of tongues*", mentioned in the Epistles of Paul and Peter (1 Cor. 14:27, 1 Pet. 4:10), is the miraculous ability to speak in a foreign and unknown language.

"And the *Word* was *made flesh*, and dwelt among us" (John 1:14).

Note 16: *Tao-Cho* (562-645) was the second patriarch of Pure Land Bud-dhism.

Daisetz Teitaro Suzuki (1870-1966) was a leading Japanese scholar who promoted Western interest in Chinese and Japanese forms of Buddhism. He published three volumes of *Essays in Zen Buddhism* between 1927 and 1933.

86: The *Paraclete* refers, in Christian tradition, to the Holy Spirit (see John 14:16, 26).

Hesychasm is the spiritual practice of certain monks of the Christian East whose aim is to attain a state of *hesychia*, or inner stillness, through the practice of the Jesus Prayer or other "prayer of the heart".

Note 18: "*God within us*": "Behold, the kingdom of God is within you" (Luke 17:21).

Mystery of the *Bodhisattva*

88: Note 2: *Brahmanism* is the doctrine of Hindu brahmins or priests.

90: Note 3: For *Nagarjuna* see editor's note for "Treasures of Buddhism", p. 4.

91: Note 6: For the *Mahā Prajñā Pāramitā Hridaya* see editor's note for "Insights into Zen", p. 61.

The *Vajracchedikā Prajñāpāramitā Sūtra* or "Diamond *Sūtra*" is a key text in *Mahāyāna* Buddhism, and especially Zen; it contains the discourse of the Buddha to a senior monk, Subhuti.

Note 7: *Christ strikes the Temple merchants*: "And Jesus went into the temple of God, and cast out all them that sold and bought in the temple, and overthrew the tables of the moneychangers, and the seats of them that sold doves, And said unto them, It is written, My house shall be called the house of prayer; but ye have made it a den of thieves" (Matt. 21:12-13; cf. Mark 11:15-17, Luke 19:45-46, John 2:13-16).

The *Scholastic* (see editor's note for "Insights into Zen", p. 60, Note 8) "double truth" distinguishes between *two kinds of truth*: a truth *secundum fidem* ("according to faith") and a truth *secundum rationem* ("according to reason"), each thought to be valid within its respective domain.

92: For "*Latter Times*" see editor's note for "The Question of Illusion", pp. 38-39.

Note 10: The *Family* (*āl*) of the Prophet Muhammad refers to the line of his descendants through his eldest daughter Fatimah and son-in-law Ali ibn Abi Talib.

The *Companions* (*sahb*) were the Prophet Muhammad's followers, that is, the early Muslims who lived in close proximity to him in Mecca and Medina in seventh century Arabia.

Note 11: *Ali* ibn Abi Talib (597-661) was the cousin and son-in-law of the Prophet Muhammad and the fourth *caliph* of Islam.

93: For *Shinran* see editor's note for "Treasures of Buddhism", p. 10.

Note 13: For *Tao Te Ching* see editor's note for "Treasures of Buddhism", p. 14.

94: In a previous life as a *Bodhisattva* named Dharmakara, the future *Amitabha Buddha* made his *"original vow"* not to enter *Nirvāna* until he had brought all who invoked his *sacred Name* into the paradise of his Pure Land.

For *Honen* see editor's note for "Treasures of Buddhism", p. 10.

95: For *Apocatastasis* see editor's note for "Cosmological and Eschatological Viewpoints", p. 43.

Note 17: *Gregory of Nyssa* (c. 330-c. 395), a bishop of the early church and an influential mystical and ascetical writer, taught that the *nous* or intellect is the fundamental reason for man's intrinsic dignity as the "image of God".

Note 18: *Jacques Bacot* (1877-1965) was a French explorer and Tibetologist.

96: Note 20: *Milarepa* (c. 1052-c. 1135) was a renowned poet, ascetic, and *yogin* who became a great sage and one of the most revered figures in the Tibetan tradition.

97: Note 23: *Chaitanya* (1486-1533), a Vaishnavite Hindu spiritual teacher and ecstatic devotee of Krishna, was regarded by his followers as an *avatāra* of both Krishna and his consort Radha (see editor's note for "Selections from Letters and Other Writings", p. 187).

98: *Manjushri* is the *Bodhisattva* of discriminating wisdom, usually portrayed brandishing a sword that cuts through the knots of ignorance.

Note 24: *Theresa of Lisieux* (1873-1897), also known as "Theresa of the Child Jesus" and as "The Little Flower", was a Carmelite nun who had been drawn to the life of prayer as a very young child.

100: Note 26: For *Shankara* see editor's note for "Treasures of Buddhism", p. 6.

Catholic tradition associates *Mary Magdalene* with three distinct figures mentioned in the Scriptures: "a woman in the city, which was a sinner", who washed Jesus' feet "with tears, and did wipe them with the hairs of her head, and kissed his feet, and anointed them with ointment" (Luke 7:37-38); "Mary called Magdalene, out of whom went seven devils" (Luke 8:2); and the sister of Lazarus and Martha, who "sat at Jesus' feet, and heard his word", whom Christ commended, saying, "One thing is needful: and Mary hath chosen that good part, which shall not be taken from her" (Luke 10:39, 42; cf. John 11:1-2).

102: For *Ramakrishna* see editor's note for "*Nirvāna*", p. 73.

For *Ramana Maharshi* see editor's note for "Treasures of Buddhism", p. 12.

For *Rama* see editor's note for "Christianity and Buddhism", p. 77.

For *Krishna* see editor's note for "*Nirvāna*", p. 74.

For the *Mother of Jesus* as "*Co-Redemptress*" see editor's note for "*Nirvāna*", p. 74.

103: *Truth "become flesh"*: "And the Word was made flesh" (John 1:14).

"*Each thing is* Ātmā": "*Ātmā* was indeed *Brahma* in the beginning. It knew only that 'I am *Brahma*'. Therefore It became all. And whoever among the gods knew It also became That; and the same with sages and men. . . . And to this day whoever in like manner knows 'I am *Brahma*' becomes all this universe. Even the gods cannot prevail against him, for he becomes their *Ātmā*" (*Brihadāranyaka Upanishad*, 1.4.10).

"*The world is false*; Brahma *is true*; the soul is not other than *Brahma*" is a summation of *Advaita Vedānta* traditionally ascribed to Shankara.

The Islamic testimony of faith (*Shahādah*) proclaims that "*There is no divinity save the one Divinity*" or "There is no god but God" (*Lā ilāha illā 'Llāh*).

The "celestial weight" of Revelation: "If We had caused this Koran to descend upon a mountain, thou (O Muhammad) verily hadst seen it humbled, rent asunder by the fear of God" (*Sūrah* "The Gathering" [59]:21).

105: The *breaking of the first Tables of the Law* refers to the two pieces of stone inscribed with the Ten Commandments revealed to *Moses on Mount Sinai*. The first tablet, inscribed by God, was smashed by Moses when he became enraged by the sight of the Israelites worshipping the Golden Calf (see Exod. 32:15-19).

"*Those who have ears to hear*": "He that hath ears to hear, let him hear" (Matt. 11:15, *passim*).

106: For *Avalokiteshvara* see editor's note for "Treasures of Buddhism", p. 7.

Kshitigarbha is a *bodhisattva* who made a vow to postpone Buddhahood until all the hells are emptied of human souls; he is the guardian of children, deceased children, and hell-beings.

Akashagarbha is a *bodhisattva* associated with infinite wisdom and compassion, and the twin brother of Kshitigarbha.

107: The *Gordian knot* stems from the legend of the Phrygian Gordias, whose son Midas tied his father's ox-cart to a post with an intricate knot which no one could untie. After Alexander the Great failed to unravel the knot, he cut through it with his sword.

"Though I speak with the tongues of men and of angels, and have not charity, I am become as *sounding brass, or a tinkling cymbal*" (1 Cor. 13:1).

Synthesis of the *Pāramitās*

109: For *Shankara* see editor's note for "Treasures of Buddhism", p. 6.

For *Nagarjuna* see editor's note for "Treasures of Buddhism", p. 4.

110: Muhyi al-Din *Ibn Arabi* (1165-1240) was a prolific and profoundly influential Sufi mystic, known in tradition as the Shaykh al-Akbar ("great master"). He is the author of numerous works, including *Meccan Revelations* and *Bezels of Wisdom*.

111: For *Shingon* see editor's note for "Treasures of Buddhism", p. 10.

For *Tendai* see editor's note for "Treasures of Buddhism", p. 10.

For *Jōdo* see editor's note for "Treasures of Buddhism", p. 10.

112: For *Apocatastasis* see editor's note for "Cosmological and Eschatological Viewpoints", p. 43.

"Form is not different from void, and void is not different from form. *Form is void and Void is form*" (*Prajnā Pāramitā Hridaya Sūtra*).

113: *Amidism*, or Pure Land Buddhism (see editor's note for "Treasures of Buddhism", p. 10), is based on the practice of the invocation of the Buddha Amitabha, especially through the formula *Namo'mitābhaya Buddhāya* (Sanskrit) or *Namu Amida Butsu* (Japanese), "I trust in the Buddha of Immeasurable Light".

Editor's Notes

Tan-Luan (476-542) was a Chinese monk, credited by Honen as the founder of Pure Land Buddhism in China.

For *Tao-Cho* see editor's note for "Christianity and Buddhism", p. 85.

Shan-Tao (613-81), an early Chinese proponent of Pure Land Buddhism, was among the first to emphasize *nien-fo*, or recitation of the Name of Amida (Amitabha) Buddha, as the most important of spiritual practices.

For *Honen* see editor's note for "Treasures of Buddhism", p. 10.

For *Shinran* see editor's note for "Treasures of Buddhism", p. 10.

114: Amidism, or the *cult of Amitabha*, places strong emphasis on *"power of the Other"* (*tariki*), that is, attaining salvation through the mercy of Amitabha Buddha, in contrast to schools such as *Zen* and *Shingon* which emphasize *"power of Self"* (*jiriki*) through meditational practices.

For the *Buddha's "Original Vow"* see editor's note for "Mystery of the Bodhisattva", p. 94.

115: The *"third Eye"* is the invisible organ of mystical perception.

116: For *Vairochana* see editor's note for "Message and Messenger", p. 27.

In *Vajrayāna* Buddhism, *Akshobhya* ("The Immovable One"), *Amitabha* ("Infinite Light", see editor's note for "Treasures of Buddhism", p. 3), *Amoghasiddhi* ("Dispassion", "Charity"), and *Ratnasambhava* ("Equanimity", "Humility") are four of the *Dhyāni* or "Meditation" Buddhas, the fifth being *Vairochana* ("The Great Illuminator").

Note 7: For *Vajradhara* see editor's note for "Elementary Remarks on an Enigma of the *Kōan*", p. 66.

Note 8: The *four Archangels* of *Islam* are Gabriel (Arabic: Jibrail), Michael (Mikhail), Raphael (Israfil), and Azrael (Izrail). See the author's chapter *"An-Nūr"* in *Dimensions of Islam* (London: George Allen & Unwin, 1969) for a more detailed treatment of this subject.

118: *Honen the Buddhist Saint*, from the fourteenth century manuscript compiled by imperial order, was first translated into English in 1925 by Rev. Harper Havelock Coates and Rev. Ryugaku Ishizuka and comprised five volumes.

Treasures of Buddhism

A Note on the Feminine Element in *Mahāyāna*

119: Note 2: The *Buddhacharita*, or "Acts of the Buddha", is a second century Sanskrit epic poem on the life of Gautama Buddha; it was written by the Indian philosopher-poet *Ashvagosha* (c. 80-c. 150), author of the influential text, *Awakening of Mahāyāna Faith.*

The *Jātaka* tales concern the previous lives of Gautama Buddha in both human and animal form.

For René *Guénon* see editor's note for "Cosmological and Eschatological Viewpoints", p. 50.

Jerome (c. 342-420), the most important Biblical scholar of the early Church, is known for his passionate attacks against Arianism, Pelagianism, Origenism, and other heresies of his day.

For *Plato* see editor's note for "Cosmological and Eschatological Viewpoints", p. 47.

Ananda K. Coomaraswamy (1877-1947), for many years curator of Indian art in the Boston Museum of Fine Arts and one of the founding figures of the perennialist school, was the author of numerous books and articles on art, religion, and metaphysics from the point of view of the primordial and universal tradition.

120: Note 4: "*One neither marries nor is given in marriage*": "For in the resurrection they neither marry, nor are given in marriage, but are as the angels of God in heaven" (Matt. 22:30; cf. Luke 20:35).

The *houris* are celestial maidens, "fair ones with wide, lovely eyes" (*Sūrah* "The Smoke" [44]:54 *passim*), who are promised as a reward to the faithful in the Muslim Paradise.

121: For some commentary on the mystery of *Eve* see the author's "The Primordial Tree", in *Esoterism as Principle and as Way* (London: Perennial Books, 1981), pp. 79-89.

For *Krishna* see editor's note for "*Nirvāna*", p. 74.

"For our conversation is in heaven; from whence also we look for the Savior, the Lord Jesus Christ: Who shall change our vile body, that it may be fashioned like unto his *glorious body*, according to the working whereby he is able even to subdue all things unto himself" (Phil. 3:20-21; see also 1 Cor. 15:35-38).

Note 5: In the *Amitāyur Dhyāna Sūtra*, one of the principal Pure Land scriptures, *Queen Vaidehi* appeals to the *Buddha* after she has been imprisoned by her brother, who in turn has killed their father, King Bimbisara. The Buddha teaches her the practices leading to liberation and re-birth in *Sukhāvatī*, the Pure Land or Western Paradise.

Amitayus, the "Buddha of Infinite Life", is essentially identical to Amitabha; in the Pure Land tradition the two were combined in the figure of Amida.

122: For *Shinran* see editor's note for "Treasures of Buddhism", p. 10.

For *Honen* see editor's note for "Treasures of Buddhism", p. 10.

For *Shingon* see editor's note for "Treasures of Buddhism", p. 10.

Dharmakara's Vow

124: "The book of the generation of Jesus *Christ, the Son of David*, the son of Abraham" (Matt. 1:1).

For the *Buddha Amitabha's* "*Original Vow*" see editor's note for "Mystery of the *Bodhisattva*", p. 94.

125: Note 5: The author's *L'Œil du Cœur* (Paris: Gallimard, 1950; Paris: Dervy-Livres, 1974) first appeared in English in revised form as *The Eye of the Heart: Metaphysics, Cosmology, Spiritual Life* (Bloomington, Indiana: World Wisdom, 1997). The chapter "*An-Nūr*" is to be found in the author's *Dimensions of Islam* (London: George Allen & Unwin, 1969), pp. 102-120.

126: In *Mahāyāna* tradition, *Dharmakara* was an ancient king who renounced his throne and became a monk, devoting himself to good deeds and the service of others and vowing, were he to become a Buddha, to establish a perfect world, a Pure Land, for all those who invoked his Buddha *name, Amitabha* (Sanskrit) or Amida (Japanese).

For *Shakyamuni* see editor's note for "Treasures of Buddhism", p. 6.

"*Each thing is* Ātmā": "*Ātmā* was indeed *Brahma* in the beginning. It knew only that 'I am *Brahma*'. Therefore It became all. And whoever among the gods knew It also became That; and the same with sages and men. . . . And to this day whoever in like manner knows 'I am *Brahma*' becomes all this universe. Even the gods cannot prevail against him, for he becomes their *Ātmā*" (*Brihadāranyaka Upanishad*, 1.4.10).

127: *"There will be more joy in Heaven over one sinner that repenteth than over ninety-nine just persons who need no repentance"* (Luke 15:7).

Note 6: *Blasphemies against the "Father" and the "Son" can be forgiven, but not those uttered against the "Holy Spirit"*: "All manner of sin and blasphemy shall be forgiven unto men: but the blasphemy against the Holy Ghost shall not be forgiven unto men" (Matt. 12:31; cf. Mark 3:29, Luke 12:10).

Prostration of the Angels before Adam: "And when We said unto the angels: Prostrate yourselves before Adam, they fell prostrate, all save Iblis. He demurred through pride, and so became a disbeliever" (*Sūrah* "The Cow" [2]:34).

128: "Thou hast ravished my heart, my *sister*, my *spouse*; thou hast ravished my heart with one of thine eyes, with one chain of thy neck. How fair is thy love, my *sister*, my *spouse*! How much better is thy love than wine, and the smell of thine ointments than all spices! Thy lips, O my *spouse*, drop as the honeycomb: honey and milk are under thy tongue; and the smell of thy garments is like the smell of Lebanon. A garden enclosed is my *sister*, my *spouse*; a spring shut up, a fountain sealed" (*Song of Songs* 4:9-12).

129: The Divine *Names of Mercy*, invoked in the Muslim *Basmalah* (*Bismi 'Llāhi 'r-Rahmāni 'r-Rahīm*), or formula of consecration, are *Rahmān*, "the Beneficent", and *Rahīm*, "the Merciful".

130: "Those who believe and leave their homes and *fight in offering their goods and their lives* in the way of God are of much greater worth in God's sight. These are they who are triumphant" (*Sūrah* "Repentance" [9]:20, *passim*).

Note 10: For *Amidism* see editor's note for "Treasures of Buddhism", p. 10.

Note 11: *Bernard* of Clairvaux (1090-1153) was a Cistercian monk and author of numerous homilies on the Song of Songs.

On Sinai, God appeared in the form of a *Burning Bush* and spoke these words to Moses: "*I am that I am*: and He said, Thus shalt thou say unto the children of Israel, I AM hath sent me unto you" (Exod. 3:14).

The three *Evangelical counsels* of *poverty*, *obedience*, and *chastity*, also known as the "counsels of perfection", gave rise to the traditional vows of the monk.

131: Note 11 (cont.): The Latin phrase *perinde ac si cadaver essent* ("as if they were a corpse") comes from the *Constitutions* of Ignatius Loyola (1491-1556), founder and first general of the Society of Jesus: "Those who live under obedience must let themselves be led and ruled by divine providence through their superiors, as if they were a corpse, which allows itself to be carried here and there and treated in any way."

Christ's invitation: "And he saith unto them, *Follow me*, and I will make you fishers of men" (Matt. 4:19, *passim*).

The Kingdom of Heaven that is "within you": "Behold, the kingdom of God is within you" (Luke 17:21).

Note 13: For *Shan-Tao* see editor's note for "Synthesis of the *Pāramitās*", p. 113.

For *Honen* see editor's note for "Treasures of Buddhism", p. 10.

For *Shinran* see editor's note for "Treasures of Buddhism", p. 10.

Initial Remarks

137: *A Shintoist divinity becomes a* Bodhisattva *without being altered in its essence since the respective names cover universal realities:* It is recorded of the Emperor Shomu that in the year 742 A.D. he sent an envoy to the Ise shrine, symbolic center for the nation of Japan, to request an oracle from the Sun Goddess Amaterasu concerning his projected building of the great Buddhist temple Todaiji at Nara; a favorable oracle was granted. Soon after that the Emperor had a dream in which the Goddess herself appeared to him saying: "This is the land of the Gods, the people should revere them. In my essence I am the (solar) Buddha Vairochana. Let my people understand this and take refuge in the Law of the Buddhas."

The *Duke of Orléans* was Louis Philippe I (1773-1850) who became King of France in 1830.

The Meaning of the Ancestors

139: *Voraussetzungsloses Denken*, "unconditional thinking", is a phrase which appears in the works of such *German philosophers* as Georg Hegel (1770-1831), Friedrich Schleiermacher (1768-1834), and Friedrich Nietzsche (1844-1900).

142: Note 2: *Jacques Maritain* (1892-1973) was a Catholic philosopher and prolific author who revived Thomist theology within the Church.

John of *Ruysbroeck* (1290-1831) was a Flemish architect, scholar, and mystic.

John *Tauler* (c. 1300-1361) was a Dominican theologian and popular preacher.

For *Teresa of Avila* see editor's note for "Originality of Buddhism", p. 16.

For *John of the Cross* see editor's note for "Originality of Buddhism", p. 16.

Mary of the Incarnation (1566-1618) founded the Discalced Carmelite Order in France. We may surmise that the author is referring to this "Mary of the Incarnation" rather than to Marie Guyart (1599-1672), the nun sent to establish the Ursuline Order in "New France", the area colonized by the French in North America, now in Canada.

Note 3: The *Apostles* were the disciples of Jesus who proclaimed his teachings. The term usually refers to the twelve apostles as identified in the synoptic Gospels (Matt. 10:1-4, Mark 3:13-19, and Luke 6:12-16).

143: "And the *Word* was *made flesh*, and dwelt among us" (John 1:14).

144: The *yamato race* is the dominant native ethnic group in Japan who founded the Imperial House of Japan, also called the "Yamato Dynasty", in the sixth century C.E.

Note 5: According to legend *Jimmu Tenno* was a descendant of the Sun Goddess Amaterasu who founded the Japanese Empire in 660 B.C.

Charles A. Eastman (1858-1939), also known as "Ohiyesa", belonged to the Santee tribe of the Sioux. He became a physician, writer, and champion of Native Americans. *The Soul of the Indian*, from which the quoted passage is taken, was first published in 1911.

145: *Motoori Norinaga* (1730-1801), a scholar of the Edo period, advocated the spirit and values of the indigenous Japanese Shinto religion against what he considered to be the negative influence of Confucianism. He belonged to the Kokugaku movement which focused attention on Japan's earliest texts.

Note 6: The opening line of the *Tao Te Ching* (see editor's note for "Treasures of Buddhism", p. 14) is "*The way* (Tao) *that can be followed is not the true Way* (Tao)".

The *Philokalia* is a collection of ascetical and mystical writings by spiritual masters of the Christian East, compiled by Saint Nikodimos of the Holy Mountain (1748-1809) and Saint Makarios of Corinth (1731-1805).

Editor's Notes

146: Note 7: *Tomobe-no-Yasutaka* (1667-1740) was a Shinto scholar of the Edo period.

Mythology of Shinto

149: For *Vishnu* see editor's note for "Treasures of Buddhism", p. 7.

For *Rama* see editor's note for "Christianity and Buddhism", p. 77.

For *Krishna* see editor's note for "*Nirvāna*", p. 74.

For *Jimmu Tenno* see editor's note for "The Meaning of the Ancestors", p. 144.

Note 2: *Genchi Kato* (1873-1965) was the author of *A Study of Shinto: The Religion of the Japanese Nation* (1926), one of the first books on Shinto to appear in English and other European languages, and now regarded as a classic work.

Michel Revon (1833-1884) was a French Japanologist and author of *Le Shintoïsme* (1907).

J.-M. Martin was a nineteenth century Christian missionary who wrote several works on oriental traditions. The work to which the author refers was re-published in 1988 as *Le Shintoïsme ancient*.

150: In Hindu tradition, *Brahmā* is the creator, *Vishnu* the preserver, and *Shiva* the transformer. *Saraswati*, the consort of Brahmā, is the Hindu Goddess of music, art, and learning; *Lakshmi*, the consort of Vishnu, is the Goddess of good fortune and the embodiment of beauty; and *Parvati*, the consort of Shiva, is the Goddess of fertility, love, and devotion, as well as of divine strength and power.

152: *The end of Jerusalem, in Christ's prophecies:* "O Jerusalem, Jerusalem, thou that killest the prophets, and stonest them which are sent unto thee, how often would I have gathered thy children together, even as a hen gathereth her chickens under her wings, and ye would not! Behold, your house is left unto you desolate" (Matt. 23:37-38; cf. Luke 13:34-35); see also Matt. 24:1-31, Mark 13:1-23, and Luke 21:5-24 for the connection between the destruction of Jerusalem and *the end of the world*.

The *Ainus* are an ethnic group of hunter-gatherers indigenous to the northern regions of Japan and Russia who are distinct from the dominant *yamato* people.

The *demiurgic* and *deifugal mystery of the serpent* is related in the *Biblical* account of the fall (see Gen. 3), where the first couple Adam and Eve are tempted by the serpent and expelled from the Garden of Eden for disobeying God's command.

Note 10: For *Motoori Norinaga* see editor's note for "The Meaning of the Ancestors", p. 145.

153: For *Lucifer and Satan* see editor's note for "Cosmological and Eschatological Viewpoints", p. 48.

Note 10 (cont.): For *Ananda K. Coomaraswamy* see editor's note for "A Note on the Feminine Element in the *Mahāyāna*", p. 119.

Denis ("Dionysius" or "Denys") *the Areopagite* (dated c. 500 by many scholars) was a disciple of Saint Paul's (Acts 17:34) and author of several important mystical works, including *On the Celestial Hierarchy*, from which this passage is quoted.

154: *Orpheus and Eurydice* were ill-fated lovers in Greco-Roman mythology.

Raimondin, a prince of Poitou, and *Melusine*, a faery, were lovers in the legends associated with the royal House of *Lusignan*.

In Greek mythology, the *Elysian fields* were the final abode of the heroic and the virtuous.

Note 13: *Osiris* is the Egyptian god of the afterlife and the underworld; in one version of the Osiris myth he is killed by his brother *Seth*.

157: In Hinduism, the *Veda* is a body of sacred knowledge revealed to ancient Indian seers and transmitted in the *Vedas*, sacred texts composed of hymns, ritual formulas, and metaphysical doctrines regarded as authoritative for both doctrine and practice. The *Rig-Veda* is amongst the most ancient of the Vedic texts.

The *Upanishads*, also referred to as the *Vedānta* since they were traditionally placed at the "end" of the *Vedas* and are seen by such authorities as Shankara as a synthesis of Vedic teaching, are Hindu scriptures containing metaphysical, mystical, and esoteric doctrine; among their number is the *Mundaka Upanishad*.

Note 16 (cont.): For *Honen the Buddhist Saint* see editor's note for "Synthesis of the *Pāramitās*", p. 118.

158: *According to the Koran, the Angels had to learn the names of all things from Adam*: "And He [God] taught Adam all the names, then showed them to the angels, saying: Inform me of the names of these, if ye are truthful. They said: Be glorified! We have no knowledge saving that which Thou hast taught us. Lo! Thou, only Thou, art the Knower, the Wise. He said: O Adam! Inform them of their names, and when he had informed them of their names, He said: Did I not tell you that I know the secret of the heavens and the earth? And I know that which ye disclose and which ye hide" (*Sūrah* "The Cow" [2]:31-33).

159: Note 22: *Masaharu Anesaki* (1873-1945) was a Nichiren Buddhist scholar of the Meiji period and the author of *Japanese Mythology*.

160: Note 24: In Greek mythology, *Pandora* opened a jar which released plagues and diseases into the human realm.

161: For a detailed interpretation of the *"Reed-pen"* and *"Ink"* of the Islamic doctrine see the author's *"An-Nūr"*, in *Dimensions of Islam* (London: George Allen & Unwin, 1969), pp. 102-120.

The *Hebraic doctrine* of the *"Upper Waters"* and *"Lower Waters"* is expounded by *René Guénon* in *Man and His Becoming According to the Vedānta* (Ghent, New York: Sophia Perennis, 2001), p. 50n: "If the symbol of water is taken in its usual sense, then the sum of formal possibilities is described as the 'lower waters' and that of the formless possibilities as the 'upper waters'. From the point of view of cosmogony, the parting of the 'lower waters' from the 'upper waters' is also described in Genesis 1:6, and 7; it is also worth noting that the word *Maīm*, which means 'water' in Hebrew, has the grammatical form of the dual number, which allows of its conveying, among other meanings, the idea of the 'double chaos' of the formal and formless possibilities in the potential state. The primordial waters, before their separation, are the totality of the possibilities of manifestation, insofar as the latter constitutes the potential aspect of Universal Being, which is properly speaking *Prakriti*. But there is also another and superior meaning to the same symbolism, which appears when it is carried over beyond Being itself: the waters then represent Universal Possibility conceived in an absolutely total manner, that is to say insofar as it embraces at the same time in its Infinity the domains of manifestation and non-manifestation alike. This last meaning is the highest of all; at the degree immediately below it, in the original polarization of Being, we have *Prakriti*, with which we have still only reached the Principle of manifestation. After that, continuing downward, the three fundamental degrees of manifestation can be considered as we have done previously: we then have, in the first two cases, the 'double chaos' before mentioned, and lastly, in the corporeal world, water as a sensible element (*Ap*), in which capacity it is already included implicitly, like all things that pertain to gross manifestation, in the realm of the 'lower waters', for the subtle manifestation plays the part of immediate principle relative to this gross manifestation."

Note 29: *L'homme et son devenir selon le Vedānta*, by René Guénon (Paris: Éditions Traditionnelles, 1925), was one of the first European studies of *Vedānta* from an integral and traditionalist perspective. It was translated into English as *Man and His Becoming According to the Vedānta* (London: Rider, 1928).

162: Note 31: The *churning of the ocean in Hindu mythology* refers to the story of the *devas* (gods) and *asuras* (demi-gods or titans) who, at the bidding of Vishnu, stir the cosmic Ocean of Milk to obtain *amrita*, the nectar of immortal life.

Julius Schwabe (1892-1980) was a Swiss philologist and scholar of traditional symbolism.

Karl Florenz (1865-1939) was a pioneering German scholar in Japanese studies.

Virtues and Symbols of Shinto

163: For *the Prophet* of Islam see editor's note for "Christianity and Buddhism", p. 77.

Note 1: Although the teachings of *Confucius*—the Latinized form of Kung Fu Tzu, "the great master Kung" (c. 552-479 B.C.)—are often thought to be of a "merely" ethical nature, the prophet-sage himself regarded his teachings as religious in character, emphasizing that "Heaven is the author of the virtue that is in me" (*Analects*, Book 7, Ch. 22).

The *"Lion Throne" of Mysore* is an elaborate throne made of figwood and ivory, embellished with precious jewels, and covered with figures of elephants, horses, flowers, chariots, and divine figures, as well as lions.

164: The *Ark of the Covenant* (see Exod. 25:10-22) was a gold-plated wooden chest that housed the tablets on which the Ten Commandments were inscribed.

Note 2: For *Kakuzo Okakura* see editor's note for "Insights into Zen", p. 59.

Regina Wineza was a French author and photographer.

Note 4: For *Genchi Kato* see editor's note for "Mythology of Shinto", p. 149.

166: *The Biblical prohibition of images of God*: "Thou shalt not make unto thee any graven image, or any likeness of any thing that is in heaven above, or that is in the earth beneath, or that is in the water under the earth" (Exod. 20:4).

167: The *"Lesser Mysteries" of Western Antiquity*, secondary to the "Greater Mysteries", were secret cultic rites associated with the Greek city of Eleusis.

169: Note 11: For *Jōdo-Shinshū* see editor's note for "Treasures of Buddhism", p. 10.

Selections from Letters and Other Writings

173: Selection 1: *Images de l'Esprit* (Paris: Flammarion, 1961), "Mythes Shin-toïques", pp. 42-43, 45.

The *bugaku* is a form of Japanese traditional *dance* performed in order to select functionaries for the imperial court.

174: For *Hokusai* see editor's note for "Treasures of Buddhism", p. 5.

175: Selection 2: Letter of September 1956.

Selection 3: Letter of January 17, 1976.

176: Selection 4: Letter of February 8, 1972.

For *the Prophet* of Islam see editor's note for "Christianity and Buddhism", p. 77.

For *Ali* see editor's note for "Mystery of the *Bodhisattva*", p. 92.

Abu Bakr (c. 573-634) was the father-in-law and companion of Muhummad, and the first Caliph of Islam.

Uways al-Qarani was a Muslim martyr, killed in the Battle of Siffin in 657.

For *Ramana Maharshi* see editor's note for "Treasures of Buddhism", p. 12.

Badayarana (first century) is accredited with authorship of the *Brahma Sūtra*, one of the foundational texts of the *Vedānta* school of Indian philosophy.

Selection 5: "Reflections Concerning a Letter", undated.

177: For *Apocatastasis* see editor's note for "Cosmological and Eschatological Viewpoints", p. 43.

Selection 6: Letter of October 7, 1960.

178: Selection 7: Letter of January 5, 1957.

For *Jōdo-Shinshū* see editor's note for "Treasures of Buddhism", p. 10.

Selection 8: Letter of February 26, 1963.

Émile *Steinilber-Oberlin* (1878-1939) was a French orientalist whose work *Les Sectes bouddhiques japonaises* was published in 1930.

179: Selection 9: Letter of September 3, 1981.

180: Selection 10: Letter of May 31, 1975.

181: Selection 11: Letter of June 9, 1982.

For the Buddha's *"flower sermon"* see editor's note for "Message and Messenger", p. 27.

Selection 12: *Spiritual Perspectives and Human Facts: A New Translation with Selected Letters*, ed. James S. Cutsinger (Bloomington, Indiana: World Wisdom, 2007), "Contours of the Spirit, 1", pp. 56-57.

182: Selection 13: Letter of August 7, 1979.

For *Shankara* see editor's note for "Treasures of Buddhism", p. 6.

For *Brahmanism* see editor's note for "Mystery of the *Bodhisattva*", p. 88.

For *Veda* see editor's note for "Mythology of Shinto", p. 157.

Shiism is an Islamic sect that looks to Ali and his descendents as the legitimate and authoritative representatives of the Prophet Muhammad.

For *Thomas Aquinas* see editor's note for "Cosmological and Eschatological Viewpoints", p. 47.

For *Gregory Palamas* see editor's note for *"Nirvāna"*, p. 67.

Selection 14: *Spiritual Perspectives and Human Facts: A New Translation with Selected Letters*, ed. James S. Cutsinger (Bloomington, Indiana: World Wisdom, 2007), "Contours of the Spirit, 1", p. 55.

Editor's Notes

183: Selection 15: *To Have a Center: A New Translation with Selected Letters*, ed. Harry Oldmeadow (Bloomington, Indiana: World Wisdom, 2015), "David, Shankara, Honen", pp. 108-109.

For *Nagarjuna* see editor's note for "Treasures of Buddhism", p. 4.

Selection 16: *Spiritual Perspectives and Human Facts: A New Translation with Selected Letters*, ed. James S. Cutsinger (Bloomington, Indiana: World Wisdom, 2007), "*Vedānta, 2*", pp. 109-110.

184: Selection 17: *The Transfiguration of Man* (Bloomington, Indiana: World Wisdom, 1995), "Reflections on Ideological Sentimentalism", pp. 13-14.

185: Selection 18: *Esoterism as Principle and as Way* (Bedfont: Perennial Books, 1981), "The Problem of Sexuality", pp. 141-142.

For *Eckhart* see editor's note for "Originality of Buddhism", p. 21.

For *Silesius* see editor's note for "Originality of Buddhism", p. 21.

Selection 19: *Christianity/Islam: Perspectives on Esoteric Ecumenism: A New Translation with Selected Letters*, ed. James S. Cutsinger (Bloomington, Indiana: World Wisdom, 2008), "Alternations in Semitic Monotheism", p. 66.

186: *"There is no change in the words of God"* (*Sūrah* "Jonah" [10]:64).

Selection 20: *In the Face of the Absolute: A New Translation with Selected Letters*, ed. Harry Oldmeadow (Bloomington, Indiana: World Wisdom, 2014), "The Complexity of Dogmatism", pp. 43-44.

Selection 21: *Roots of the Human Condition* (Bloomington, Indiana: World Wisdom, 1991), "*Mahāshakti*", pp. 37-38.

For *Kwan-Yin—the Kwannon of Japanese Buddhism*—see editor's note for "Treasures of Buddhism", p. 7.

For *the* Bodhisattva *Avalokiteshvara* see editor's note for "Treasures of Buddhism", p. 7.

For *Tara* see editor's note for "*Nirvāna*", p. 74.

187: For the Virgin *Mary* as "*Co-Redemptress*" see editor's note for "*Nirvāna*", p. 74.

The third of the Ecumenical Councils, meeting in Ephesus (431), declared that the Blessed Virgin Mary is rightly called the *Theotokos* or "*Mother of God*".

Sita, an incarnation of the Goddess Lakshmi, was abducted by the demon king Ravana and taken from India to the island of Lanka, where she was eventually rescued by her husband, Rama, the seventh *Avatāra* of the Hindu God Vishnu; after rescuing her, however, Rama began to doubt her fidelity and ordered her banished to the forest and killed; spared by the executioner, she was finally able to convince Rama of her devotion, though her own heart was now broken.

In Hindu tradition, *Radha* was one of the *gopīs,* or cowherd girls, who loved Krishna, the eighth of the incarnations of Vishnu, and she was the one whom he especially loved in return; although not an *avatāra,* she is understood to be the *shakti,* or radiant power, of Krishna and an embodiment of *Ānanda.*

For *Rama* see editor's note for "Christianity and Buddhism", p. 77.

For *Krishna* see editor's note for *"Nirvāna",* p. 74.

Selection 22: *From the Divine to the Human: A New Translation with Selected Letters,* ed. Patrick Laude (Bloomington, Indiana: World Wisdom, 2013), "The Message of the Human Body", pp. 76-77.

188: For *Amidism* see editor's note for "Treasures of Buddhism", p. 10.

Selection 23: *Roots of the Human Condition* (Bloomington, Indiana: World Wisdom, 1991), "Man in the Face of the Sovereign Good", p. 70.

Selection 24: *Stations of Wisdom* (Bloomington, Indiana: World Wisdom, 1995), "Complexity of the Concept of Charity", p. 107n.

The Christian must love his enemies: "But I say unto you, Love your enemies, bless them that curse you, do good to them that hate you, and pray for them which despitefully use you, and persecute you" (Matt. 5:44; cf. Luke 6:27-31).

189: "For he (God) maketh his sun to rise on the evil and on the good, and *sendeth rain on the just and on the unjust"* (Matt. 5:45).

Selection 25: *Survey of Metaphysics and Esoterism* (Bloomington, Indiana: World Wisdom, 1986), "Anonymity of the Virtues", p. 205n.

The *Magnificat* (Luke 1:46-55), also known as the "Song of Mary", is a canticle sung by the Blessed Virgin after being greeted by her cousin Elizabeth as the mother of Christ; it is thus named after the first word of the hymn in the Vulgate text: "And Mary said, My soul doth magnify the Lord (*Magnificat anima mea Dominum*)." The *Magnificat* includes *fulminations* such as:

"He hath shown strength with His arm; He hath scattered the proud in the imagination of their hearts. He hath put down the mighty from their seats, and exalted them of low degree. He hath filled the hungry with good things; and the rich He hath sent empty away" (Luke 1:51-53).

The *Sermon on the Mount* (see Matt. 5-7) is the most extended Gospel account of the teachings of Jesus and includes the Beatitudes (Matt. 5:3-12) and the Lord's Prayer (Matt. 6:5-13), as well as *fulminations* such as the following: "Whosoever is angry with his brother without a cause shall be in danger of the judgment . . . and whosoever shall say, Thou fool, shall be in danger of hell fire" (5:22); "If thy right eye offend thee, pluck it out, and cast it from thee: for it is profitable for thee that one of thy members should perish, and not that thy whole body should be cast into hell" (5:29); "And when thou prayest, thou shalt not be as the hypocrites are: for they love to pray standing in the synagogues and in the corners of the streets, that they may be seen of men. Verily I say unto you, They have their reward" (6:5); "The light of the body is the eye: if therefore thine eye be single, thy whole body shall be full of light. But if thine eye be evil, thy whole body shall be full of darkness. If therefore the light that is in thee be darkness, how great is that darkness!" (6:22-23); "Enter ye in at the strait gate: for wide is the gate, and broad is the way, that leadeth to destruction, and many there be which go in thereat" (7:13); "Every tree that bringeth not forth good fruit is hewn down, and cast into the fire" (7:19); "Many will say to me in that day, Lord, Lord, have we not prophesied in thy name? and in thy name have cast out devils? and in thy name done many wonderful works? And then will I profess unto them, I never knew you: depart from me, ye that work iniquity" (7:23). For the author's commentary on the Lord's Prayer see "Our Father Who Art in Heaven", in *To Have a Center: A New Translation with Selected Letters*, ed. Harry Oldmeadow (Bloomington, Indiana: World Wisdom, 2015), pp. 97-103; this can also be found in *The Fullness of God: Frithjof Schuon on Christianity* (Bloomington, Indiana: World Wisdom, 2004), ed. James S. Cutsinger, pp. 31-37.

Selection 26: *Spiritual Perspectives and Human Facts: A New Translation with Selected Letters*, ed. James S. Cutsinger (Bloomington, Indiana: World Wisdom, 2007), "Contours of the Spirit, 1", p. 61.

Selection 27: *To Have a Center: A New Translation with Selected Letters*, ed. Harry Oldmeadow (Bloomington, Indiana: World Wisdom, 2015), "To Have a Center", p. 28.

190: Selection 28: *Language of the Self* (Bloomington, Indiana: World Wisdom, 1999), "Principles and Criteria of Art", pp. 91-92.

For the author's numerous commentaries on *the Buddhist conception of art* see the posthumous compilation, *Art from the Sacred to the Profane: East and West* (Bloomington, Indiana: World Wisdom, 2007), ed. Catherine Schuon, "Buddhist Art" and "Far Eastern Art", pp. 91-105.

The stūpa *of Piprahwa*, near present-day Birdpur in Uttar Pradesh, northern India, was *built immediately after the death of Shakyamuni* and is said to contain a portion of the Buddha's ashes given to his Shayka clan.

191: "And the *Word* was *made flesh*, and dwelt among us" (John 1:14).

Selection 29: *The Transfiguration of Man* (Bloomington, Indiana: World Wisdom, 1995), "The Ternary Rhythm of the Spirit", p. 73n.

Selection 30: *From the Divine to the Human: A New Translation with Selected Letters*, ed. Patrick Laude (Bloomington, Indiana: World Wisdom, 2013), "The Message of the Human Body", p. 86.

192: Selection 31: *To Have a Center: A New Translation with Selected Letters*, ed. Harry Oldmeadow (Bloomington, Indiana: World Wisdom, 2015), "David, Shankara, Honen", pp. 110-111.

"*Faith that moves mountains*": "If ye have faith as a grain of mustard seed, ye shall say unto this mountain, Remove hence to yonder place; and it shall remove; and nothing shall be impossible unto you" (Matt. 17:20).

For *Shinran* see editor's note for "Treasures of Buddhism", p. 10.

For *Honen* see editor's note for "Treasures of Buddhism", p. 10.

193: Selection 32: *Form and Substance in the Religions* (Bloomington, Indiana: World Wisdom, 2002), "Truth and Presence", pp. 8-10.

194: Note 8: *Aishah*, the daughter of Abu Bakr and youngest of the wives of Muhammad, is quoted as the source for many *ahādīth*, especially those concerning the Prophet's personal life.

195: For *Bodhidharma* see editor's note for "Message and Messenger", p. 27.

In the Amidist tradition, *Vasubandhu* (fl. fourth century C.E.), author of the influential *Treatise on the Sūtra of Immeasurable Life*, is considered to be the second of the Pure Land Patriarchs.

Selection 33: *Form and Substance in the Religions* (Bloomington, Indiana: World Wisdom, 2002), "Insights into the Muhammadan Phenomenon", pp.

94-95n.

Abd al-Qadir al-Jilani (1077-1166) was a gifted preacher and teacher, and the founder of the Qadiriyya Sufi order.

Selection 34: *Spiritual Perspectives and Human Facts: A New Translation with Selected Letters,* ed. James S. Cutsinger (Bloomington, Indiana: World Wisdom, 2007), "Contours of the Spirit, 1", p. 56.

Note 9: For the *Tendai, Shingon,* and *Kegon schools* of Buddhism see editor's notes for "Treasures of Buddhism", p. 10.

GLOSSARY OF FOREIGN TERMS AND PHRASES

Ādi-Buddha (Sanskrit): in Buddhist cosmology, the universal or primordial Buddha, in whom is personified supreme suchness or emptiness, and from whom come forth both the *Dhyāni-Buddhas* and the historical Buddhas, including Siddhartha Gautama.

Advaita (Sanskrit): "non-dualist" interpretation of the *Vedānta*; Hindu doctrine according to which the seeming multiplicity of things is regarded as the product of ignorance, the only true reality being *Brahma*, the One, the Absolute, the Infinite, which is the unchanging ground of appearance.

A fortiori (Latin): literally, "from greater reason"; used when drawing a conclusion inferred to be even stronger than the one already put forward.

Ahadīyah (Arabic): the supreme Divine Unity of the pure Absolute; see *Wāhidīyah*

Ahimsā (Sanskrit): "non-violence", a fundamental tenet of Hindu ethics, also emphasized in Buddhism and Jainism.

Ānanda (Sanskrit): "bliss, beatitude, joy"; one of the three essential aspects of *Apara-Brahma*, together with *Sat*, "being", and *Chit*, "consciousness".

Antarakalpa (Sanskrit): a lesser cycle between the beginning and end of a greater cycle.

Apara-Brahma (Sanskrit): the "non-supreme" or penultimate *Brahma*, also called *Brahma saguna*; in the author's teaching, the "relative Absolute".

A posteriori (Latin): literally, "from after"; subsequently; proceeding from effect to cause or from experience to principle.

A priori (Latin): literally, "from before"; in the first instance; proceeding from cause to effect or from principle to experience.

Apsarā (Sanskrit): in Hinduism, a celestial maiden in Indra's heaven skilled in the performance of music and dance.

Arahant (Pali) or *Arhat* (Sanskrit): in Buddhism, a perfected saint who has realized enlightenment.

Asankhyeya (Sanskrit): "innumerable" or "uncountable"; a period of indefi-

235

nite extent in Hindu and Buddhist theories of cosmic cycles.

Asmā' (Arabic, singular *ism*): literally, "names"; in Islam, the Divine Names of God, traditionally numbered at ninety-nine, and including the supreme Names of the Essence (*Dhāt*) and the non-supreme Names of the Qualities (*Sifāt*).

Asura-Loka (Sanskrit): the realm of the *asura*s or wicked deities, titans, giants, evil spirits, demons; contrasted with the *deva*s or gods. Hindu and Buddhist mythology represents the *asura*s as rebelling against the *deva*s, symbolizing the centrifugal and subversive tendencies within manifestation.

Ātmā or *Ātman* (Sanskrit): the real or true "Self", underlying the ego and its manifestations; in the perspective of *Advaita Vedānta*, identical with *Brahma*.

Avatāra (Sanskrit): a divine "descent"; the incarnation or manifestation of God, especially of Vishnu in the Hindu tradition.

Avidyā (Sanskrit): "ignorance" of the truth; spiritual delusion, unawareness of *Brahma*.

Baqā' (Arabic): "permanence", "subsistence"; in Sufism, the spiritual station or degree of realization following upon "extinction" (*fanā'*), in which the being is reintegrated or united with God.

Barakah (Arabic): "blessing", grace; in Islam, a spiritual influence or energy emanating originally from God, but often attached to sacred objects and spiritual persons.

Basmalah (Arabic): traditional Muslim formula of blessing, found at the beginning of all but one of the *surah*s of the Koran, consisting of the words *Bismi 'Llāhi 'r-Rahmāni 'r-Rahīm*, "In the Name of God, the Clement (*Rahmān*), the Merciful (*Rahīm*)".

Bhagavat (Sanskrit): "blessed one", "world-honored one"; in Buddhism, an epithet for a Buddha.

Bhakta (Sanskrit): a follower of the spiritual path of *bhakti*; a person whose relationship with God is based primarily on adoration and love.

Bhakti, bhakti-mārga (Sanskrit): the spiritual "path" (*mārga*) of "love" (*bhakti*) and devotion.

Bodhi (Sanskrit, Pali): "awakened, enlightened"; in Buddhism, the attainment of perfect clarity of mind, in which things are seen as they truly are.

Glossary

Bodhisattva (Sanskrit, Pali): literally, "enlightenment-being"; in *Mahāyāna* Buddhism, one who postpones his own final enlightenment and entry into *Nirvāna* in order to aid all other sentient beings in their quest for Buddhahood.

Brahmā (Sanskrit): God in the aspect of Creator, the first divine "person" of the *Trimūrti*; to be distinguished from *Brahma*, the Supreme Reality.

Brahmā-Loka (Sanskrit): "domain of *Brahmā*"; Hindu heaven in the company of God as creator.

Brahma or *Brahman* (Sanskrit): the Supreme Reality, the Absolute.

Brāhmana (Sanskrit): "Brahmin"; a member of the highest of the four Hindu castes; a priest or spiritual teacher.

Brahma nirguna (Sanskrit): *Brahma* considered as transcending all "qualities", attributes, or predicates; God as He is in Himself; also called *Para-Brahma*.

Brahma saguna (Sanskrit): *Brahma* "qualified" by attributes and predicates; God insofar as He can be known by man; also called *Apara-Brahma*.

Buddhānusmriti (Sanskrit): "remembrance or mindfulness of the Buddha", based upon the repeated invocation of his Name; central to the Pure Land school of Buddhism; known in Chinese as *nien-fo* and in Japanese as *nembutsu*.

Buddhi (Sanskrit): "Intellect"; the highest faculty of knowledge, to be contrasted with *manas*, that is, mind or reason.

Bugaku (Japanese): a form of Japanese traditional dance performed in order to select functionaries for the imperial court.

Bushidō (Japanese): literally, the "way of the warrior"; in Japan, the exacting code of conduct of the military samurai class, strongly influenced by Buddhist, Shinto, and Confucian ideals.

Carte blanche (French): literally "blank document"; freedom to think and act as one chooses.

Circulus vitiosus (Latin): literally, "vicious circle".

Dākinī (Sanskrit): in Tibetan Buddhism, a female spirit who attends and inspires the *yogin*, transmitting to him secret teachings in dreams.

Darshan or *Darshana* (Sanskrit): a spiritual "perspective", point of view, or school of thought; also the "viewing" of a holy person, object, or place, together with the resulting blessing or merit.

Deva (Sanskrit): literally, "shining one"; in Hinduism, a celestial being; any of the gods of the *Vedas*, traditionally reckoned as thirty-three.

Dharma (Sanskrit): in Hinduism, the underlying "law" or "order" of the cosmos as expressed in sacred rites and in actions appropriate to various social relationships and human vocations; in Buddhism, the practice and realization of Truth.

Dharmas (Sanskrit): in Buddhism, the elementary qualities of the being.

Dharmakāya (Sanskrit): literally, "*dharma* body"; in *Mahāyāna* Buddhism, the supreme and non-manifest form of the Buddhas, personified as the *Ādi-Buddha*; see *Sambhogakāya* and *Nirmānakāya*.

Dhāt (Arabic): the supra-personal Divine Essence; see *Ahadīyah*.

Dhikr (Arabic): "remembrance" of God, based upon the repeated invocation of His Name; central to Sufi practice, where the remembrance is often supported by the single word *Allāh*.

Dhyāna (Sanskrit): literally, "meditation", "contemplation"; one of the six *pāramitās* or spiritual virtues of the *Bodhisattva*; also the term from which *Ch'an* (Chinese) and *Zen* (Japanese) Buddhism derive their name.

Dhyāni-Buddha (Sanskrit): Buddha "of meditation"; a Buddha, such as Amitabha (Amida in Japanese), who appears to the eye of contemplative vision, but is not accessible in a historical form.

Ex cathedra (Latin): literally, "from the throne"; in Roman Catholicism, authoritative teaching issued by the pope and regarded as infallible.

Fanā' (Arabic): "extinction, annihilation, evanescence"; in Sufism, the spiritual station or degree of realization in which all individual attributes and limitations are extinguished in union with God; see *baqā'*.

Fard (Arabic): "alone"; in Sufism, one who realizes the truth on his own and without membership in a *tarīqah*, or even without belonging to a revealed religion, receiving illumination directly from God.

Force majeure (Latin): "overmastering force" or "overwhelming fate".

Gandharva (Sanskrit): celestial musician; in Hinduism, the male counterpart of the female *apsarā* in Indra's heaven, also skilled in the performance of music and dance.

Gnosis (Greek): "knowledge"; spiritual insight, principial comprehension, divine wisdom.

Gopī (Sanskrit): literally, "keeper of the cows"; in Hindu tradition, one of the cowherd girls involved with Krishna in the love affairs of his youth, symbolic of the soul's devotion to God.

Grosso modo (Italian): "roughly speaking".

Guna (Sanskrit): literally, "strand"; quality, characteristic, attribute; in Hinduism, the *gunas* are the three constituents of *Prakriti*: *sattva* (the ascending, luminous quality), *rajas* (the expansive, passional quality), and *tamas* (the descending, dark quality).

Hadīth (Arabic, plural *ahādīth*): "saying, narrative"; an account of the words or deeds of the Prophet Muhammad, transmitted through a traditional chain of known intermediaries.

Hīnayāna (Sanskrit): "lesser or small vehicle"; in Buddhism, the early monastic way comprised of branches including the *Theravāda, Mahāsānghika,* and *Sarvāstivāda;* the *Theravāda* is today prevalent in regions such as Sri Lanka, Burma, Thailand, Cambodia, and Laos; see *Mahāyāna.*

Hiranyagarbha (Sanskrit): in Hindu cosmogony, the "golden embryo" from which the world proceeds.

Hypostasis (Greek, plural *hypostases*): literally, "substance"; in Eastern Christian theology, a technical term for one of the three "Persons" of the Trinity; the Father, the Son, and the Holy Spirit are distinct *hypostases* sharing a single *ousia,* or essence.

In divinis (Latin): literally, "in or among divine things"; within the divine Principle; the plural form is used insofar as the Principle comprises both *Para-Brahma,* Beyond-Being or the Absolute, and *Apara-Brahma,* Being or the relative Absolute.

Īshvara (Sanskrit): one who "possesses power"; God understood as a personal being, as Creator and Lord; manifest in the *Trimūrti* as Brahmā, Vishnu, and Shiva.

Jannat adh-Dhāt (Arabic): the Paradise of the supra-personal Divine Essence.

Jātaka (Pali): a "birth story" of the Buddha's previous lives; numbering 547 in total, they form part of the *Sutta-pitāka* in the Buddhist canon.

Jiriki (Japanese): literally, "power of the self"; a Buddhist term for spiritual methods that emphasize one's own efforts in reaching the goal of liberation or salvation, as for example in Zen; in contrast to *tariki*.

Jīvan-mukta (Sanskrit): one who is "liberated" while still in this "life"; a person who has attained a state of spiritual perfection or self-realization before death; in contrast to *videha-mukta*, one who is liberated at the moment of death; see *krama-mukta*.

Jnāna or *jnāna-mārga* (Sanskrit): the spiritual "path" (*mārga*) of "knowledge" (*jnāna*) and intellection; see *bhakti* and *karma*.

Jnānī or *Jnānin* (Sanskrit): a follower of the path of *jnāna*; a person whose relationship with God is based primarily on sapiential knowledge or *gnosis*.

Jōdo (Japanese): "pure land"; the untainted, transcendent realm created by the Buddha Amida (Amitabha in Sanskrit), into which his devotees aspire to be born in their next life; see *Sukhāvatī*.

Jōdo-shinshū (Japanese): "true pure land school"; a sect of Japanese Pure Land Buddhism founded by Shinran, the disciple of Honen, based on faith in the power of the Buddha Amida and characterized by use of the *nembutsu*.

Jōdo-shū (Japanese): "pure land school"; a sect of Japanese Pure Land Buddhism founded by Honen, based on faith in the power of the Buddha Amida and characterized by use of the *nembutsu*.

Kalpa (Sanskrit): in Hinduism, a "day in the life of Brahmā", understood as lasting one thousand *mahāyuga*s or fourteen *manvantara*s.

Kami (Japanese): variously described as "deities", "spirits", and "energies" that pervade natural phenomena and which are worshipped in the Shinto tradition; may also refer to the spirits of the deceased.

Karma (Sanskrit): "action, work"; one of the principal *mārga*s or spiritual "paths", characterized by its stress on righteous deeds (see *bhakti* and *jnāna*); in Hinduism and Buddhism, the law of consequence, in which the present is explained by reference to the nature and quality of one's past actions.

karma-mārga, karma-yoga (Sanskrit): the spiritual "path" (*mārga*) or method of "union" (*yoga*) based upon right "action, work" (*karma*); see *bhakti* and *jnāna*.

Karma-yogī (Sanskrit): a practitioner of *karma-yoga*, or the "way of works".

Glossary

Kōan (Japanese): literally, "precedent for public use", case study; in Zen Buddhism, a question or anecdote often based on the experience or sayings of a notable master and involving a paradox or puzzle which cannot be solved in conventional terms or with ordinary thinking.

Krama-mukta (Sanskrit): one who obtains "deferred" or "gradual liberation"; one who is liberated by intermediate stages through various posthumous states; see *jīvan-mukta*.

Logos (Greek): "word, reason"; in Christian theology, the divine, uncreated Word of God (cf. John 1:1); the transcendent Principle of creation and revelation; in its created aspect, the various prophets insofar as they transmit the Word of God to humanity.

Mahākalpa (Sanskrit): a great "day in the life of Brahmā"; see *kalpa*.

Mahāprajnāpāramitā (Sanskrit): "supreme transcendent wisdom"; the *shakti* or consort of the supreme *Ādi-Buddha*.

Mahāpralaya (Sanskrit): in Hinduism, the "great" or final "dissolving" of the universe at the end of a *kalpa*, or "day in the life of Brahmā", understood as lasting one thousand *yugas*.

Mahāyāna (Sanskrit): "great vehicle"; the form of Buddhism, including such traditions as Zen and *Jōdo-shinshū*, which regards itself as the fullest or most adequate expression of the Buddha's teaching; distinguished by the idea that *nirvāna* is not other than *samsāra* truly seen as it is; prevalent today in regions such as China, Tibet, Mongolia, Vietnam, Korea, and Japan; see *Hīnayāna* and *Theravāda*.

Mahāyuga (Sanskrit): literally, a "great age"; in the Hindu theory of cosmic cycles as derived from the *Mānava-Dharma-Shāstra*, a period of four *yugas*.

Maitrī (Sanskrit): kindness, benevolence, love of one's neighbor.

Mandala (Sanskrit): "circle"; in Hinduism and Buddhism, a symbolic representation of the universe, used in religious ceremonies and meditation.

Mantra or *mantram* (Sanskrit): "instrument of thought"; a word or phrase of divine origin, often including a Name of God, repeated by those initiated into its proper use as a means of salvation or liberation; see *Buddhānusmriti*

Mantra-yoga (Sanskrit): the spiritual path or method of "union" (*yoga*) based upon the recitation of a divine Name or word or phrase (*mantra*) of divine origin.

Manvantara (Sanskrit): in the Hindu theory of cosmic cycles as derived from the *Mānava-Dharma-Shāstra*, a period of seventy-one *mahāyugas*; see *yuga*.

Materia prima (Latin): "first or prime matter"; in Platonic cosmology, the undifferentiated and primordial substance that serves as a "receptacle" for the shaping force of divine forms or ideas; universal potentiality.

Materia secunda (Latin): "secondary matter", existence; in Platonic cosmology, the secondary material forms of the physical world, as distinguished from *materia prima*, primordial and formless substance.

Māyā (Sanskrit): universal illusion, relativity, appearance; in *Advaita Vedānta*, the veiling or concealment of *Brahma* in the form or under the appearance of a lower, relative reality; also, as "productive power", the unveiling or manifestation of *Ātmā* as "divine art" or theophany. *Māyā* is neither real nor unreal, and ranges from the Supreme Lord to the "last blade of grass".

Metatron (Hebrew): in Jewish Kabbalah, the Universal Spirit; also characterized as Universal Man and Prince of the Angels.

Mudrā (Sanskrit): in the Hindu and Buddhist traditions, a ritual gesture usually made with the hands, but sometimes involving other parts of the body or the breathing; also a "seal" or "mark" of iconographical authenticity.

Mutatis mutandis (Latin): literally, "those things having been changed which need to be changed".

Nabī (Arabic, plural *anbiyā'*): prophet.

Namomitābhaya Buddhaya (Sanskrit) or *Namu-Amida-Butsu* (Japanese): literally, "praise to Amida Buddha"; a common formulation of the *nembutsu* in Pure Land Buddhism.

Natura naturata (Latin): literally, "nature natured"; the phenomena of the physical world considered as the passive effect or production of an inward and invisible causal power; a term associated with the Dutch philosopher Spinoza; see *natura naturans*.

Natura naturans (Latin): literally, "nature naturing"; nature as an active principle of causality that constitutes and governs the phenomena of the physical world; a term associated with the Dutch philosopher Spinoza; see *natura naturata*.

Nembutsu (Japanese): "remembrance or mindfulness of the Buddha", based upon the repeated invocation of his Name; same as *buddhānusmriti* in San-

Glossary

skrit and *nien-fo* in Chinese.

Nirmānakāya (Sanskrit): the "earthly body" or "body of supernatural meta-morphosis" of the Buddha; see *Dharmakāya* and *Sambhogakāya*.

Nirvāna (Sanskrit): literally, "blowing out" or "extinction"; in Indian tradi-tions, especially Buddhism, the extinction of suffering and the resulting, blissful state of liberation from egoism and attachment; extinction in relation to universal manifestation; see *parinirvāna*.

Noblesse oblige (French): literally, "nobility obliges"; the duty of the nobility to display honorable and generous conduct.

Nothelfer (German): "helpers in need"; in Roman Catholicism, apotropaic saints or "holy helpers" whose intercession is thought to be particularly effective.

Nubuwwah (Arabic): prophecy.

Nūr (Arabic): light, in particular the uncreated Divine Light considered as the principle of Existence (cf. Koran *Sūrah "An-Nūr"* [24]:35).

Paramātmā (Sanskrit): the "supreme" or ultimate Self; see *Ātmā*.

Pāramitās (Sanskrit): literally, "that which has reached the other shore"; the six virtues or disciplines characteristic of the *Bodhisattva*, namely *dāna* ("charity"), *shīla* ("renunciation"), *kshānti* ("patience"), *vīrya* ("virility"), *dhyāna* ("contemplation"), and *prajnā* ("wisdom").

Parinirvāna (Sanskrit): "supreme extinction", "extinction without residue"; complete extinction in relation to universal manifestation and to Being, espe-cially at the moment of death; see *nirvāna*.

Philosophia perennis (Latin): "perennial philosophy".

Prajnā (Sanskrit): "wisdom, intelligence, understanding"; in Hinduism, the self-awareness of *Ātmā*; knowledge of things as they truly are; in Buddhism, one of the six *pāramitās* or virtues of the *Bodhisattva*.

Prakriti (Sanskrit): literally, "making first" (see *material prima*); the funda-mental, "feminine" substance or material cause of all things; see *Purusha*.

Pralaya (Sanskrit): "dissolution"; Hindu teaching that all appearance is sub-ject to a periodic process of destruction and recreation; see *mahāpralaya*.

Pranidhāna (Sanskrit): literally, "vow"; especially the "original vow" of *Bod-*

243

hisattva Dharmakara—the future Amitabha Buddha—not to enter *Nirvāna* until he had brought all who invoked his sacred Name into the paradise of his Pure Land.

Pratyeka-Buddha (Sanskrit): "independent Buddha"; in Buddhism, one who attains enlightenment without a teacher and who makes no attempt to instruct disciples.

Proothoi (Greek): in Eastern Christian theology, the non-supreme Divine "Processions" or "Energies" (*dynameis*), as distinguished *in divinis* from the supreme Divine Essence (*uparxis*).

Purusha (Sanskrit): literally, "man"; the informing or shaping principle of creation; the "masculine" demiurge or fashioner of the universe; see *Prakriti*.

Rajas (Sanskrit): in Hinduism, one of the three *gunas*, or qualities, of *Prakriti*, of which all things are woven; the quality of expansiveness, manifest in the material world as force or movement and in the soul as ambition, initiative, and restlessness.

Rasūl (Arabic, plural *rusul*): "messenger, apostle"; in Islam, one whom God sends with a message for a particular people and who is thus a founder of a religion.

Rūh (Arabic): "Spirit"; in Sufism, either the uncreated Spirit of God or the spirit of man.

Salāt 'alā 'n-Nabī (Arabic): a formula of blessing upon the Prophet Muhammad; in Sufism, often recited as part of a rosary during devotional worship.

Sambhogakāya (Sanskrit): the "beatific body" or paradisal "body of bliss" of the Buddha; see *Dharmakāya* and *Nirmānakāya*.

Samsāra (Sanskrit): literally, "wandering"; in Hinduism and Buddhism, trans-migration or the cycle of birth, death, and rebirth; also the world of apparent flux and change.

Samyaksambodhi (Sanskrit): literally, "plenary enlightenment"; see *bodhi*.

Samyaksam-Buddha (Sanskrit): literally, "fully awakened one"; a fully enlight-ened Buddha with the function of enlightening others through preaching the *Dharma*; equivalent to a major *avatāra* in Hinduism and a *rasūl*, or messenger of God who founds a religion, in Islam.

Glossary

Sat-Chit-Ānanda or *saccidānanda* (Sanskrit): "being-consciousness-bliss"; the three essential aspects of *Apara-Brahma*, that is, *Brahma* insofar as it can be grasped in human experience.

Satori (Japanese): in Zen Buddhism, the sudden experience of enlightenment; a flash of intuitive insight often gained through the employment of a *kōan* during *zazen* or "sitting meditation"; see *bodhi*.

Sattva (Sanskrit): in Hinduism, one of the three *gunas*, or qualities, of *Prakriti*, of which all things are woven; the quality of luminosity, manifest in the material world as buoyancy or lightness and in the soul as intelligence and virtue.

Scientia sacra (Latin): the "sacred knowledge" at the heart of all orthodox religious traditions; see *philosophia perennis*.

Secundum fidem (Latin): literally, "according to faith"; the Christian Scholastic "double truth" distinguished a truth "according to faith" from a truth "according to reason" (*secundum rationem*), each thought to be valid within its respective domain.

Secundum rationem (Latin): literally, "according to reason"; the Christian Scholastic "double truth" distinguished a truth "according to reason" from a truth "according to faith" (*secundum fidem*), each thought to be valid within its respective domain.

Shahādah (Arabic): the fundamental "profession" or "testimony" of faith in Islam, consisting of the words *lā ilāha illā 'Llāh, Muhammadan rasūlu 'Llāh*: "There is no god but God; Muhammad is the messenger of God."

Shakti (Sanskrit): creative "power", expressed in Hinduism in the form of divine femininity.

Sharīf (Arabic, plural *shurafa'*): literally, "noble"; the descendents of the Prophet Muhammad through his daughter Fatima and son-in-law Ali.

Shāstra (Sanskrit): "command, rule"; traditional Hindu book of law.

Shekhinah (Hebrew): in Judaism, the dwelling-place or presence of God in the world; the Divine immanence.

Shramana (Sanskrit): in Buddhism, a monk or ascetic.

Shrāvaka (Sanskrit): "hearer" or "disciple"; in early Buddhism, a disciple of the Buddha, or a disciple of a disciple of the Buddha, who attained to enlightenment and became an *arahant* or perfected saint; in later Buddhism, a disciple who accepts the essential precepts of the Buddhist *Dharma*.

Shūnya (Sanskrit): "void" or "empty"; in *Mahāyāna* Buddhism, the true nature of all phenomena, devoid of all independent selfhood or substance; giving rise to the concept of *shūnyatā*, ultimate "emptiness" or "voidness".

Shūnyamūrti (Sanskrit): "the form or manifestation of the void"; traditional epithet of the Buddha, in whom is "incarnate" *shūnyatā*, ultimate "emptiness", that is, the final absence of all definite being or selfhood.

Sifāt (Arabic, singular *Sifah*): the Divine Qualities; see *Dhāt*.

Sub specie aeternitatis (Latin): literally, "under the gaze of eternity", that is, from an eternal perspective.

Sukhāvatī (Sanskrit): "place of bliss"; the Western Paradise, or Pure Land, of Amitabha Buddha.

Sukshma sharīra (Sanskrit): in Hinduism, the "subtle body" surrounding or enveloping *Ātmā* and comprised of thinking, feeling, and desiring; intermediate between the *kārana sharīra* ("blissful body") and the *sthūla sharīra* ("gross body").

Sūtra (Sanskrit): literally, "thread"; a Hindu or Buddhist sacred text; in Hinduism, any short, aphoristic verse or collection of verses, often elliptical in style; in Buddhism, a collection of the discourses of the Buddha.

Tamas (Sanskrit): in Hinduism, one of the three *gunas*, or qualities, of *Prakriti*, of which all things are woven; the quality of darkness or heaviness, manifest in the material world as inertia or rigidity and in the soul as sloth, stupidity, and vice.

Tārā (Sanskrit): literally, "she who saves"; the title of a number of Tibetan female *Bodhisattvas* and Hindu goddesses.

Tariki (Japanese): "power of the other"; a Buddhist term for forms of spirituality that emphasize the importance of grace or celestial assistance, especially that of the Buddha Amida, as in the Pure Land schools; in contrast to *jiriki*.

Tathāgata (Sanskrit): literally, "thus gone" or "thus come"; according to Buddhist tradition, the title the Buddha chose for himself, interpreted to mean: he who has won through to the supreme liberation; he who has come with the supreme teaching; he who has gone before and found the true path.

Tathatā (Sanskrit): "thusness", "suchness"; in *Mahāyāna* Buddhism, the nondual and supremely blissful nature of reality as seen by the enlightened mind;

the "positive" complement to *Shūnyatā.*

Tennō (Japanese): "heavenly sovereign"; a title of the Japanese emperor.

Theravāda (Pali): "teaching of the elders"; the oldest surviving school of Buddhism; see *Hīnayāna* and *Mahāyāna.*

Tomoye or *tomoe* (Japanese): ancient Shinto symbol representing the interplay of the cosmic forces.

Torii (Japanese): open gateway demarcating the sacred precincts of a Shinto shrine and signaling the presence of *kami,* or spirits.

Trimūrti (Sanskrit): literally, "having three forms"; in Hindu tradition, a triadic expression of the Divine, especially in the form of Brahmā, the creator, Vishnu, the preserver, and Shiva, the transformer.

Trishnā (Sanskrit): "thirst, craving, desire"; in Buddhism, the cause of suffering as stated in the second noble truth.

Tülku (Tibetan): literally "transformation body"; in Tibetan Buddhism, a person who is recognized at a young age and through various miraculous signs as the custodian of a specific lineage of teachings.

Upanishad (Sanskrit): literally, "to sit close by"; hence, any esoteric doctrine requiring direct transmission from master to disciple; in Hinduism, the genre of sacred texts that end or complete the *Vedas;* see *Vedānta.*

Uparxis or *hyparxis* (Greek): in Eastern Christianity theology, the supreme Divine Essence, as distinguished *in divinis* from the non-supreme Divine "Energies" (*dynameis*) or "Processions" (*proothoi*).

Upāya (Sanskrit): "means, expedient, method"; in Buddhist tradition, the adaptation of spiritual teaching to a form suited to the level of one's audience.

Upekshā (Sanskrit): impassivity.

Vairochana (Sanskrit): literally, "he who is like the sun"; the "solar" Buddha.

Vajrayāna (Sanskrit): "diamond vehicle"; a mysterious form of *Mahāyāna* Buddhism prevalent in Tibet emphasizing meditative and tantric practices.

Veda (Sanskrit): "knowledge"; in Hinduism, the body of sacred knowledge held to be the basis of orthodoxy and right practice.

Vedānta (Sanskrit): "end or culmination of the *Vedas*"; one of the major schools of traditional Hindu philosophy, based in part on the Upanishads;

see *advaita.*

Videha-Mukta (Sanskrit): one who is liberated at the moment of death; see *jīvan-mukta.*

Vijnāna (Sanskrit): consciousness.

Virāj (Sanskrit): in Hindu cosmology, the cosmic Intellect that governs the sensible world.

Wāhidīyah (Arabic): the non-supreme Divine Unicity of the "relative Absolute"; see *Ahadīyah.*

Walī (Arabic): literally, "friend"; in Islam, a saint.

Wilāyah (Arabic): sainthood.

Yin-Yang (Chinese): in Chinese tradition, two opposite but complementary forces or qualities, from whose interpenetration the universe and all its diverse forms emerge; *Yin* corresponds to the feminine, the yielding, the moon, liquidity; *Yang* corresponds to the masculine, the resisting, the sun, solidity.

Yoga (Sanskrit): literally, "yoking, union"; in Indian traditions, any meditative and ascetic technique designed to bring the soul and body into a state of concentration; one of the six orthodox *darshana*s, or perspectives, of classical Hinduism.

Yogī or *yogin* (Sanskrit): one who is "yoked" or "joined"; a practitioner of *yoga*, especially a form of *yoga* involving meditative and ascetic techniques designed to bring the soul and body into a state of concentration.

Yuga (Sanskrit): an "age" in Hinduism, one of the four periods into which a cycle of time is divided.

Zazen (Japanese): literally, "sitting meditation"; in Zen Buddhism, a contemplative practice, often used in conjunction with the *kōan*, and seen as the most direct path to enlightenment.

For a glossary of all key foreign words used in books published by World Wisdom, including metaphysical terms in English, consult: www.DictionaryofSpiritualTerms.org. This on-line Dictionary of Spiritual Terms provides extensive definitions, examples, and related terms in other languages.

INDEX

metaphysics, 10, 26, 28, 31, 69, 106, 182, 183, 218, 259
Metatron, 73, 242
Middle Ages, the, 33, 110, 142, 168, 207
Milarepa, 95, 96, 214
Mirror, the, 163, 165, 166
misogyny (of Buddhism), 187
modernism, 167
Mongols, the, 119, 143
Monotheism, 80, 105, 106, 229, 229
Mosaic Law, 78, 211
Moses, 77, 105, 163, 166, 210, 211, 215, 220
Motoori Norinaga, 145, 152, 222, 224
Muadh Ar-Razi, 209
mudrā, 181
Muhammad. *See* Prophet (Muhammad), the

Nagarjuna, 26, 90, 109, 183, 197, 203, 213, 216, 229
natura naturata, 49, 154, 160, 242
natura naturans, 154, 242
nembutsu, 99, 115, 237, 240, 242
Neoplatonism, 87
Nichiren, 10, 13, 198, 225
Nirmānakāya, 98, 108, 119, 126, 177, 238, 243, 244
Nirvāna, 5, 8, 11, 12, 14, 18, 19, 21, 25, 31, 39, 65, 67, 68, 72, 73, 89, 90, 92, 93, 94, 95, 96, 97, 99, 100, 101, 102, 103, 104, 108, 111, 112, 114, 120, 122, 124, 125, 126, 127, 128, 130, 178, 183, 184, 185, 186, 188, 197, 208, 214, 215, 218, 223, 228, 229, 230, 237, 243, 244
non-theism, viii, ix, 16, 18, 190

Omar Khayyam, 21, 202

Original Vow (of Dharmakara), the, 114, 124, 217, 219
Orléans, Duke of, 137, 221
Orpheus and Eurydice, 154, 224
orthodoxy, viii, 15, 16, 60, 78, 158, 193, 247
Osiris, 154, 157, 224

Pandora, 160, 225
Paraclete, the, 86, 212
Paradise, 53, 67, 68, 69, 70, 71, 93, 94, 98, 118, 126, 142, 178, 197, 218, 219, 239, 246
pāramitās, 111, 112, 113, 114, 115, 117, 119, 238, 243
Parinirvāna, 68, 70, 78, 97, 99, 101, 243
Parvati, 150, 223
Pascal, Blaise, 27, 203
patience, 91, 112, 113, 115, 117, 118, 153, 163, 168, 243
Paul (Apostle), 52, 60, 80, 224
Philokalia, 145, 222
philosophia perennis, 36, 139, 245
Piprahwa, *stūpa* of, 190, 232
pity, 25, 81, 95, 96
Plato, 47, 119, 205, 218, 259
power of self, 9, 114, 188, 192, 193, 194, 195, 217. See also *jiriki*
power of the Other, 114, 117, 192, 193, 194, 195, 217. See also *tariki*
prajnā, 95, 111, 112, 115, 117, 119, 120, 122, 243
Prajnaparamita, 119, 122
Prajnā Pāramitā Hridaya Sūtra, 207, 216
Prakriti, 75, 126, 127, 128, 149, 150, 151, 153, 161, 225, 239, 243, 244, 245, 246
pralaya, 43
Pratyeka-Buddha(s), 8, 88, 90, 91,

Shankara, ix, 6, 53, 78, 100, 109, 110, 182, 183, 197, 211, 214, 215, 216, 224, 228, 229, 232
Shan-Tao, 113, 118, 131, 217, 221
sharīfs, 163
Shekhinah, 74, 210, 245
Shiism, 182, 228
Shingon, 10, 11, 27, 111, 114, 117, 122, 195, 199, 216, 217, 219, 233
Shinran, 10, 13, 93, 94, 113, 122, 131, 192, 193, 194, 195, 198, 199, 214, 217, 219, 221, 232, 240
Shinshū. See *Jōdo-Shinshū*
Shinto, vii, xi, xii, 65, 135, 137, 141, 143, 144, 145, 146, 147, 149, 150, 152, 154, 155, 156, 157, 161, 162, 163, 165, 166, 167, 168, 169, 174, 222, 223, 226, 227, 228, 237, 240, 247
Shiva, 150, 198, 210, 223, 239, 247
Shotoku Taishi, 13, 200
Shrāvaka, 88, 91, 245
Shūnya, 5, 14, 27, 184, 204, 246
shūnyamūrti, 5, 27
shūnyatā, 18, 117, 197, 246
Silesius, Angelus, 21, 185, 202, 229
Sita, 187, 230
Son (second Person of the Christian Trinity), 70, 124, 127, 219, 220, 239
Song of Songs, the, 128, 220
Sovereign Good, the, 179, 230
Steinilber-Oberlin, Émile, 178, 228
suffering, x, 19, 21, 25, 39, 77, 87, 89, 91, 92, 164, 182, 183, 195, 196, 243, 247
Sukhāvatī, 93, 94, 114, 121, 197, 199, 219, 240, 246. *See also* Pure Land
sukshma sharīra, 43

Susano-wo-no-Mikoto, 151, 154, 156, 157, 159, 161, 162
Suzuki, Daisetz Teitaro, 85, 212
Sword, the, 163, 164, 165

Ta-Hui, 207
Takamimusubi-no-Kami, 150
Tamas, 151, 246
Tan-Luan, 113, 217
Tantrism, 110, 120
Tao-Cho, 113, 212, 217
Taoism, x, xi, 5, 10, 65, 87, 137, 149, 200
Tao Te Ching, 14, 93, 145, 200, 214, 222
Tara, 74, 119, 186, 187, 210, 229
tariki, 9, 10, 192, 193, 217, 240, 246
Tathāgata, 7, 11, 27, 101, 105, 108, 117, 121, 122, 246. *See also* Buddha, the
Tauler, John, 142, 222
tea ceremony, the, 58, 59, 64, 195
Tendai, 10, 11, 27, 111, 195, 199, 216, 233
Tennō, 137, 149, 163, 164, 247
Teresa of Avila, 16, 142, 201, 222
theology, Apophatic, 211; Areopagitic, 208; Palamite, 208; Patristic, 67, 208
theophany, 130, 188, 242
Theravāda, x, 9, 11, 26, 89, 109, 191, 239, 241, 247
Theresa of Lisieux, 98, 214
third Eye, the, 115, 217
Thomas Aquinas, 182, 205, 207, 228
Thomism, 47, 205
Tomobe-no-Yasutaka, 223
tomoye, 174
tongues, gift of, 85, 212
torii, 143
transmigration, x, 18, 42, 44, 80, 87,

BIOGRAPHICAL NOTES

Frithjof Schuon

Born in Basle, Switzerland in 1907, Frithjof Schuon was the twentieth century's pre-eminent spokesman for the perennialist school of comparative religious thought.

The leitmotif of Schuon's work was foreshadowed in an encounter during his youth with a marabout who had accompanied some members of his Senegalese village to Basle for the purpose of demonstrating their African culture. When Schuon talked with him, the venerable old man drew a circle with radii on the ground and explained: "God is the center; all paths lead to Him." Until his later years Schuon traveled widely, from India and the Middle East to America, experiencing traditional cultures and establishing lifelong friendships with Hindu, Buddhist, Christian, Muslim, and American Indian spiritual leaders.

A philosopher in the tradition of Plato, Shankara, and Eckhart, Schuon was a gifted artist and poet as well as the author of over twenty books on religion, metaphysics, sacred art, and the spiritual path. Describing his first book, *The Transcendent Unity of Religions*, T. S. Eliot wrote, "I have met with no more impressive work in the comparative study of Oriental and Occidental religion", and world-renowned religion scholar Huston Smith said of Schuon, "The man is a living wonder; intellectually apropos religion, equally in depth and breadth, the paragon of our time". Schuon's books have been translated into over a dozen languages and are respected by academic and religious authorities alike.

More than a scholar and writer, Schuon was a spiritual guide for seekers from a wide variety of religions and backgrounds throughout the world. He died in 1998.

Harry Oldmeadow was, until his recent retirement, the Coordinator of Philosophy and Religious Studies at La Trobe University Bendigo, in southeast Australia. A widely respected author on the *sophia perennis* and the perennialist school, his publications include *Traditionalism: Religion in the Light of the Perennial Philosophy* (2000) and *Frithjof Schuon and the Perennial Philosophy* (2010). He has edited several anthologies for World Wisdom, the most recent being *Crossing Religious Frontiers* (2010), and has contributed to such journals as *Sophia* and *Sacred Web*. In addition to his studies of perennialism, he has written extensively on the modern encounter of Eastern and Western traditions in works such as *Journeys East: 20ᵗʰ Century Western Encounters with Eastern Religious Traditions* (2004) and *A Christian Pilgrim in India: The Spiritual Journey of Swami Abhishiktananda* (2008).